"Many investors have substantial business expertise, and experience in specific capital markets. But such knowledge is not enough. Success requires an integrated view of the investment problem, and of the full range of investment products. Peter Stanyer's excellent guide to investment strategy provides exactly this, summarising the latest thinking in a concise, readable format."
John Campbell, Professor of Economics, Harvard University

"Peter Stanyer uses both his practical investment experience and recent developments in financial economics to tackle many of the more important and complex decisions faced by investors. Don't expect to find simple answers; do expect to be stimulated."
Richard Brealey, Emeritus Professor of Finance, London Business School

"This book provides a thoughtful and incisive appraisal of the optimal approach to long-term investment, drawing on historical data, the latest academic studies and best practice among institutional investors. It will be essential reading for investment advisers and private bankers as well as individual investors seeking to preserve and grow wealth."
John Calverley, Chief Economist and Strategist, American Express Bank

"Investing today grows more complex by the day, and it is important to take a step back and simplify the foundation of the principles that guide the desired results. This guide does just that in a practical and accessible manner."
Christopher Hyzy, Investment Strategist, U.S. Trust

"Peter Stanyer has used the full breadth of his experience to construct a guide which is practical but also insightful. The style is that of a knowledgeable friend, telling interesting stories, patiently explaining difficult points, but never talking down. Both the professional investor and the interested amateur will quickly find much useful and relevant information in this book."
Chris Hitchen, Chief Executive, Railways Pension Trusteee Co Ltd

"Wealth management has been traditionally associated with expensive lunches, bespoke tailoring and not much else. Peter Stanyer's excellent, accessible guide brings the techniques of quantitative finance to wealth management, giving the subject a structure and content that has been sorely needed."
Dr Steve Satchell, Reader of Financial Econometrics, Cambridge University; Fellow, Trinity College, Cambridge

Peter Stanyer is one of the most knowledgeable investment professionals I encountered during my three decades at Merrill Lynch. Peter has utilised sound academic research, but he has also listened to investors over the years. The result is a clear, practical and authoritative book on investing in today's markets that will be useful for both high net worth investors and their financial advisers. I highly recommend it.
Winthrop H. Smith Jr, Chairman of the Advisory Board of Overture Financial Services, former Executive Vice President of Merrill Lynch & Co. and Chairman of Merrill Lynch International, Inc.

GUIDE TO INVESTMENT STRATEGY

OTHER ECONOMIST BOOKS

Guide to Analysing Companies
Guide to Business Modelling
Guide to Business Planning
Guide to Economic Indicators
Guide to the European Union
Guide to Financial Markets
Guide to Management Ideas
Numbers Guide
Style Guide

Dictionary of Business
Dictionary of Economics
International Dictionary of Finance

Brands and Branding
Business Consulting
Business Ethics
Business Miscellany
Business Strategy
China's Stockmarket
Dealing with Financial Risk
Economics
Future of Technology
Globalisation
Headhunters and How to Use Them
Successful Mergers
The City
Wall Street

Essential Director
Essential Economics
Essential Investment
Essential Negotiation

Pocket World in Figures

GUIDE TO INVESTMENT STRATEGY

How to understand markets, risk, rewards
and behaviour

Peter Stanyer

THE ECONOMIST IN ASSOCIATION WITH
PROFILE BOOKS LTD

Published by Profile Books Ltd
3A Exmouth House, Pine Street, London EC1R OJH
www.profilebooks.com

Copyright © The Economist Newspaper Ltd, 2006

Text copyright © Peter Stanyer, 2006

The greatest care has been taken in compiling this book.
However, no responsibility can be accepted by the publishers or compilers
for the accuracy of the information presented.

This publication contains the author's opinions and is designed to provide accurate
and authoritative information. It is sold with the understanding that the author,
the publisher and *The Economist* are not engaged in rendering legal, accounting,
investment-planning, or other professional advice. The reader should seek the
services of a qualified professional for such advice; the author, the publisher and
The Economist cannot be held responsible for any loss incurred as a result of specific
investments or planning decisions made by the reader.

Where opinion is expressed it is that of the author and does not necessarily coincide
with the editorial views of The Economist Newspaper.

Typeset in EcoType by MacGuru Ltd
info@macguru.org.uk

Printed in Great Britain by
Creative Print and Design (Wales), Ebbw Vale

A CIP catalogue record for this book is available
from the British Library

ISBN-10: 1 86197 851 0
ISBN-13: 978 1 86197 851 6

To Alex

Contents

List of figures

List of tables

Acknowledgements

I owe a debt of gratitude to many individuals who helped me with this book. Foremost is my wife Alex for encouraging me to have the courage of my convictions and to resign from Merrill Lynch, so as to find time to write it. Elroy Dimson and Steve Satchell provided invaluable nuggets of advice and moral support along the way. Paul Barrett, Nick Bucknell and Stephen Collins provided important advice and suggestions on the draft. Helpful contributions on particular issues or chapters were provided by Mohammad Baki, Chris Bartram, Graham Birch, Jeff Bryan, Mike Casel, Jon Chesshire, Mark DeSario, Simon Des-Etages, Cory Easter, Matt Feinstein, Hugh Ferry, Karen Froehlich, Masood Javaid, Samir Kabbaj, Truman Lam, Tim Lund, Yoram Lustig, Nick Miller Smith, Paul Polries, Afroz Qadeer, Katy Reynolds, Fabio Savoldelli, Andrew Schmuhl and Clifford Smout. I am most grateful to each of them.

I also owe a substantial debt to many colleagues and former colleagues at Overture Financial Services, Merrill Lynch, Mercury Asset Management and Railpen Investments, and to the clients and trustees of those organisations, whose perceptive insights and experiences are reflected in this book.

The book contains numerous tables and charts, and I am grateful to those firms whose data I have used for granting their permission.

Lastly, I would like to thank Stephen Brough at Profile Books for his support and Penny Williams, who edited the book.

Please note that this book aims to help inform the process of seeking and giving professional advice, but that it cannot be a substitute for that advice.

It draws on and summarises research and investor perspectives on a wide range of issues, but it is not punctuated with footnotes citing sources for facts or opinions. Although important areas of debate are flagged with references to leading researchers, in other areas ideas which are more commonly expressed are presented but not attributed. Sources which were particularly important for each chapter are listed in Appendix 4.

Since writing this book, I have been appointed chief investment officer of Overture Investments LLC. It goes without saying that any views expressed in this book represent my views, at the time of writing, and not necessarily those of Overture.

Foreword

Investors walk a tricky tightrope of risk and performance. Those who choose too little risk may fail to reach their goal. Those who choose too much may lose their balance, with potentially disastrous results. How should investors decide what level of risk exposure is suitable for them? For many advisers, the solution is to ask their clients to indicate how much risk they can tolerate, and then to design a portfolio that meets their risk preferences. But individuals are not usually investment experts. Furthermore, it is extremely hard to elicit a person's appetite for risk: what investors say they want is not necessarily what they really want. Investors may be ill-informed and their behaviour may be less than rational.

Individuals face an even tougher challenge than pension funds and insurance companies. For many institutions there are opportunities to mitigate poor investment performance. In contrast, individual investors face fewer remedies for poor returns. They might wish to live as well as possible, but it is not clear how to accomplish this objective. If the appropriate strategy for individuals is more problematic than for investment institutions, how can one best help individual investors?

Peter Stanyer's solution is to educate investors. He wants to extend their knowledge, to inform them about relevant theory and evidence, and to accomplish this without resorting to complicated mathematics. The result is a clear exposition of the arguments for and against different investment approaches. The author is not afraid to express a firm opinion based on his interpretation of current thinking. Whether the reader is interested in the big picture or wants to learn about individual asset classes, there is something for everyone in this book. The surveys of each of the main assets provide a helicopter tour of key topics: the discussion of equity investment in chapter 6 is an excellent example of this. The statistics in this volume are up to date, and many of the graphics employ data that appeared as recently as the beginning of 2006.

The author is well qualified to steer us through the investment maze. After more than a decade in varied roles with the Bank of England and IMF, Peter Stanyer was appointed at the age of only 33 to be head of investments of one of the top five pension funds in the UK: the British Rail Pension Fund. While there, he drafted the National Association of

Pension Funds' commission of enquiry on investment performance. Six years later he joined Mercury Asset Management, where he headed the performance and risk team, and later on, after MAM became part of Merrill Lynch, the team responsible for investment allocation for international private clients. It is this breadth of experience – public sector finance in the 1980s, pension fund management in the 1990s, private client investment in the 2000s – coupled with an enduring interest in new ideas, that underpins his extensive knowledge and varied perspectives. I can think of few experts better qualified than Peter Stanyer to guide us through the challenge of investing for our futures.

Elroy Dimson
April 2006

Introduction

There are many popular investment books, but relatively few provide a dispassionate introduction to the controversies that surround the management of wealth. Even though there are plenty of important articles that take these controversies forward, few of the investment guides pull the different sides of the arguments together in one place. That is what this book seeks to do, in a way which is intended to be of practical use.

Investment advisers are often left to themselves to reconcile competing arguments in investment controversies. This is not surprising as there will always be unresolved debates. Investors and their advisers do not need to align themselves strongly with either side of a dispute between academics; instead they need to think through how unresolved debate influences the uncertainty that accompanies their proposals for investment strategy. One of several examples is the question of whether good times in the stockmarket predictably follow bad (in the jargon, whether equity markets mean revert), because if they do, long-term equity investors might find the stockmarket to be a less risky place than short-term investors do. The current academic position (see Chapters 3 and 5) is broadly that such a process appears to occur, to some uncertain extent. Nevertheless, equities must still be regarded as risky for long-term investors, particularly in comparison with the alternative of inflation-linked government bonds. Investors' circumstances change and reactions to those changes, and to market opportunities and developments at different points in time, influence attitudes to risk-taking by long-term investors. It might be the case that equity risk could be less risky for long-term than for short-term investors, but whether it is in practice is a different matter.

In other areas there is little place for substantial debate. The correct approach is agreed, but nevertheless it is frequently ignored in practice. An example of this is the practice of treating long-term private investors as if they were short-term investors whose principal focus in risk management should be the danger of losing money. The focus of much strategic advice is anchored on an investor's apparent tolerance for suffering varying degrees of negative investment returns. In these exercises, short-term investors are generally expected to be less tolerant of short-term losses, and long-term investors are expected to be more tolerant of such reversals. This may be how many investors instinctively behave, but that does not mean that it is in their interests to do so. This common approach confuses risk-taking with the time horizon of an investor, and the focus on negative investment returns misses the appropriate focus of a long-term investor, which should be the risk of jeopardising future income.

This picks up a theme that is reflected in various places in the book. In Chapter 2, the contrast between the framework of traditional finance, which, loosely, describes how investors "ought" to behave, and the insights of modern behavioural finance, which describe how investors "do" behave, is emphasised as a challenge for advice-giving. In Chapter 4, the discussion of the time horizon introduces (or rather borrows) the concepts of "good" and "bad" volatility. This distinguishes between a fall in price caused by a rise in interest rates, which is good for long-term savers, and a loss caused by a decline in earnings prospects for the economy or a company, which is bad for all investors. Understanding this difference is fundamental to long-term investment success and can be reinforced by providing simple management information (see Appendix 2) that can be used, at times of negative market returns, to encourage informed discussion rather than inappropriate reactions. As much as anything, that is the objective of this book.

PART 1
THE BIG PICTURE

1 Setting the scene

Other people's dreadful experiences can provide useful cautionary tales. So it is instructive to start a discussion of managing wealth with some historic examples of institutions or individuals who got things badly wrong.

Spectacular losses of financial wealth can be put into three categories. The first is where investors fully understand the risks they are taking, and against their better judgment, they deliberately gamble and the gamble fails. They regret what they did, they know it was ill-considered and they can blame only themselves for their misfortune. A good example of this behaviour is the often told story of Sir Isaac Newton's financial ruin.

In the spring of 1720, Sir Isaac Newton, "a scientist and presumably rational", sold his investment in the South Sea Company, collecting £7,000, a 100% profit on his investment and a substantial sum of money, equivalent to as much as £7m today. He wrote that the stock price had by then become irrationally inflated by "the madness of people". The South Sea Company itself contained a toxic mix of government sponsorship, endorsement by the great and the good of the day, and management by energetic fraudsters. In the subsequent months its price climbed yet further. Newton could have profited more during that summer of 1720. Then, perhaps overcome by regret at missing these additional profits, he invested heavily – £20,000 – at the top of the market. However, as the speculation unravelled, he lost it all. "Although the most imperturbable of men, [he] could never bear to hear the South Sea referred to for the rest of his life. Intelligence was no protection."

The second category of spectacular losses is where a concentrated position is established because of faith in a particular investment story, while the benefits of diversification are dismissed as holding back the prospects for rapid wealth accumulation – but then the concentrated position turns sour. A celebrated episode that conforms to this pattern is the attempt by Bunker Hunt, his brother, Herbert, and a few other investors to establish and maintain enormous positions in the 1970s silver market. One irony is that the Hunt brothers shared with Paul Volcker, the newly appointed chairman of the Federal Reserve, the view that inflation was getting dangerously out of control and embedded as a malaise in the US economy (and elsewhere) . "A billion dollars ain't what it used to be,"

Bunker Hunt complained, and he was right, as in the 1970s US consumer prices more than doubled. Hunt's reaction was to put his faith in long-term holdings of a real asset, silver, for which demand was outstripping new production and supply was consequently squeezed. Volcker's reaction to entrenched inflation was to squeeze the money supply, with a dramatic effect on short-term interest rates. This was to be a once-in-a-generation shift in policy that ushered in a 20-year period of disinflation. Bunker Hunt, through concern about the same macroeconomic trends as Volcker, ended up on the wrong side of those momentous events. He was also a victim of a change in commodity exchange rules, which were deliberately adjusted to relieve supply shortages.

In this second category are included the concentrations of pension savings of employees in the stock of a number of failed US corporations and some well-publicised, ill-fated concentrations of institutional investment which have caused acute embarrassment to particular funds. In the 1980s and 1990s, Boston University suffered an enormous financial setback through having invested nearly 20% of its investment portfolio in one biotech company, Seragen; and in the early 19th century, Yale University lost more than 90% of its endowment when its efforts to sponsor banking competition by founding a local bank failed. When such misfortune affects an institution, the consequences are public, because the fiduciary structure carries with it exposure to public scrutiny. This accountability helps to enforce diversification (see Chapter 6 for a discussion of the role of the "prudent person" obligations on fiduciaries). However, instances of unnecessary concentrated risk-taking are probably a more common threat to financial well-being in the private world of family wealth than in institutional investment.

The third category of spectacular losses is where investors did not know, but should have known, the risks that they were taking, and would probably have altered their risk exposure if only they had had adequate information. Instead, they were taken by surprise and suffered the consequences. Investors should not take risks that are not expected to be rewarded, and uncertainty caused by poor information is never likely to be rewarded. No investor needs to take this risk, though it may be reasonable to accept less than full transparency for a small part of an investment strategy, for example part of a hedge fund allocation.

Examples of this third category include those equity investors who did not appreciate the full extent of their exposure to technology, media and telecom stocks in early 2000, and who might have curtailed those positions during the bull market if they had been aware. Similar comments can be made of the ignorance (because of deception) of the management of Barings Bank of the speculative derivatives exposures that led to the bank's failure in January 1995. Other examples exist in the financial sector, but this example is particularly relevant to a discussion of wealth management as most of the bank's equity was owned by the Baring Foundation, the philanthropic arm of the Baring family. The foundation was, in the words of its chairman, "grievously wounded" by the bank's collapse and the scale of its charitable work was curtailed thereafter.

The message is that all investors should worry about the information that they need before worrying about issues of investment strategy. This is an unavoidable first step for any investor who wishes to sleep easy at night. If investors are going to risk losing large amounts of money, it is inexcusable for them not to know in advance that this might happen (see Appendix 2 for an illustration of the sort of information that investors should review).

Think about risk before it hits you

Risk attracts much discussion. Risk is about bad outcomes. What constitutes a bad outcome is far from simple. It is determined by each investor (and not by the textbooks). It varies from one investor to another and from investment to investment. If an investor is saving for a pension, or to pay off a mortgage, or to fund a child's education, the bad outcome that matters is the risk of a shortfall from the investment objective. This is different from the risk of a negative return. In Chapter 4, the distinction is drawn between threats to future income (which is of concern to a pensioner) and threats to the value of investments (which may be critical to a cautious short-term investor). This shows that the risk of losing money cannot be a general measure of risk. This means we need to be cautious in the use we make of common metrics such as the standard deviation or volatility of investment returns.

Risk relates to the danger of failing to meet particular objectives. But risk is also the chance of anything happening at intermediate dates which undermines an investor's confidence in that future objective being met. Since those working in the investment business are uncertain about market relationships, it is reasonable for investors to be at least as uncertain. It is also reasonable for their confidence to be shaken by disappointing developments along the way, even if those developments are not surprising to a quantitative analyst. Investors' expectations are naturally updated as time evolves and as their own experience (and everyone else's) grows. So far as the investor is concerned, the perceived risk of a bad outcome will be increased by disappointments before the target date is reached, undermining confidence in the investment strategy.

Recent research by Mark Kritzman and Don Rich on risk measurement has explored this theme – the pattern of investment returns along the way matters to investors, not just the final return at some target date in the future. This focus on the risk of suffering unacceptable losses at any stage before an investor's target date has highlighted the dangers of mismeasuring risk. An investor might accept some low probability of a particular bad outcome occurring after, say, three years. However, the likelihood of that poor threshold being breached at some stage before the end of the three years will be much higher than the investor might expect. The danger is that the investor's attention and judgment are initially drawn only to the complete three-year period. As the time period is extended, the risk of experiencing particularly poor interim results, at some time, can increase dramatically. Advisers should ensure that investors are aware of this danger.

The insights from behavioural finance (see Chapter 2) on investor loss aversion are particularly important here. Disappointing performance disproportionately undermines investor confidence. The risk of this, and its repercussions for the likelihood of achieving longer-term objectives, represents issues that investors need to discuss regularly with their advisers, especially when they are considering moving to a higher-risk strategy.

Research findings on behavioural finance emphasise that investors often attach different importance to achieving different goals. The risk of bad outcomes should be removed, as far as possible, from objectives which the investor regards as most critical to achieve, and, ideally, any high risk of missing objectives should be focused on the nice-to-have but dispensable targets. Investors may then be less likely to react adversely to the disappointments that inevitably accompany risk-based strategies. They will know that such targets are less critical objectives.

A separate issue is whether a bad outcome is itself a measure of risk. An investor who is taken by surprise by a disappointing performance might say, "I had no idea we were running that sort of risk". The simple answer is that performance itself is not a measure of risk. It is easy, but human, to extrapolate from the performance of an investment the risk of that outcome occurring.

The important message is that risk is about the chance of disappointing outcomes. Risk can be managed but disappointing outcomes cannot, and surprising things sometimes happen. However, measuring the volatility of performance, as a check on what the statistical models say is likely, can be helpful in coming to an independent assessment of risk. But it will always be based on a small sample of data. Thus we can attempt to measure only perceived risks. Risks that exist but that we do not have the imagination to perceive will always escape our metrics. There is no solution to this problem of measuring risk, which led Glynn Holton to write: "It is meaningless to ask if a risk metric captures risk. Instead, ask if it is useful."

More often than not, the real problem is that unusual risk-taking is rewarded rather than penalised. We need to avoid drawing the wrong conclusions about the good times as well as the bad times. This theme is captured by a photo at the front of Frank Sortino's and Stephen Satchell's book *Managing Downside Risk in Financial Markets*. It shows Karen Sortino on safari in Africa, petting an intimidating rhino. The caption underneath the photo reads: "Just because you got away with it, doesn't mean you didn't take any risk."

Know your niche

The style of involvement in decision-making is one of the most important issues that investors need to decide. How hands-on or hands-off do they wish to be, and what are their preferences and special areas of investment expertise? This is a natural starting point for discussions for any investor with a new investment adviser.

Some investors like to devote much time and personal effort to their investments. Others prefer to delegate as much as possible to someone they trust. Neither policy is inherently superior, so long as keen investors have grounds for believing that their interventions are likely to add value (or to save value), and disinterested investors are sure that their invest-ment objectives are properly understood by their advisers and that a reliable process of review has been established.

Successful entrepreneurs often have specialist skills that put them in a privileged position in the assessment of new business opportunities in their specialist areas. This role as potential informed investors is likely to open doors to investment opportunities that are not available to other investors. But it will be unclear how these investments should fit into an overall investment strategy and how the entrepreneur should weigh the risks.

Hindsight is a useful guide here. A private investor with specialist knowledge in the technology sector is unlikely to have been able to protect investments in this sector during the bear market of 2000–02. Neither the skills of the investor nor the quality of the venture capital investments would have protected them from that downturn, even if they have subsequently recovered. An even bleaker example can be provided when niche expertise is concentrated on a particular foreign market which may be subject to marked currency risk. Each specialist investor will best be able to assess these risks individually. Such investors need to consider whether and how far to diversify away from their niche area to provide a downside layer of protection, or a safety net for at least part of their wealth.

How much should be allocated to such rainy-day investments will depend on personal circumstances, preferences and willingness to tolerate extreme disappointment. For example, there is great scope for disappointment from individual venture capital investments, even when skilfully selected. For successful venture capitalists, it is likely that the risk of an individual investment failing is greater than the likelihood of that investment being a runaway success. But one runaway success will more than pay for several failures. One temptation for specialist investors will be to try to diversify into related areas. In these cases, a quiet review of the behavioural biases that commonly affect decision-making could prove invaluable (see Chapter 2). Investors should always ask themselves the following questions:

- Am I moving away from my natural habitat where I am confident of my "edge"?
- Do my skills and specific expertise translate to this new market?
- Will I have the same degree of control?
- Do I have the same degree of confidence in my access to information and in my feel for these new businesses?

If an investor cannot be confident of replicating the ingredients of success which were successfully employed in the original niche, there will be no basis for expecting the extra performance needed to justify the risk that goes with this pattern of concentrated private investments. In any event, an investor should ask whether this new venture provides the diversification of risk that is being sought. It may be better to seek a professionally managed approach to financial investments for part of the overall wealth. If all goes well, it is most likely that the "natural habitat" investments will perform better than the diversified investments. But this simply reflects the old saying that to become wealthy, it is necessary to concentrate expertise, but that to conserve wealth, it is necessary to diversify. However, risk concentration where there is no information advantage is a recipe for ruin.

Wealthy individuals are often entrepreneurs, and their own businesses will often represent the bulk of their wealth. Although the risks and opportunities of each business will vary considerably, when considering overall investment risk, it is usually appropriate to treat the business, which will typically be a private company, as if it represents a concentrated exposure to equity-market risk. A mistake that is often made is to allow familiarity with a business to cloud perceptions of that business's intrinsic risk. Just because it is not possible to observe the volatility of the stock price of a private company does not mean that its value is not highly volatile. Whether a company is quoted or unquoted, an investor's familiarity with it – even the knowledge that the company is well managed – is no guide to its lack of volatility or risk as an investment. Successful entrepreneurs often have such investments dominating their risk profile. Allowances need to be made for this when setting investment policy for financial investments that are held separately from the business. Typically, and depending upon financial needs, this will result in cautious recommendations for such investments, even if the investor is tolerant of financial uncertainty. Not surprisingly, most investors are concerned to conserve as well as to accumulate, to have a layer of downside protection as well as upside potential.

War chests and umbrellas

Where financial investments are being managed alongside business investments, they may constitute a liquid war chest to help fund future new opportunities, which may arise at short notice. In this case, the time horizon is likely to be short, with a premium put on the stability of capital values.

Alternatively, a family with a volatile business may wish to build up a rainy-day umbrella fund, either to help the business through tough times which the family expects to be short-lived, or to provide an alternative source of income should the business fail. Many family business investors do not trust the umbrella of loan facilities willingly extended by banks during good times to be available when it starts raining seriously and have therefore arranged financial "umbrellas" from their own resources. In such cases, a low-risk umbrella investment strategy would be expected to include a significant allocation to investment-grade bonds, and possibly inflation-linked government bonds.

Base currency

Most investors have no difficulty in defining their base currency. This is the currency of their home country: the currency in which they measure their wealth and in which they formulate their expenditure plans. Anything outside this base represents foreign currency and entails a risk of adverse fluctuations against the base currency.

The position is more ambiguous for many investors. Most private investors in Latin America, the Middle East and parts of East Asia use the US dollar as the accounting currency for their investments. But a convenient accounting currency is not necessarily a base currency. For many of these investors, the role of the US dollar will be different from the role it plays for a purely domestic US investor. Meanwhile, there are now tens of thousands of expatriate international executives, many of whom have earnings and residency in one currency and nationality and perhaps also retirement plans in another. This ambiguity alters the benchmark for measuring success or disappointment from investment returns. It is also particularly important in constructing cautious investment strategies needed to meet particular commitments in a range of currencies. Consider, for example, a European working in New York, subject to severe earnings volatility and with alimony payments in euros, or a financially constrained foundation with commitments to support projects in more than one country. In both cases, the concept of base currency and currency risk management need addressing.

Discussions with international investors whose investments are typically accounted for in US dollars suggest that this currency ambiguity is rarely considered an important issue in Latin America, is recognised as a potential issue in the Middle East, and is regarded as a material concern by many in Asia. Asian investors may have their investments reported and measured in US dollars, but they are concerned by any marked depreciation of the US dollar against the yen and other Asian currencies. One practical and easy way to address this is to manage the investments, in particular the cash and fixed-income investments, through a basket of currencies that approximately meets their particular needs. For example, the Monetary Authority of Singapore has for many years pursued a policy of stabilising the value of the Singapore dollar against a basket of currencies of Singapore's major trading partners and competitors. In other words, account is taken of fluctuations in the yen, the euro, sterling, other Asian currencies and the US dollar.

The intention is not to reflect views on which currencies are likely to strengthen or weaken, but rather to have a view, which may be revised from time to time, as to what investors feel to be financially safe. However, they will still need to accommodate the accounting impact of exchange rate swings on their investments in their reporting currency.

2 Understand your behaviour

Insights from behavioural finance

The opportunity to hold wide-ranging investment seminars with wealthy families or institutional investors is one of the privileges that can go with the role of an investment strategy adviser. They are invaluable opportunities to listen and to learn from investors about their goals, experiences and preferences. But sometimes it is possible to hear something and still not understand. On the wall of my office is a framed 500,000 Reichsmark note, which was issued by the German central bank in 1923 during the hyper-inflation that destroyed much of the private wealth of German families. It was given to me by an investor whose family decided to implement an equity-oriented strategy for their new foundation, despite my strong advice that it should have a significant anchor of fixed income. "Peter," I was told, "you simply do not understand the perils of inflation."

In this case I had heard but not grasped the depth of the family's concern about inflation – in other words, their strong preference to avoid exposure to long-term inflation risk. In recent years, the introduction of inflation-linked government bonds has made the hedging of inflation risk easier. However, advances in behavioural finance also provide a framework that enables us to better explore and understand investor preferences, and to delve into the biases that affect how we take decisions and how these may cause us to deviate from the textbook assumptions of how rational investors ought to behave. An appreciation of these influences is a prerequisite for ensuring that appropriate investment strategies are adopted by investors.

These behavioural insights have emerged from the application in finance and economics of insights from experimental psychology. Traditionally, economics and finance have focused on models that assume rationality. There is a well-known story about economists that highlights a key message of the efficient markets hypothesis, which itself underlies what can be called traditional finance:

> An economist [was] strolling down the street with a companion. They come upon a $100 bill lying on the ground, and as the companion reaches down to pick it up, the economist says: "Don't bother – if it were a genuine $100 bill, someone would have already picked it up."

The economist's theoretical prior belief tells him that the anomalous observation must be a data problem. The behaviourist, however, would want to examine the evidence, in other words to conduct an experiment before concluding that the bill was probably a fake, without any prior belief one way or the other. This is a profound difference in approach which has important implications for investment advice.

Traditional models in finance can be caricatured as follows: *"If investors are rational, and if markets are efficient, then investors ought to be behaving as follows."* Almost all investors have been shown these models, for example in the "risk" and "return" trade-offs of an "efficient frontier" analysis, which implicitly assume that markets are "well behaved" and "efficient", and that investors should prefer diversified to undiversified portfolios of risky investments. These models remain useful (and are used to provide illustrations of policy alternatives in Chapter 4), but investors should have some understanding of their potential weaknesses. A simple illustration will suffice. Many people buy lottery tickets; they expect to lose money, but they hope to gain riches. Traditional finance implicitly finds this behaviour inefficient. Nevertheless, it can be rational as it provides the best legal way to have at least some chance (however remote) of securing riches in the short term. If you do not buy a lottery ticket, it is certain that you will not win.

Behavioural finance uses research from psychology that describes how individuals actually behave, and applies those insights to finance. This has led to two major streams of research. The first concerns how investor behaviour might not accord with the textbook concept of the efficient rational investor. The other is how less than fully rational investors may cause market prices to deviate from their fundamental values. The first strand of work, how investors behave, is used to look at how investment strategy should accommodate what investors want. The second strand of work, how investors' behaviour may affect how markets function, is used in Chapter 6 to look at whether active investment managers are likely to find it easier to outperform (for which the short answer is "no").

Recognition of the contribution that behavioural analysis is now making in financial economics was reflected in 2002 with the award of the Nobel Prize in economics to a professor of psychology, Daniel Kahneman (who won it jointly with Vernon Smith). This work has grown out of a series of experiments that have led to strong conclusions about the biases that affect how individuals take decisions and how they form preferences. A good understanding of investor preferences is critical in giving investment advice, and an understanding of investor biases is important in understanding how investors may respond to particular events or developments. For a psychologist, if biases are weaknesses which could injure the interests of an investor, investment advisers should not pander to them. This indicates, for example, a need for investor education. But investors and their advisers should be aware of these biases since they will help determine reactions to a range of predictable market developments.

Investor biases

Psychologists have documented systematic patterns of bias in how people form views and take decisions. Although the primary research did not usually involve investors or investment decisions, it is directly applicable to investments. These biases influence how we form investment opinions, and then how we take investment decisions. For example, the observation that most car drivers think that they are better than average drivers reflects a general characteristic of optimism and wishful thinking. It would be naive to think that this characteristic did not affect our investment views. Furthermore, people are systematically overconfident in the reliability of their own judgments, for example in assessing the chance of something happening or not happening. Overconfidence in turn is reflected in self-attribution, for example attributing to their own innate ability and unusual skill any success that they enjoy. For example, individuals who are unusually well paid might interpret this as evidence of their own unusual ability.

Correspondingly, self-attribution leads to a natural tendency to attribute any disappointment to bad luck rather than a lack of skill. Investment examples of this would be provided by most accounts of investment manager underperformance that an investor might have heard: outperformance reflects skill, while underperformance reflects bad luck. This is also associated with hindsight bias, whereby individuals are sure, after the event, that they expected whatever happened to happen: "It was obvious it was going to happen, wasn't it?" Or, if the outcome was a bad outcome: "It was a disaster waiting to happen."

A similar bias is representativeness and sample size neglect, whereby individuals are too quick to conclude that they understand developments on the basis of too little information. For example, in 100 years of stock and bond market performance history, five separate (non-overlapping) 20-year periods can be observed (which is a small sample). Subject to the periodicity of the data, any number of overlapping 20-year periods can also be constructed – for example, 20 years to last year, 20 years to the year before last, and so on. This will help to slice and dice the data more finely and enable more fancy statistical analysis. Despite this, the inescapable fact is that we do not have many 20-year observations of performance to conclude much (purely using performance numbers) about, for example, the likelihood of stocks outperforming bonds over 20-year periods. There are more sophisticated techniques that can be used to get a handle on the same issue (see Chapter 3), but it remains common to draw strong conclusions from small data sets when that is the only evidence available. In such circumstances, it is safer to be circumspect about any conclusions drawn from limited data.

Another bias (probably just displayed) is conservatism, which arises when it is widely recognised that the available data are insufficient to support strong conclusions. In this case, it is a common error to place too little weight on the available evidence, or even to disregard it and to rely solely on prior expectations.

Lastly, there is belief perseverance which concerns the evidence that people cling to prior opinions for too long when confronted with contrary evidence that would be sufficient to convince equally talented newcomers to the field. In this way, individuals demonstrate a reluctance to search for evidence that contradicts their previous views, because they are reluctant to write off past investments in their own human capital, despite it being clear that they are partly obsolescent.

Even when investors are able to sit back and consider each of these potential biases dispassionately, there is no escape from the danger of regret risk. Regret is the emotion individuals feel if they can easily imagine having acted in a way that would have led to a more favourable outcome. Early behavioural studies emphasised that regret from taking action which was subsequently unprofitable is usually felt more acutely than regret from decisions to take no action which were subsequently equally costly. The classic investment example is the different reactions to a fall in the price of investments. If it is a recently acquired investment, there is generally more regret than if it is a long-standing investment. For investors, this leads to the common dilemma of how and when to implement new invest-ment decisions, even if investment risk arguments point to the desirability of immediate implementation (see Chapter 5 for a discussion about the issues involved in implementing investment strategy changes).

Recent studies have also found that aggressive investors may regret losses (or missed opportunities) from inaction more than losses from action. However, cautious investors may experience anxiety about the possible consequences of making different policy choices. This can lead to procrastination and inaction, even when an investor agrees that a particular course of action is necessary. This is the tendency to avoid taking any action for fear that it will turn out to have been less than ideal, for example in terms of timing.

An important theme of new research is that regret about a disappointing outcome following a change in strategy was found to be reduced if the decision was justified. This has led to a distinction between regret about bad decisions and regret about bad outcomes. These do not always go together: sometimes bad decisions do not lead to bad outcomes. For example, a drunk driver may drive home without an accident but still regret and blame himself for his irresponsibility. In investment, the parallel is with instances when undue risk-taking happens to be rewarded. The fact that an investor got away with it does not mean that the risks were reasonable, nor that it was a good decision. Sometimes a bad outcome results from a good decision, for example if the drunk takes a taxi home but by chance the taxi is involved in an accident. The drunk regrets getting into that particular taxi but does not blame himself for his decision to take a taxi. If an unprofitable investment decision was unjustified, the investor will blame himself (or the adviser). If an investment decision was justified, the investor may regret the decision or its timing but will understand why it was taken.

Thus good process should not only lead to more considered (and, hopefully, better) decision-making, but should also support stability and confidence in the existence of a "steady hand at the tiller". This should help control the potentially harmful effect of some of the biases that can influence investment decision-making. One of the best ways to manage the impact of these may be to draw attention to them and discuss their potential impact before important investment decisions are taken.

Investor preferences

If investor biases should be managed, investor preferences should be respected and reflected in investment strategy, in so far as it is both feasible and sensible (after discussing the various issues with an investment adviser).

There are two particular areas of investor preference that have been highlighted by behavioural finance. The first (perhaps not surprisingly) is loss aversion, which in behavioural finance fills the role of risk aversion in traditional finance. The second is mental accounting, which reflects the way in which investors assign sums of money to different actual or notional accounts for different purposes with varying degrees of risk tolerance depending upon the importance of achieving the particular objective. For example, an individual's summer vacation money will be in a different mental account (and probably a different actual account) from pension savings.

Loss aversion

Traditional finance assumes that investors behave rationally and evaluate the risk and potential return of investment strategies in terms of their expected utility or satisfaction. There are different ways of calibrating utility, but they all have the characteristic that they represent assumptions about how investors should be expected to express preferences. They have the additional characteristic that they can be modelled mathematically, which is convenient for modellers. Much less convenient is the widespread evidence that these rational utility models do not reflect how people view the prospect of financial gains or losses.

This has been reflected in prospect theory, which is built upon a wide range of experiments showing that people will take quite large risks to have some chance of avoiding otherwise certain losses, but that they are quick to bank any winnings. Investment banks tap into this investor preference through sales of highly profitable principal-protected structured products, which provide downside protection with the prospect of some combination of leveraged positive returns. In other words, they offer a seductive combination of "little fear and much hope". This relationship between the disutility or dissatisfaction that comes from losses and the utility or satisfaction that comes from gains is captured in the so-called coefficient of loss aversion, which across a wide range of experiments has come out at a value of around two. This measures how much more highly investors weigh losses than they weigh gains.

These experiments have highlighted the importance of how a question is framed or asked as a determinant of the reaction to it. This is of fundamental importance in managing private wealth because there is an inconsistency between the widespread desire to have stable, or at least protected investment values, and the desire to have a stable income which is financed by those investments (see Chapter 4). These wishes are incompatible, because only long-dated government bonds, which are volatile, can guarantee a stable income over time. This highlights the need for investors to be educated as well as asked the appropriate questions, framed in an appropriate way. The classic investment example of the importance of framing is the difference in participation rates in voluntary 401(k) defined contribution corporate pension plans in the United States. Plans that automatically enrol new employees, while giving them the right to opt out, show significantly higher employee participation rates than plans where individuals have to opt in to participate.

Mental accounting and behavioural portfolio theory

A division of investments between safety-first accounts or portfolios to meet basic needs and more aggressive "aspirational" accounts to meet more speculative, less critical, or simply more distant objectives is one of the predictions of the mental accounting framework of behavioural finance. This approach is not found anywhere in the traditional finance textbooks but it is common (some would say common sense) in everyday experience, as the following examples illustrate.

The subsistence farmer. Subsistence farmers often grow two types of crops: food for the family and cash crops with volatile prices. Growing food represents the safety-first portfolio. The allocation of land to growing food is determined first by basic needs, such as family size. The remaining land is allocated to the cash crop, which is the more speculative opportunity to raise living standards – in other words, the aspirational portfolio.

The champion poker player. Greg "Fossilman" Raymer gives this account of how he and his wife kept their "aspirational account" separate from their essential "safety-first" cash when he started out on his successful career at the poker table:

> I started getting steady wins, but I was now married, and [my wife] was becoming increasingly concerned about the time I was spending on it. She'd also hear horror stories about players bankrupting their families. In the end we made a deal: I was allowed a $1,000 poker bankroll on condition it stayed separate from our savings. And if I lost it all, I'd never play again. It never got to that.

The individual investor in traded options. Such segmentation is widespread in the management of personal wealth. The point is illustrated by a money manager who had an agreement with his wife that he could buy financial options for his personal account, up to a level set by the level of interest income on their family cash holdings plus his accumulated investment gains (from option trading). There is evidence that many individual investors in options use interest income from cash to fund purchases of options, thus providing another illustration of a separation of accounts for downside protection and upside potential layers in personal finances.

The central bank foreign exchange reserve manager. Even central banks demonstrate this layering of investment resources. The first purpose of a central bank's foreign exchange reserves is to fund whatever market intervention might be necessary to defend the exchange rate of the national currency. This means investing in high-quality, highly liquid, short-dated securities, in particular US treasury securities. This is the safety-first portfolio. For more conservative central banks, this downside protection layer would also include, if appropriate, investment holdings designed to hedge any foreign currency borrowing for which the central bank is responsible. Historically, many central banks have also held substantial reserves of gold bullion. These were intended to have a different, longer-term capital preservation and confidence-building role, which set them apart from short-term liquid reserves.

In recent years a number of central banks have accumulated unprecedented levels of foreign exchange reserves, far in excess of the likely need to support their currencies in the short term. This part of their reserves represents an endowment fund for future generations, as well as an insurance policy against the threat of humiliating currency crises. At the same time, there has been a move towards investing this part of the reserves in a separate fund, with different objectives from short-term liquidity. This often represents the aspirational portfolio. The investment of the reserves of these central banks parallels the layered pyramid of behavioural portfolio theory.

The pension plan. In the late 1980s when I joined a major UK pension fund, its near-term pension benefit payments were secured through a portfolio of short-dated government bonds that we called the Seven Year Cash Certain Fund. This was the pension fund's safety-first portfolio. At that stage the bulk of other assets were held in a number of equity-oriented balanced funds, which might be described as having provided the pension fund's aspirational portfolio.

Investment strategy and behavioural finance

Each of these examples, from the champion poker player to the pension plan, shows a natural process of segmentation of risk-taking, with separate allocations to different accounts, each with distinctive risk tolerances and time horizons dictated by particular objectives. Above all, this segmentation provides an easy-to-monitor, keep-it-simple management information system for individuals and institutions.

This mental accounting also helps to discipline future behaviour by highlighting deviations from decisions that have already been taken. For example, in a family context, someone might say, "no, we will not use that money to buy a new car, it's our pension savings"; or, in an institution, "no, we can't use that cash to finance a private equity opportunity, we need it to pay pensions; go and check if we have enough liquidity left in the private equity account". Traditional finance does not segment financial resources in this way. It treats all a family's financial resources or all a pension plan's resources as a unified whole and seeks a total wealth-efficient solution to considering risk, return and investment strategy. It also considers money to be fungible (cash in this account is the same as cash in another account if it is owned by the same person). Furthermore, and this is of great importance, traditional finance considers the relationships that may exist between the investments and the objectives or obligations of the different accounts. Separate accounting, with separate strategies designed independently for each account, would ignore these relationships. This can be a major inefficiency in the widespread practice of mental accounting, which should therefore be adopted with caution.

Mental accounting helps financial resources to be targeted for different purposes. Each person will have a different risk tolerance for achieving different objectives. Some goals are critical, but others are just nice to have. And decisions will be influenced by regulations that impinge on taxed and tax-exempt accounts, current-generation resources and trust or other tax-efficient accounts for future generations, and philanthropic accounts.

A more general example of mental accounting is quoted by Meir Statman and Vincent Wood in *Investment Temperament*, when they describe the pattern of responses to the following question in the Fidelity Investments Asset Allocation Planner:

> *If you could increase your chances of improving your returns by taking more risk would you:*
> 1 *Be willing to take a lot more risk with all of your money*
> 2 *Be willing to take a lot more risk with some of your money*
> 3 *Be willing to take a little more risk with all of your money*
> 4 *Be willing to take a little more risk with some of your money*

Overwhelmingly, the responses indicated a willingness to take either a lot or a little more risk with some of their money. This indicates a preference to segment or layer risk-taking. This is generally considered to be at odds with the traditional risk–return trade-off commonly presented to investors addressing the performance and risk of the total portfolio, which would presume taking either a little or a lot more risk with all of the money. However, if a traditional efficient portfolio comprises a mixture of a holding of risk-free assets and an allocation to market risk, these responses would make sense in terms of being willing to shift some resources out of a safe haven investment into a market risk portfolio. In other words, the responses could be consistent with traditional finance as well as behavioural portfolio theory.

Parameter uncertainty and behavioural finance

Investors often like to test the reasonableness of major decisions from different perspectives before committing themselves. This is a rational way to proceed with decision-making when faced with uncertainty about the reliability of models or approaches. One of the themes that pervade this book is that the parameters used in financial models are subject to marked degrees of uncertainty, with some elements more uncertain than others. There is nothing new about this.

One consequence is that even in the traditional model of rational markets and rational investors, investors have not generally faced a unique solution to their investment problems, although that may be what they were offered. The exception is the case of a minimum risk-hedging strategy (see Chapter 3). For all other strategies, quantitative analysis may provide supposedly unique answers to asset allocation problems. But the investment markets have never provided such clear answers. Instead, our understanding of the uncertain relationships between markets has always involved a trade-off between broadly appropriate alternative investment strategies which appear to lie within the range of what is best described as the "fuzzy frontier". This means that in any particular situation there will always be strategies that are demonstrably inefficient or that involve a clearly inappropriate risk profile. But there will also be a range of strategies that are each broadly appropriate, given our current state of knowledge of markets and the risk tolerance of investors. This can give a surprisingly wide scope for the investment preferences of principals or fiduciaries to be reflected in investment strategy, while still staying consistent with the overriding desire to adhere to their goals and objectives. It also makes it more likely that investors will find that independent ways of presenting strategy, such as the behaviourist-layered pyramid approach, provide intuitively attractive cross-checks on the traditional quantitative approach.

The idea of a fuzzy frontier can be traced back to work on uncertainty in scientific measurement dating from the 1960s. Much of the uncertainty in measurement that we know exists cannot be adequately captured by statistics. This has potential applications in many different fields. One of its starting points is that we often do not know precisely how to categorise items that are being analysed. In the United States in the 1990s, this was reflected in the debate about whether US quoted multinational corporations with US boards of directors but extensive overseas operations were really US companies. This was captured in the title of a 1990 article in the *Harvard Business Review*, "Who Is Us?", by Robert Reich, a former US labour secretary. In reality, this is an issue that the operations staff of any investment firm wrestle with every day. For example, should the common equity of an Israeli firm listed on NASDAQ be classified as a US stock or an emerging-market stock? For some accounting systems, should a convertible bond be classified as debt or as equity? In finance, these classification issues are routinely put to one side in investment analysis and yet they undermine the precision with which policy conclusions can be drawn.

Traditional finance, behavioural finance and evolution

In the past few years steps have been taken towards synthesising traditional finance with the insights from behavioural finance, but there is much further to go before an integrated approach is agreed which combines both the comprehensiveness of "traditional" finance with the more recent insights from behavioural finance.

Some things are already clear. First, it is important for investors and their advisers to benefit from the insights of behavioural finance in order to better understand the influences on their own behaviour and preferences. Advice and strategy can then be adapted to accommodate that. This does not provide an excuse for ignoring the fundamental principles of diversification, correlations between different investments or the need to tailor policies to the time horizon of investment objectives. Equally, it would be arrogant to suggest that it is always poor practice for individuals to want to purchase the investment equivalent of lottery tickets, as this may be an efficient way of maximising the chances of acquiring riches. Furthermore, behavioural finance helps advisers gain a better understanding of why investors' portfolios are structured as they are, how investors are likely to respond to any instance of disappointing performance and the nature of their strong preferences.

As Meir Statman writes in *Behavioral Portfolios: Hope for Riches and Protection from Poverty*: "We might lament the fact that people are attracted to lotteries, or we might accept it, and help people strike a balance between hope for riches and protection from poverty."

Andrew Lo, Harris & Harris Group professor and director of the Laboratory for Financial Engineering at MIT, puts it more starkly when he writes in *The Adaptive Markets Hypothesis* that "for all financial market participants, survival is the only objective that matters".

Against this background, the most important first step may be to start discussions of investment strategy with an assessment of whether an investor has sufficient wealth to guarantee survival. In other words, does the investor have sufficient resources to hedge against the risk of shortfall from critical objectives by investing in liability- or objective-matching government bonds? If the answer is yes, the investor can choose between objectives, and if so wished, pursue a high-risk strategy to have some chance, however remote, of achieving the least critical objectives. This theme is developed further in the next chapter.

3 Market investment returns: will the markets make me rich?

You know the answer. If you are a portfolio manager or, even better, a hedge fund manager, the answer is quite possibly "yes". Otherwise, the likely answer is "no". Skill, luck, and investment manager fees, particularly hedge fund fees, are discussed in Chapter 9. This chapter looks at expectations and uncertainties for future market returns. This matters in designing an investment strategy, as well as in assessing how saving and wealth planning exercises are undertaken by investment advisers.

This chapter has two strong messages: that equity returns are likely to be less favourable in the 21st century than they were in the 20th, but that – barring a resurgence of inflation – government bond returns should be more favourable (particularly because of the innovation of inflation-linked government bonds). The main qualification to this is that, within wide ranges, we just do not know how markets are going to behave, even over extended periods of time.

Sources of investment performance

Investment performance can be described as coming from six sources:

1 Treasury bill yield. The short term (less than one year, and typically 1–6 months) risk-free rate of interest.

2 Inflation-indexed government bond yield. The long-term inflation-risk-free rate of interest. It is unclear whether these inflation-indexed bonds need to offer a premium return over Treasury bills, but they probably will.

3 Conventional Treasury bond yield. The long-term nominal risk-free rate of interest. This rate of interest is subject to the risk of unexpectedly high inflation. It will include a premium over inflation-linked bonds to compensate for expected inflation, and probably also a margin above this for the uncertainty of that inflation (see below).

4 Market risk premium. The compensation that any rational saver should seek in return for putting money or future income at risk of loss. The market provides this reward for bearing "market risk". This is most obviously reflected in the equity risk premium (the amount by which equities are expected to outperform bonds or cash) and the credit risk premium (the extra yield paid on corporate bonds to compensate for the risk that a company might default). Less obviously, market risk premiums appear systematically to be offered in return for accepting various types of insurance risk and for different types of equity risk (for example, small company risk separately from equity market risk). These last two are discussed in Chapter 7 (equity investing), Chapter 9 (hedge funds) and Chapter 11 (real estate).

5 Investment manager skill. Generates investment performance (or alpha) that is separate from the performance of the market (or beta). Frequently, investment performance that managers attribute to their skill (which is an expensive, scarce commodity) gets jumbled up with different aspects of market investment performance (which can normally be accessed easily and inexpensively). One example is where managers who are responsible for asset allocation between stocks and bonds might normally overweight equities, because equities are expected to outperform bonds. This, though, is a reward for greater risk-taking, not a reward for skill.

6 Noise. What unskilful managers introduce to the performance of investors' portfolios. Noise is often described as "alpha" when it is positive. (Sceptics have described alpha as "the average error term".) Distinguishing noise from skill is one of the most difficult tasks for investors. There are always likely to be more unskilled "noise" managers with marketable track records than skilled managers who, in addition to being skilled, also have a marketable record at any point in time. Noise will normally bring some extra volatility; it will also incur fees and distract investors, wasting their valuable time.

The first three sources can be accessed easily and inexpensively by anyone, through direct holdings of government securities. Equity market risk can be accessed inexpensively through index funds or exchange traded funds. Some investment markets and some aspects of market risk premiums (for example, private equity) can be accessed only if the investor is willing to take a view on investment manager skill. The sources of hedge fund performance are discussed in Chapter 9.

The pattern of returns from exposure to market risk can also be re-engineered through "structured products" which contain combinations of embedded options with exposure to particular markets. These do not generate performance, but they can provide insurance against the risk of disappointing outcomes in ways which may suit the investors.

Safe havens that provide different kinds of shelter

If investors take no risk, they should not expect to receive a premium return. But what is risk-free for one investor may be risky for another:

- For a short-term investor, Treasury bills represent the zero risk investment that provides the highest level of guaranteed income, and capital protection over the short term.
- For an insurance company, which has particular amounts to pay at certain dates in the future, an investment in Treasury bills would risk exposure to a future fall in interest rates which would cause a shortfall from the amounts that were due to be paid. For this insurance company, a tailored mixture of conventional Treasury bonds would provide the lowest-risk investments. Ideally, the bonds should be zero coupon, or pure discount bonds, which mature on the dates the insurance company needs to make its payments. (See Appendix 1 for a definition.) In this case, perfect matching could be achieved.
- For an individual, a pension fund or an endowment, concerned to protect future income, inflation-linked Treasury bonds provide the low-risk investment, insuring against adverse inflation and adverse real interest rate surprises. Taxation complicates the position, and investors need to consider which investments, and if appropriate, which investment objectives, should be targeted with taxable accounts and which with tax-exempt accounts (see Chapter 6).

Each of these investors has a different safe-haven investment: Treasury bills for the short-term investor; conventional fixed-income Treasury bonds for the insurance company; and inflation-linked government bonds for the prospective pensioner (or endowment). Each investor would be taking a risk to venture outside their own safe haven – and they should not do so unless they expect to be rewarded for taking that risk.

Which government bonds will perform best?

In the examples above, the insurance company does not need to be paid a premium yield by the taxpayer to be persuaded to hold Treasury bonds, nor does the pension fund or endowment to hold inflation-linked government bonds. This means that it is unclear how much premium return, if any, should be expected from bonds, whether indexed or not, over cash. Cautious long-term investors should be aware that it is common for bond managers erroneously to assume that a long-dated government bond benchmark suggests a high degree of tolerance for risk-taking by the investor.

This means that different groups of investors have their own separate natural or preferred habitats in different segments of the government bond market. From time to time this can affect the shape of the yield curve (that is, the pattern of government bond yields). This can sometimes make it hard to rationalise the differences in interest rates that are paid to different groups of investors by the government. The barriers that can limit attempts to arbitrage away apparent pricing anomalies are looked at in Chapter 6.

The normal pattern for the relationship between different maturities of government bonds, in other words the normal shape of the yield curve, has been an area of extensive, and often inconclusive, research in macroeconomics. The historical pattern is clear on two things. First, there has normally been an upward-sloping yield curve – in other words, longer-dated Treasury bonds have offered higher yields and returns than shorter-dated government bonds, in particular Treasury bills. (See Appendix 1 for definitions of Treasury bonds and Treasury bills.) Second, the extent of this premium varies over time. This is often described as the term premium that short-term investors need to be offered to tempt them to buy longer-dated bonds (because such bonds are subject to price volatility). But insurance companies do not need to be paid a term premium because longer maturities provide their "natural habitat".

More recently, since the introduction (see below) of the markets in inflation-linked government bonds, there has been growing emphasis on this premium in conventional government bond yields as an inflation risk premium. Pensioners should not normally buy conventional bonds unless they offer compensation not only for the expected rate of inflation, but also for the risk that the actual rate of inflation might be higher than the rate that is expected. This is the inflation risk premium. (This ignores taxation issues, which are important in deciding between different types of government bonds.)

If this inflation risk premium is present, the difference between the yield on nominal government bonds and the yield on inflation-linked bonds might increase as the maturity of bonds increases (though this might not happen in practice because of other influences, such as taxation). This is because uncertainty about price levels always increases as we look further into the future. A market expectation for inflation can be deduced from the difference between yields on conventional government bonds and the yields on these indexed bonds. This is the so-called "break-even" inflation rate. (If inflation turns out at this rate, an investor will get, approximately, the same return from holding indexed government bonds as from conventional treasuries of the same maturity.) But whether the break-even rate really is a market forecast for inflation is controversial.

Is the break-even inflation rate the market's forecast?

Inflation-indexed government bonds are now available in each major financial market. They were introduced in the UK in 1981 and since then they have been made available in Australia (1985), Canada (1991), Sweden (1994), the United States (1997), France (1998) and most recently Japan (2004). A number of emerging markets, including Brazil, Israel and South Africa have also made extensive use of inflation-linked bonds. They now represent an instrument whose characteristics investors in each country should understand. In the US these bonds are known as Treasury Inflation Protected Securities, or TIPS, and that acronym is used here to refer to any inflation-linked government bond, not just those issued by the US government.

Those unfamiliar with inflation-indexed bonds are advised to check the difference in yields from conventional and index-linked issues of government bonds. Tables showing yields and break-even inflation rates in different markets are regularly published in the *Financial Times*, but they can be deduced from any table of government bond prices and yields. TIPS are indicated by the letter "i" in tables of US Treasury bond yields (for example, in the *Wall Street Journal*). The same classification rule is used for French government issues linked to the euro-zone inflation rate (early issues are linked to the French price level).

The difference between the yield on inflation-linked and conventional government bonds of the same maturity is known as the break-even rate of inflation. (In principle, it should be the difference in yield between two zero-coupon bonds of the same maturity.) This is affected by a number of technical factors which may mean that it is not a true market forecast for inflation. These include the following:

- An inflation risk premium. This would cause the break-even rate to be higher than the market's forecast for inflation.
- Taxation differences. These can distort the relationship between inflation-linked

and conventional government bonds. Tax treatment of inflation-linked bonds differs among countries. In the United States, for example, taxable investors must pay tax on both the real yield and the inflation accrual. So when inflation (or expected inflation) increases, a fall in bond prices is needed to keep the after-tax real yield unchanged, and vice versa for reductions in inflation expectations. By contrast, in the UK income tax is levied only on the coupon of inflation-linked government bonds, not on the inflation compensation on the outstanding principal. So UK taxable investors have an incentive to hold shorter-dated index-linked bonds as their tax treatment is more favourable than that of short-dated conventional bonds. To the extent that the prices of inflation-linked bonds are driven by taxable investors rather than tax-exempt investors, this can influence the break-even inflation rate.

◪ Regulation and valuation rules for tax exempt pension funds and insurance companies. These can cause concentrations of demand for particular segments of the conventional and inflation-linked markets, leading to valuation anomalies which require particularly long time horizons to arbitrage. This can be reflected in differences in break-even inflation rates over different maturities (and can represent investment opportunities for long-term investors who are guided by their own financial needs rather than arbitrary rules or benchmarks). It may also be a reflection of the lesser liquidity of inflation-linked rather than conventional government bond markets (see Chapter 6).

◪ Biases in the measurement of inflation by the official indices used in calculating the uplifted value of indexed bonds. In principle, these biases would be reflected in the break-even rate of inflation. For example, if it was believed that indexed bonds were more than compensated for inflation because of biases in the index, their price would be bid up (and their yield bid down) and the recorded break-even rate of inflation would be higher than the expected rate of inflation.

These factors can cause the break-even rate to differ from an inflation forecast and such differences might vary between countries and between maturities of bonds. But as a first approximation, the break-even rate is the best "rule of thumb" there is for a market forecast of inflation. If a long-term investor has strong views that the break-even rate is likely to prove either overoptimistic or overpessimistic, these views should reasonably influence how the investor moves away from the safety of inflation-linked bonds in implementing strategy. Investors whose risk-free investment is an inflation-linked government bond should have a strategic position in conventional government bonds if they expect conventional bonds to provide an adequate reward for expected inflation and a risk premium above it. In other words, such investors should regard the insurance offered by inflation linked bonds as too expensive.

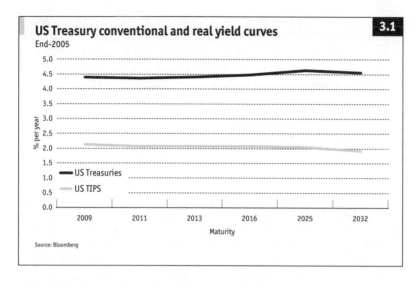

US Treasury conventional and real yield curves `3.1`
End-2005

Source: Bloomberg

What premium return should bond investors expect?

It is not normally in doubt that the government will make the payments it is obliged to on its debt, but how those payments on different types of government debt relate to each other is still unclear.

We know that during the 20th century US long-dated bonds delivered a premium return over Treasury bills of 0.7% a year and that the international average was 0.5%, although this may well have been less than investors were expecting in advance. However, it is unclear how much premium, if any, should be expected from inflation-linked government bonds over Treasury bills. The experience to date is strongly influenced by the monetary policy background and the tax regime in the countries concerned and is simply too short to be conclusive. John Campbell, Morton L. and Carole S. Olshan professor of economics at Harvard University, and Robert Shiller, Stanley B. Resor professor of economics at Yale University, in their study before the introduction of the TIPS market in the United States, said that their "best guess" for the inflation risk premium in conventional government bonds yields "might be 50–100 basis points for a five-year zero-coupon nominal bond" and that "long-term indexed debt ... does not seem likely to have a large risk premium and might even have a negative risk premium". In other words, inflation-linked bonds might, normally, be expected to underperform conventional government bonds by 0.5–1% a year, and over long periods they may perform little or no better (conceivably even worse) than Treasury bills.

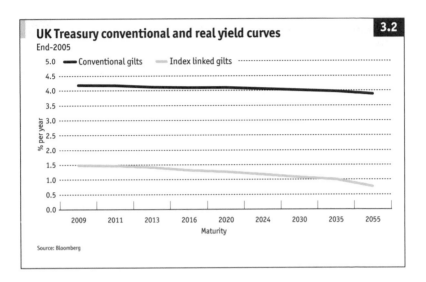

UK Treasury conventional and real yield curves
End-2005

3.2

Source: Bloomberg

The conclusions in deriving assumptions for modelling investment strategy can be summarised as follows:

- Inflation-linked bonds should provide a benchmark for long-term investors just as Treasury bills provide a benchmark for short-term investors.
- They may provide only a modest premium return over Treasury bills. A reasonable working assumption would be 0.25% a year.

Conventional bonds are likely to provide an inflation risk premium over inflation-linked bonds of perhaps on average 0.75% a year, but this will be lowest when inflation is low. The most cautious long-term investors may have an anchor holding of inflation-linked bonds, but at times of lesser inflation uncertainty (or greater confidence in the monetary authorities' ability to restrict the range of future inflation), high-quality conventional bonds are likely to replace inflation-linked bonds as the core holdings of many long-term investors. This reflects both the expected premium return and the convenience of their greater regular income distribution. But this should happen only after reviewing inflation risk and taking into account how this fits in with investors' tolerance for short-fall risk (as well as the tax implications of such a move).

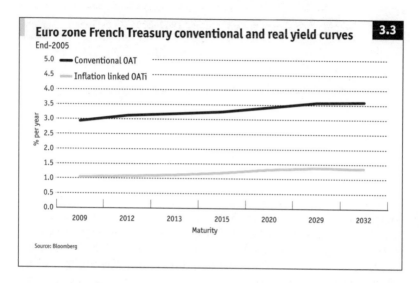

Euro zone French Treasury conventional and real yield curves 3.3
End-2005

Source: Bloomberg

The equity risk premium

It is likely that equities will produce lower returns in this century than they did in the previous one. It is therefore important that investors have an understanding of how much they should expect to be rewarded for investing in equities. This is an area of great controversy, and therefore uncertainty. This uncertainty matters and needs to be reflected in the design of investment strategy.

In recent years a substantial volume of academic research into historic market performance has been published. The original pioneers in this were studies by Roger Ibbotson, a professor in the practice of finance at Yale School of Management, and Rex Sinquefield, co-founder of money managers Dimensional Fund Advisors, in publishing long-run databases of carefully constructed returns data for the United States back to 1926. In the past few years this has been substantially extended, most notably by Elroy Dimson, Paul Marsh and Mike Staunton at London Business School, for 17 international markets, including the United States, back to 1900.

The data conclusively show that in all countries for which long runs of data exist, equities have outperformed both government bonds and Treasury bills and so risk-taking has been rewarded.

Nevertheless, there have been long periods when equities have not outperformed cash or bonds. This is illustrated in Figures 3.4 and 3.5 on page 33, which show the range of 20-year excess returns from equities over Treasury bills (or deposit rates) and conventional government bonds

Table 3.1 **Long-run investment market returns,**[a] **1900–2005 (% per year**[b]**)**

	US	UK
Treasury bills	1.0	1.0
Long-dated government bonds	1.9	1.4
Equities	6.5	5.5

a After inflation but before fees and expenses. b Geometric annualised returns.
Source: Dimson, E., Marsh, P. and Staunton, M.

from the 17 countries (Australia, Belgium, Canada, Denmark, France, Germany, Ireland, Italy, Japan, Netherlands, Norway, South Africa, Spain, Sweden, Switzerland, Portugal, UK, United States) covered by the Dimson, Marsh and Staunton research. The markets represented by the maxima or minima can change from one year to another. The position of the United States is also plotted. These figures show the extremes of experience and indicate, for example, that most of the time there has been at least one country whose equity market has been underperforming relative to its own Treasury bills or Treasury bonds over the previous 20 years. At the end of 2005, four of the countries showed domestic equities lagging behind domestic bonds over the preceding 20 years. Although it is the norm for equities to outperform bonds and cash, history can provide examples of long-term disappointing returns from equities. There is nothing extraordinary about equity markets underperforming bonds or even cash over periods as long as 20 years. And this is before allowing for the higher fees typically paid for equity management and for possible investment manager underperformance.

So much for history: what matters for setting strategy is what we expect for the future. The majority (but not consensus) view is that the 20th century was kinder to equity investors than they should reasonably have expected. This view is captured in the title of the major data study in this area by Dimson, Marsh and Staunton: *Triumph of the Optimists*. Or, in the words of Jeremy Siegel, Russell E. Palmer professor of finance at Wharton School at the University of Pennsylvania: "The abnormally high equity premium since 1926 is certainly not sustainable." The principal reason for this is that there was a re-rating of equities over the 20th century, which is reflected in an increase in the price/earnings ratio and in a decrease in the dividend yield on the market. This contributed to the superior performance and may occur

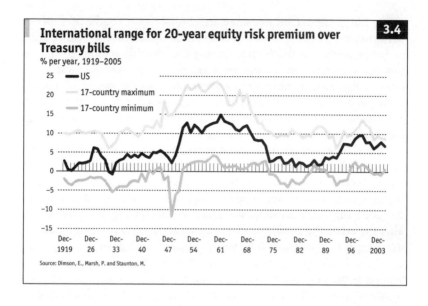

3.4

International range for 20-year equity risk premium over Treasury bills

% per year, 1919–2005

Source: Dimson, E., Marsh, P. and Staunton, M.

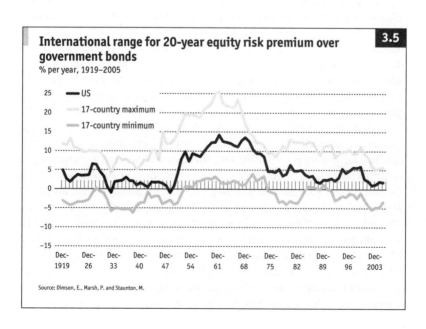

3.5

International range for 20-year equity risk premium over government bonds

% per year, 1919–2005

Source: Dimson, E., Marsh, P. and Staunton, M.

again, but it cannot be sustained indefinitely as a source of superior performance. In effect, stock prices were bid up to reflect an expectation of lower returns in the future. Among the possible reasons for this is that investors can now manage their exposure to market risk more easily than in the past, thanks to innovations such as the spread of mutual funds, and in particular market-matching index funds. In other words, 20th-century investors enjoyed the fruits of performance which was in part borrowed from the 21st century, and now it is pay-back time.

One counter argument is that it is easy to be misled by the dividend yield, which may come to be seen as artificially reduced by the end of the 20th century by a combination of tax disincentives and market and managerial incentives not to pay dividends. It is likely, for example, that the 2003 cut in US dividend tax and a change in corporate behaviour after the accounting scandals of 2001 and 2002, with company management eager to underscore the quality of their earnings by making larger dividend distributions, mean that in future more of an investor's return will come from dividends than in the past. Possibly there will be a period of adjustment as the share of corporate earnings that is distributed as dividends to shareholders increases rapidly, before stabilising at a new higher level.

The plausibility of this scenario is important for equity market prospects, and how far short of historical experience investment performance is likely to be in future. Ibbotson and Peng Chen, in their 2003 survey of the alternative methods for analysing capital market returns, estimated the US equity risk premium to be 4.0% in excess of long-dated US Treasuries on a geometric basis and 5.9% on an annual average arithmetic basis. This is towards the higher end of published estimates. Siegel expects the premium over bonds to be "in the range of 2–3%, about one-half the level that has prevailed over the past 70 years" but "all the evidence still indicates that equities will significantly outperform fixed-income investments over the long run". Dimson, Marsh and Staunton conclude their study by saying: "The result is a forward-looking, geometric mean risk premium [over government bonds] for the United States, United Kingdom and world of around 2.5–4% and an arithmetic mean risk premium for US, UK and world equities that falls within a range from a little below 4% to a little above 5%." At the opposing end of the argument from Ibbotson and Chen are Robert Arnott, editor of the *Financial Analysts Journal*, and Peter Bernstein, author of *Against The Gods: The Remarkable Story of Risk*, who can both be described as dividend growth and valuation pessimists. They wrote in early 2002 that "the long-term forward-looking risk premium is nowhere near the level of the past; today it may well be near zero, perhaps even negative".

The standard MBA corporate finance textbook by Richard Brealey and Stewart Myers provides a sceptical view of this debate. They point out that "many financial managers and economists believe that long-run historical returns are the best measure available ... out of this debate only one firm conclusion emerges: Do not trust anyone who claims to know what returns investors expect."

This debate does not much affect the likelihood of next year's equity market performance being disappointing. However, it does have a large impact on the prospects for wealth accumulation from equities over longer periods, particularly the potential for disappointing returns from equity markets over extended periods.

Equity risk: don't bank on time diversifying risk

The size of the equity risk premium would be of less concern if it was true that equities are "less risky" for long-term investors than for short-term investors. This is a separate area of debate with strong differences of opinion – and therefore much confusion – among investors. But what are the experts saying?

The longer the time horizon the more likely it is that stockmarket indices will outperform bonds or cash, simply because on average stocks are expected to perform better. Furthermore, the longer the period the more likely it is that this cumulative outperformance will translate into an increasingly large proportion of the initial investment. Long-term investors in equities should expect to do better on average than investors in bonds or cash, and the longer the period of time, the better in monetary terms they should expect, on average, to do. So long as equity investors are offered a positive risk premium, which more than outweighs the extra investment management fees they pay, this should be uncontroversial.

The real issue is the risk of disappointing results over longer periods of time and how this can compound into an increasingly large shortfall, and how strongly investors should be assumed to want to avoid the pain caused by such shortfalls. This has always been a central focus of finance, and it has been brought into even sharper focus through the work on "loss aversion" in behavioural finance. The experimental work on loss aversion discussed in Chapter 2 suggests that investors are probably twice as sensitive to the prospect of losses as they are to gains.

For long periods (up to 20 years or so), the risks of equities under-performing bonds and cash are not negligible, even though equities are, on average, expected to outperform bonds and cash by a wide margin. Figures 3.4 and 3.5 on page 33 show this vividly and more persuasively than would a quantitative model whose assumptions will always be subject to debate, and therefore doubt.

Table 3.2 shows the results of just such a modelling exercise in which 2,000 possible outcomes for equity markets have been simulated by replicating the summary characteristics of how the US markets have behaved since 1900. Of course, actual experience is only one of very many possible outcomes. The table shows a range of outcomes, from the disappointing 5th percentile outcome, through the median or 50th percentile outcome to the favourable 95th percentile outcome, and it shows these simulated results over five, ten and twenty years.

Table 3.2 shows that in at least half of the modelled scenarios equities far outperform stocks and bonds over each period, with the potential in strongly favourable markets for substantial outperformance. Nevertheless, the 5th percentile unfavourable outcome for equities is shown lagging behind cash and bonds over each period.

In recent years, there has been growing agreement that the standard statistical assumptions underlying Table 3.2 understate short-term risk (crashes happen more often than the models assume) and may overstate long-term equity risk. This is because academic research increasingly supports the widely held view that, to some extent, markets "overreact" (in relation to the standard assumptions underlying the table) and are mean reverting. If this is true (that markets mean revert), if investment returns have been above average, they are likely subsequently to come down, and if they have been below average, they are likely to increase. A result of this is that equity markets would vary less over time than traditional models would suggest. If this is true, stockmarket volatility measured over, say, decades or 20-year periods would be "less" than would be expected if you were simply to extrapolate short-term volatility. The degree to which it is the case is controversial, but there is evidence to support it.

The simple, easy-to-use modelling that underlies Table 3.2 (and almost all savings planning exercises) has been widely criticised. But these approaches continue to be used, partly because there is no agreement on how to replace them. However, the weakness of these models needs to be reflected in how wealth planning is presented. An expectation that a risk-based strategy is likely, but not certain, to achieve an objective is often reassuring enough. If an investor wants more certainty (for the "downside protection layer" – see Chapter 2), the underlying investment strategy needs to be based on hedging using tailored inflation-linked or

Table 3.2 **Does time diversify away the risk of disappointing equity markets?**

	100% Treasury bills as low-risk strategy			100% Treasury bonds as low-risk strategy		
	5 years	10 years	20 years	5 years	10 years	20 years
$100 in low-risk strategy becomes, after inflation[a]	105	110	121	110	121	146
$100 in all equity strategy becomes[b]						
95th percentile	267	492	1,352	267	492	1,352
50th percentile	138	191	363	138	191	363
5th percentile	71	74	98	71	74	98

a 50th percentile outcomes for bonds and Treasury bills shown.
b Using the North American convention of counting percentiles for the most disappointing outcomes.
Source: Author's calculations based on historical risks and returns using Dimson, Marsh and Staunton data for returns, after inflation, for US stocks, bonds and cash, 1900–2005

conventional government bonds. Often the honest message is that the price of such insurance is high, and many investors have little choice but to live with a significant degree of uncertainty. Spuriously precise wealth-planning models should not be used to disguise that uncertainty.

At present, the best guide to the risk of equities underperforming cash or bonds is given by examining the historical data. The prevailing view of finance academics is that the decades ahead are likely to be less favourable to equity markets than the 20th century was, and that some allowance needs to be made for the drag of investment fees and transaction costs and, most importantly for taxable accounts, for tax. So a reasonable assumption would be that the incidence of disappointing equity markets will be rather worse than the average shown by the experience of the past 100 years.

The international pattern for equities underperforming bonds over rolling five-year and 20-year periods is shown in Figures 3.6 and 3.7 overleaf. These show that across 17 countries over the past 106 years, stocks have underperformed bonds over 30% of rolling five-year periods. For periods of 20 years, the frequency of equities underperforming bonds falls to 14%. However, the record of the United States, as the largest and probably best diversified national equity market in both 1900 and 2000, is particularly important. Its record of underperformance versus bonds is in line with the international average over rolling five-year periods, but it

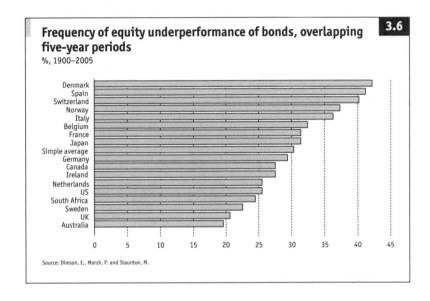

3.6

Frequency of equity underperformance of bonds, overlapping five-year periods
%, 1900–2005

Source: Dimson, E., Marsh, P. and Staunton, M.

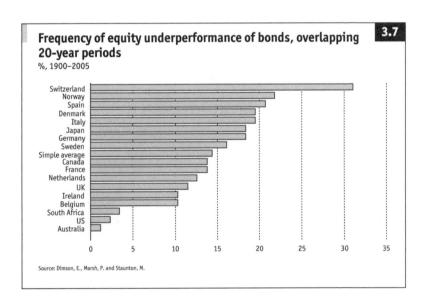

3.7

Frequency of equity underperformance of bonds, overlapping 20-year periods
%, 1900–2005

Source: Dimson, E., Marsh, P. and Staunton, M.

is much lower than the average over 20 years. The historical experience of the United States may give a misleading basis for extrapolating into the future because it was flattered by the exceptional performance of equities and by the poor performance of bonds over long periods as a result of the corrosive impact of unanticipated inflation. This is a risk that should be manageable in the decades ahead because of the existence of TIPS, but this makes it more likely that there will be prolonged periods of US equity underperformance of TIPS, if only because these bonds will not be eroded by inflation.

The risk of equity strategies underperforming safe-haven investment strategies over long periods therefore needs to be taken seriously. These are not remote events to be dismissed as exceptional bad luck: these things happen.

4 The time horizon and the shape of strategy: start with no frills and few thrills

Short-term investment strategies

For short-term investors, the safest strategy is to have 100% of their investments in cash. The "war chest" or "umbrella" fund might be considered a short-term fund (see Chapter 1). Short-term investors are absolute-return investors. Their focus is immediate and they have no need to hedge against risks in the future. Or, at a minimum, they are content to pass up the opportunity to hedge any such risks. Although the textbook benchmark against which success should be judged is the performance of Treasury bills, the reality is, always has been and always will be that achieving a positive investment return provides a line in the sand that matters above all else to short-term investors.

So what do model allocations look like for short-term or absolute-return investors? Moving strategy away from the safe haven of cash (Treasury bills) brings both the hope of a better performance and the fear of a disappointing outcome. Initially, it is simplest to constrain investment choices to the traditional areas of stocks, bonds and cash.

The chance of a bad outcome may be higher than you think

What is a "bad outcome" or "minimum acceptable return" (MAR) for short-term investors? A cautious short-term investor will be less tolerant of short-term losses than an aggressive investor. For unaggressive short-term investors, this chapter arbitrarily assumes that the measured risk of a negative return of worse than –5% in any particular year should be no greater than one in 20. This is the target MAR. For moderate risk short-term investors, the MAR is assumed to be –10% and for aggressive short-term investors –15%. In principle, any figure can be selected, but whatever it is, the calculated probability of breaching may be only one in 20 in any particular calendar year; however, over five years, for example, the probability of breaching the guideline in at least one of these five years will be more than one in five. If, as is most probable, the investor's portfolio is monitored more frequently than once a year, say at the end of each month, the probability of at least one breach, measured on the basis of rolling 12-month periods, will be closer to 50%. (Note that the MAR probability refers to the chance of an outcome worse than the specified parameter in a particular calendar year.) These things happen and are not surprising, even if you think that a one in 20 risk is a low risk.

Having selected these tolerances for losses, in theory, we can design short-term model strategies that give the best prospect for wealth generation, given these guidelines. These would be the conventional efficient portfolios that are optimal for each indicated level of risk-taking by short-term investors. Efficient portfolios give the best possible trade-off of expected risk and expected return. For any given level of risk-taking there is, in theory, only one optimal portfolio. It would be impossible to achieve higher expected returns with no increase in risk and it would be inefficient to pursue the same returns, but at higher risk. In practice, the uncertainties discussed in Chapter 3 mean that this does not work since we cannot precisely model the future. We may expect that a particular outcome is unlikely, but we generally do not know with any precision how unlikely that result is.

These indicated MAR risk figures can support a range of very different strategies, and the intention would often be to manage the strategy to a lower level of risk-taking than indicated by the MAR. Consider the three illustrative short-term strategies, using only stocks, bonds and cash, shown in Table 4.1 overleaf, which have allocations to stocks increasing from 20% to 50% and then to 75%. The allocation of non-equity investments is divided between over ten-year US Treasury bonds and cash.

Table 4.1 shows the average return for each strategy based on the performance of market indices, before all fees and expenses, since 1991. It also shows, based on historical relationships, the sort of returns that might be expected in a disappointing year. For example, the moderate strategy indicates that a return of –4.6%, or worse, should be expected with no more than a one-in-20 chance in any particular year. The back-testing of results to 1991 shows that larger negative returns would have been recorded in the recent past with such a "moderate" strategy, with market indices pointing to a negative return of 8.5% in the 12 months to July 2002.

This illustrates that actual experience can from time to time be much worse than would be suggested by the historical statistics for overall returns and volatility, which are derived from that same experience of history. The more comforting figures are provided by routinely used modelling exercises. These suffer from severe averaging difficulties that

Table 4.1 **Model short-term investment strategies, with only stocks, bonds and cash: historical US$ perspective, January 1991–December 2005**

	Unaggressive strategy	Moderate strategy	Aggressive strategy	Treasury bills	Lehman Bros Long Term Government Bond Index	MSCI US Equity Total Return Index
Asset allocation						
Equities	20	50	75	0	0	100
Bonds[a]	20	50	25	0	100	0
Cash[a]	60	0	0	100	0	0
Performance Dec 1991–Dec 2005 (% per year)[b]	6.7	10.8	11.5	3.9	9.3	12.3
Volatility	3.7	9.2	12.2	0.5	9.4	15.9

"Value at risk" (apparent 1 in 20 chance of return of this, or worse, in any one calendar year)[c]

	0.9	−4.6	−7.2	3.1	5.7	−12.2

Extreme results since 1991	Unaggressive strategy	Moderate strategy	Aggressive strategy	Treasury bills	Lehman Bros Long Term Government Bond Index	MSCI US Equity Total Return Index
Worst 12-month result	−2.1	−8.5	−17.9	0.9	−11.8	−27.0
Best 12-month result	16.6	34.6	42.7	6.2	30.9	53.0

a Indicative allocations between bonds and cash for short-term investors are very sensitive to duration of bond benchmark.
b Geometric averages.
c See text comments on risk of more frequent occurrences of disappointing returns.
Source: Underlying data sourced from Lehman Brothers Inc and MSCI Barra

Table 4.2 **Model short-term investment strategies, with only stocks, bonds and cash: forward-looking perspective**

	Unaggressive strategy "capital protection"	Moderate strategy	Aggressive strategy	Treasury bills	Long-term government bonds	US equities
Asset allocation						
Equities	20	50	75	0	0	100
Bonds[a]	20	50	25	0	100	0
Cash[a]	60	0	0	100	0	0
Expected return[b]	4.7	6.5	7.5	3.5	4.5	8.5
Historic volatility	3.7	9.2	12.2	0.5	9.4	15.9
"Value at risk" (apparent 1 in 20 chance of return of this, or worse, in any one calendar year)[c]						
Based on "expected relationships"	−1.1	−7.9	−11.9	2.7	−10.4	−15.9

a Indicative allocations between bonds and cash for short-term investors very sensitive to duration of bond benchmark.
b See text for derivation of expected returns.
c See text comments on risk of more frequent occurrences of disappointing returns.
Source: Author's calculations

suggest, for example, that stockmarket volatility stays at one average level. It doesn't, and the worst news arrives when this is least true. More particularly, the risk figures are undermined by the "surprising" frequency of extreme returns – by trending or momentum in markets, and by the fact that at times of stress, "normal" relationships between different markets may not hold.

Table 4.2 replaces the historical statistics with forward-looking statistics, based upon standard assumptions that flow from Chapter 3. The expected returns are anchored on the ten-year government bond yield, taken as 4.5%. (Cash is expected to yield 1% less than ten-year bonds and equities are expected to earn an arithmetic average return of 4% above ten-year bonds. Correlations and volatilities have been estimated using data since 1991.)

The lower slope of the line in Figure 4.1 indicates the slower future rate of accumulation of financial wealth that is being anticipated by most financial experts, whereas the higher slope shows average performance since 1991. These differences have a significant impact on the likelihood of achieving distant objectives.

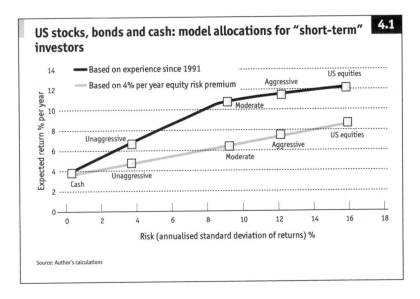

US stocks, bonds and cash: model allocations for "short-term" investors `4.1`

Source: Author's calculations

No all-seasons short-term strategy

A focus on managing short-term negative return risk has to respond to changes in the level of interest rates. The rate of interest provides a performance cushion which is reduced when rates are low. Thus short-term investing is made easier by higher interest rates when (somewhat) more aggressive strategies can be pursued with no increase in measured risk of incurring a negative return. In this particular context, investing is made more hazardous by low interest rates, when it will be natural to stay closer to the safety zone (cash).

This means that there is a tension between standard "one size fits all" model asset allocations (such as those indicated above) and the focus of short-term investors on their absolute performance. The problem with the standard approach is not that groups of clients do not face similar investment risks and opportunities – they do. It is rather that a "one size fits all" approach takes no account of market conditions. At higher rates of interest, it is appropriate for an unaggressive short-term investor to consider accepting more investment volatility. This means that the illustrative short-term stylised model allocations should be seen for what they are: allocations which might be appropriate if bond yields are around 4.5%, but otherwise they should be considered subject to revision, particularly for unaggressive investors.

Table 4.3 **Unaggressive or "capital protection" strategy: negative return risk varies as interest rates move (%)**

Ten-year Treasury yield	2	3	4	5	6	7	8
Calculated probability of a negative return[a]	29.0	20.3	12.8	7.5	3.7	2.0	0.8

a Calculated probability of a negative return in a given individual calendar year for an unchanging, unaggressive ("capital protection") strategy, described in Table 4.2. See comments in text about risk of underperformance.
Source: Author's calculations

Do bonds provide insurance for short-term investors?

The answer is sometimes yes, and sometimes no. The normal pattern is for equity markets and bond markets to be positively correlated with each other. When equities do very well, bonds tend to do at least quite well. At times of crisis and flight to quality, however, the relationship has often broken down as investors flee to government bonds. During the 2000–02 equity bear market the volatility of long-term government bonds provided an invaluable lever to offset the declines in equity markets. But the scale of the insurance "pay-out" depended critically on the size of the allocation to bonds and the duration of those bonds. Cash, the safe haven for short-term investors, provided almost no help. But at other times in the past, for example during the sustained increase in inflation expectations during the 1960s, equities did well while bonds were eroded by inflation and suffered a gradual increase in yields. There have been several years when fixed income suffered negative returns while equities performed strongly.

In times of crisis, bonds normally appreciate, but (even for longer maturities) not necessarily by much, and not by as much as equities fall. The historic record since 1980 is summarised in Tables 4.4 and 4.5 overleaf. In Table 4.4, which shows US bond market performance in months of sharp equity market setbacks, the two months of weak equity prices and poor or indifferent US Treasury prices (March 1980 and August 1990) occurred against a background of sharp increases in oil prices.

The message regarding the insurance role for bonds is that it sometimes works, but not always. The lessons of any period are "distorted" by whatever the background macroeconomic trends happen to have been. Table 4.5 looks "quite good" for supporting the insurance role of bonds. But the scale of the performance of bonds in 2000, 2001, 2002 also had a lot to do with the final stages of a 20-year process to squeeze inflation out of the economy, and with concerns that the new threat was actual deflation, or declines in consumer prices. The correction to the stockmarket euphoria of the late 1990s coincided

Table 4.4 **Bond diversification in months of equity market crisis**[a]

	MSCI US Index	MSCI EAFE® index	Lehman Bros Long Term Govt Bond Index	Lehman Bros Intermediate Term Govt Bond Index	Lehman Bros Aggregate Bond Index
Oct 1987	−21.2	−14.0	7.3	3.0	3.6
Aug 1998	−13.9	−12.4	4.4	1.9	1.6
Sep 2002	−11.3	−10.7	4.1	1.7	1.6
Aug 1990	−9.1	−9.7	−4.3	−0.4	−1.3
Feb 2001	−8.9	−7.5	1.6	0.9	0.9
Mar 1980	−8.8	−10.6	0.1	0.9	0.1

a Data sorted by worst monthly performance of MSCI US equity index, January 1976–December 2005.
Sources: MSCI Barra, Lehman Brothers Inc

Table 4.5 **Bond diversification in years of extreme equity market performance**[a]

	MSCI US Index	MSCI EAFE® index	Lehman Bros Long Term Govt Bond Index	Lehman Bros Intermediate Term Govt Bond Index	Lehman Bros Aggregate Bond Index
Dec 2002	−22.7	−15.7	17.0	9.6	10.3
Dec 2000	−12.5	−14.0	20.3	10.5	11.6
Dec 2001	−12.0	−21.2	4.3	8.4	8.4
Dec 1995	38.2	11.6	30.9	14.4	18.5
Dec 1997	34.1	2.1	15.1	7.7	9.7
Dec 1985	32.8	56.7	31.5	18.0	22.1

a US equity and bond performance during the best and worst three years for the MSCI US equity index between 1976 and 2005.
Sources: MSCI Barra; Lehman Brothers Inc

with this but was essentially different in nature and cause. In other words, don't necessarily expect the same pattern of bond market behaviour in the next equity bear market.

The other message is that the relationship between different maturities of bonds is generally predictable, with the longest dated (and most volatile) US Treasuries appreciating most in periods of stockmarket crisis. But this does not always happen. When it does not, the shape of the bond yield curve can shift markedly, which argues for diversified exposure to bond maturities. Long-dated bonds are unquestionably much further away from a short-term investor's safety zone than short-term bonds and so are much more risky. But the pay-out of short-term bonds is much less when fixed-income markets are providing insurance.

So the process, if you are a short-term investor, should be first to decide how much risk you want to take, and then to make sure that risk-taking is itself diversified across asset classes. Offset equity exposure with at least some fixed-income exposure; not in this case for income but for insurance. But do so knowing that this is one of those insurance policies with loopholes in the small print.

Are you in it for the long term?

The purpose of wealth, however large or small, is to fund expenditure in the future. This might be tomorrow or it might be in 40 years' time, but the time horizon for most investment objectives cannot be described as short term. For long-term investors who are concerned to target a minimum standard of living, or, for an endowment, a minimum level of disbursements, the strategy should not target a particular level of wealth. Wealth is a means to an end, but not the end in itself. The sufficiency of wealth is best examined from the perspective of the level of income that the wealth can support.

Time horizon for private and institutional wealth

The income that a defined-benefit pension fund or an insurance company is obliged to disburse can be modelled years in advance with a reasonable degree of accuracy by actuaries. There are issues with the uncertainty surrounding these projections and whether this has increased with corporate change and with greater life expectancy. But these issues are of an order of magnitude different from the uncertainty surrounding the spending of much private wealth.

The obligations of endowments and charities are again different in nature. Their spending is constrained by what they have, by the bequests that they receive, and by the need to balance the interests of today's beneficiaries with those of tomorrow. This need to ensure equitable treatment in making allocations between different generations of beneficiaries is a particular concern for "perpetual" endowments, such as college foundations, whose investment strategy needs to assume that the foundation will last "for ever".

The increase in wealth of tax-exempt endowments with both professional investment management and successful fund-raising offers the prospect of accumulation that is bounded only by their endowments' fund-raising capacity. David Swensen, chief investment officer at Yale University, gives a revealing account of the differing evolution of the Yale, Harvard and Carnegie Institution investment funds since the early 20th century. In 1911, Carnegie and Harvard had funds of around $23m while Yale had around $12m. By June 2003, the Carnegie Institution's investment portfolio, which devotes itself to supporting scientific research, had more than kept pace with inflation, with an endowment of $532m. However, this was dwarfed by Harvard's $19.3 billion and Yale's $11 billion. The reason for this scale of difference is not superior investment management but the much greater access of the university foundations to new bequests.

Private wealth is different. Families continue from generation to generation, but family wealth gets spent. There is little scope for the inter-generational exponential wealth accumulation that may be enjoyed by educational foundations. Private wealth is consumed, dissipated in fees, paid in taxes, or donated (as with the Carnegie family wealth) to chari-table foundations. If this did not happen, the parsimonious among the wealthy could become stupendously wealthy. For example, in the 105 years to December 2004, the cumulative return from US equities after inflation, but before all costs, taxes and fees, was 6.6% a year. This implies that a most wealthy family with perhaps $20m in 1900, equivalent to around $500m in today's prices, could have an inherited fortune of over $400 billion if it had been invested in the diversified US stockmarket, and if that family had consumed nothing apart from what they earned inde-pendently of that wealth, and had contrived to pay no taxes or invest-ment management costs. Such a scale of inherited wealth does not seem to exist. Wealth is inherited, but it is also spent or disbursed.

There is often little predictability in the spending plans of individual family members. This creates asset planning issues that do not affect insti-tutions. By contrast, the purpose and strategic direction of endowments and institutions is legally fixed by trust deeds or equivalent documents. With families, strategic objectives and actual disbursement of wealth can evolve at short notice, sometimes in surprising directions. This introduces uncertainty into the time horizon for the management of private wealth, which has few parallels for endowments or institutional investors. However, a change in regulations for pension funds and insurance companies (there have been many in the past ten years around the world) can have a sudden impact on the time horizon of institutions.

In setting strategy, the importance of different points on the time horizon for an investor needs to be clarified. For family wealth the objective is not normally precisely defined. Sometimes there are clear dates associated with particular financial goals which can easily be benchmarked using government bonds, and in other cases, wealth is explicitly needed for opportunities (or contingencies) which may arise in the short term. But usually this is not the case and plans often need to evolve as circumstances change and as more information becomes available. However, this should not be used as an excuse for assuming that such investors are, by default, short-term investors, as the adoption of a medium- or longer-term investment strategy could well help protect the purchasing power of their investments.

The time horizon is the period over which success in meeting objectives will be measured. It should not be sufficient to earn a positive return over this period. The hurdle rate of return should be the performance that could have been earned at no risk on Treasury bills for short-term objectives, and government bonds and, particularly, inflation-linked government bonds for longer-term objectives (see Chapter 3).

For longer-term savings plans, the risk of not being able to meet particular objectives, such as providing a desired standard of living in retirement or a level of disbursements for a foundation, is a more fundamental measure of risk than changes in the short-term market value of a portfolio.

Long-term investors
Long-term investors have much greater flexibility than short-term investors to make adjustments to improve the likelihood of meeting financial objectives. Long-term investors are not just at the mercy of the investment markets and their initial choice of investment strategy. Depending on the investor's circumstances, financial disappointment "along the way" often leaves time to elicit a response, which provides extra degrees of freedom that reduce risk in the ability to meet objectives. For example, there may be time for a revision to the investment strategy, or for an individual to postpone retirement or to reduce current expenditure. For an endowment, there may be time for a drive to raise additional bequests, and for a pension fund, time to raise the level of regular pension contributions. These options provide flexibility for the long-term investor that is not available to the short-term investor. For any individual or foundation (or perhaps pension plan) that relies on a regular injection of savings or contributions to fund future financial needs, variations in these sources of income are often a much bigger source of risk and opportunity to meet expected commitments than are market conditions.

Financial planning and the time horizon

Short-term investors have a clear focus on total return as a measure of success of their investment strategy. Long-term investors, particularly individual long-term investors, will often focus on the same metric. But as discussed in Chapter 3 this is wrong. For example, it is common for individuals to have a target for accumulated savings before they feel able to retire. Over quite short time periods an amount that was broadly appropriate can become inadequate if long-term interest rates fall. The key is not the absolute amount of savings, but the ability of that amount, if cautiously invested, to support the intended level of retirement income. This leads to a focus on shortfall risk rather than the risk of generating a negative return. The benchmark for measuring shortfall is the performance of the appropriate safety strategy, and so shortfall risk is the risk of underperforming that strategy.

This is well understood and reflected in financial advice and the "laddered" bond portfolios of many cautious private investors in North America. It is much less common, however, in the generic advice given to investors elsewhere. Internationally, it is common for private wealth holdings of bonds to be of quite short duration. Often this reflects concerns about the potential impact of inflation and a desire to avoid the risk of short-term negative returns from volatile assets, even if they are government bonds guaranteed to deliver a set amount at a given date in the future. Outside the United States, it is widely believed that long-term bonds are inappropriate as investments for cautious private investors for whom the emphasis should, it is argued, be on controlling absolute volatility and short-term capital preservation. In fact, this is the appropriate focus only for cautious short-term investors. An error that often accompanies failure to design risk-taking strategies appropriate to an investor's time horizon is to confuse this time horizon with risk tolerance. The two should be treated separately. There are cautious long-term investors and there are aggressive short-term investors.

This focus on controlling volatility often involves restricting interest rate exposure in investment portfolios. Bond market developments in recent years show how this approach can put at risk the spending power of long-term investors. The flip side of the succession of profitable opportunities to refinance fixed-rate mortgages around the turn of the century was the much less publicised but more important phenomenon for retirement saving: the sequence of increases in the cost of purchasing continuing flows of income whether in the form of government bonds or life annuities from insurance companies. Meanwhile, the cost of buying inflation-proof income through inflation-linked government bonds has also increased. For example, US long-term real interest rates fell from over 4% in late 1999 to under 2% in early 2004 (and were still at those levels in early 2006). For an endowment, or for a family wishing to transfer an unchanged level of real wealth to the next generation, this represents more than a halving in the level of "real" income that can, with full confidence, be supported by that fixed level of wealth. "Wealth planning" should not target wealth accumulation and would better be renamed "income planning". This is not a trivial distinction for any long-term investor, whether an individual planning for retirement or the best endowed foundation planning its support for philanthropic giving.

"Safe havens", benchmarking, risk-taking and long-term strategies
The ability of government bonds to "lock-in" objectives (by avoiding the danger of having to suffer less favourable interest rates at a later date) means that they have a benchmarking role in setting strategy for long-term investors. This applies as much in the context of any recommendation for a behavioural "safety-first" portfolio as for a conventional investment strategy. Where financial objectives can be precisely specified, the benchmark is a series of government bonds that would provide a stream of income to match the objective. Where they are long term, but not specified, the best benchmark and "safe haven" is a long-dated government bond.

A "safe-haven" investment strategy quantifies how much wealth is needed today to secure or to "hedge" with reasonable certainty a particular objective at a chosen date in the future. Alternatively, it can tell you how much can, with confidence, be accumulated by that date with a given level of initial investment. It establishes a benchmark increase of financial wealth over time. This safe haven is an intuitive starting point for considering investment strategy, wealth and income planning.

If this reveals an incompatibility between an investor's aspirations and what a low-risk strategy can provide, the investor should, if possible, prioritise objectives, distinguishing between those objectives that it might be appropriate to secure using government bonds and those that are less critical, or more "aspirational". This is an iterative process which can also help adjust expectations for sustainable objectives and tolerance for disappointment.

The stylised "subsistence farmer" of behavioural finance described in Chapter 2 provides the logic for this approach. The most cautious approach is to plant cash crops only after being assured that enough food can be grown for the family. This ignores the scope for buying food with the proceeds of at least some of the cash crop, so it is quite likely that this safety-first approach will lead to a lower standard of living, on average, than a greater focus on the volatile cash crop might have provided. The equivalent investment approach is to hedge away retirement standard-of-living risk (for example) by purchasing sufficient inflation-linked government bonds at prevailing interest rates, or an inflation-linked life annuity, to ensure that a chosen standard of living is guaranteed. This subsistence approach would then allow an aspirational portfolio to be established with any additional financial resources.

In pulling together themes from traditional and behavioural finance, Zvi Bodie, professor of finance and economics at Boston University School of Management, argues in an article, "Thoughts on the Future: Life-Cycle Investing in Theory and Practice", in the *Financial Analysts Journal* (January/February 2003) that an appropriate combined strategy could be provided by a core, safety-first portfolio of hedging investments in government bonds (ideally, TIPS), combined with residual investments in a series of call options on a broad stockmarket index. From time to time, profitable call options could be sold to purchase more government bonds, to lock in a higher level of retirement income. This is Bodie's escalating life annuity, which has a number of attractive characteristics. It meets the demand for a safety-first insurance portfolio, which is properly matched to the time horizon of the investor. It provides the prospect of a higher standard of living if the markets perform well. It is also easy to understand and should be inexpensive to provide.

The focus of long-term investors on dates in the future should also lead to a focus on shortfall risk. This is the risk that the chosen strategy may underperform the safe-haven government bond strategy, and the risk of not being able to meet expenditure objectives that could have been supported by following such a cautious strategy. Investors should pursue an alternative, more risky strategy only if it is expected to generate surplus over and above that low-risk strategy.

For a long-term investor, therefore, the emphasis needs to change from the short-term investor's familiar focus on the risk of losing money or the traditional trade-off between absolute return and volatility. Instead, it needs to focus on the opportunities and risks of seeking to generate surplus beyond the more certain outcome of a policy of, for example, investing 100% in inflation-linked government bonds of an appropriate maturity.

For cautious long-term investors, long-term bonds should dominate the investment strategy. For more aggressive investors, the holding may be much smaller, but government bonds, particularly inflation-linked government bonds, will still provide a benchmark for comparative measurement of the chosen investment strategy. If the investor is reasonably confident that there will not be adverse inflation surprises, the bond holdings may be conventional government bonds. Otherwise, particularly for extended maturities over which cost-of-living uncertainty always increases, inflation-linked government bonds should be considered.

This core role for longer-dated highest-quality bonds is needed because they enable cautious long-term investors to hedge the risk to their future income and standard of living from adverse movements in interest rates. Reductions in interest rates should be of little concern to a pensioner, or to someone approaching retirement, who has followed a sufficiently funded and properly implemented cautious long-term investment strategy.

The danger of keeping things too simple

However, for many investors, an overriding desire to "keep things simple" may encourage them to indicate that they are content to be considered as short-term investors, even though their objectives are longer term. This is the option to be treated as "absolute return" investors, for whom the safe-haven investment strategy is to be 100% invested in cash.

The danger is that these investors will miss two important differences between short-term and long-term investing. The first is the focus that long-term investors must have on the price level and inflation uncertainty. The second is that such investors will also miss the distinction that is drawn below between good and bad volatility by failing to distinguish between a reduction in the price of future security (a fall in government bond prices) and a reduction in the market's assessment of an investment's quality. So investors should ask themselves: are our investments for the short term or long term? The answer makes a big difference.

Good and bad volatility

Sometimes you can be sure that a financial loss can be reversed. Pensioners living off the income generated from a well-constructed ladder of government bonds can respond to a fall in the market value of their investment portfolio following an increase in bond yields with composure. It should be of no concern. The government will keep them in the style to which they are accustomed. However, individuals who suffer a similar fall in investment value as a result of a downgrade in the creditworthiness of a corporate bond, on which they are relying for pension income, might reasonably suffer sleepless nights, because there is no assurance that they will get paid.

This highlights a problem of being fixated on the total return or the avoidance of losses in the market value of portfolios. Long-term investors should view losses caused by an increase in interest rates (and consequent fall in government bond prices) differently from losses which result from a downward revision of earnings potential for a company. The former indicates the guarantee of a subsequent recovery performance because of the higher rate of discount. No further revision of market views is needed for this. The latter indicates a market assessment that there is now a greater chance that the security will fail to deliver its expected payment schedule. For a short-term investor who is concerned to realise objectives in the near term, either reversal should be viewed as if it might be a permanent loss which could need to be realised. For a long-term investor, only the credit downgrade should be of concern. It might be said that it is not the credit downgrade that should concern the pensioner, since it is only a default that leads to a loss of income. But this is a classic case of the dangers of mismeasuring risk. Investors lose sleep over their ability to support their future standard of living a long time before most downgraded corporate bonds default. A bond ladder comprising corporate debt that stretches many years into the future is more likely to suffer worrying credit downgrades at some stage than actual default.

Volatility which is reflected in a reduction in government bond prices reduces the cost of buying future income. This is unambiguously good news for anyone saving for a pension or a college education, or an endowment investing new money to fund future good works. It is, for example, good news for pension saving plans because it means that more pension entitlement can be bought with each new dollar of pension saving.

To achieve success as a long-term investor, it is essential that this distinction between good and bad volatility is accepted and reflected in how an investor responds to financial reverses. This is invaluable for private investors, who often regard any loss as if it is bad news, when in fact it may represent an opportunity to lock in access to higher future income. It is equally valuable for some groups of pension fund investors whose attitude has sometimes been (more so before 2000 than since) an uncritical response that short-term losses do not concern them as they are long-term investors who should be able to "look through" the peaks and troughs of the stockmarket.

A lack of clarity about financial goals can encourage investors to focus on inappropriate time horizons. The one predictable consequence of this is inefficiency in the implementation of strategy. An example of this occurs if private investors, whose appropriate focus is on the long term, behave as short-term investors. They will fail to appreciate their vulnerability to changes in long-term interest rates and to the gradual erosion of inflation. Any change in long-term interest rates is likely to be misinterpreted, with positive performance arising from only partial exposure to falling interest rates being seen as "good performance" (it is not, it is poor, because it only partially hedged the fall in interest rates and should have been better) and negative performance owing to partial exposure to rising interest rates being seen as "poor", when in fact underexposure to the safe haven of long-term bonds may (depending on the interest rate sensitivity of existing investments) offer an opportunity to secure a higher future income with existing resources.

A financially disciplined endowment fund or institution managing cash flow obligations over a number of years is less likely to make these errors. The issue is that where the financial constraints are not naturally tight (as may be the case with wealthy families), Adam Smith's "invisible hand" of market competition is not available to ensure that wealth is efficiently managed. Instead it requires deliberate decision-making and appropriate governance to ensure that a proper focus is maintained on the objectives that are suitable for the time scale of each investor.

Unexpected inflation: yet again the party pooper

The distinction between good and bad volatility, which draws on recent academic research on equity markets discussed in Chapter 7, is a useful device to help long-term investors understand the importance of the passage of time for the success of the investment strategy. It also helps differentiate clearly between short-term and long-term investors. Strictly, "good volatility" should only be used in the context of the volatility of government inflation-linked bond yields, such as TIPS. The reason is that a fall in conventional government bond prices which reflects an increase in inflation expectations (rather than an increase in real interest rates) is not good news for an investor, for it indicates an expected irrecoverable devaluation in the worth of all nominal bond investments. This is the process that explains why in most countries for which there are data, bonds provided disappointing returns in the 20th century. All comments in this chapter about good volatility should be understood as applying to inflation-linked government bonds and to conventional government bonds in the absence of a surprising increase of inflation expectations.

"Keep-it-simple" long-term asset allocation models

"Diversify, diversify," asset allocators often say. In fact, in designing low-risk strategies, which should always be the starting point for asset allocation, the first step should be to design the best hedge to neutralise risks of failing to meet objectives. For some investors it is conceivable that this could be achieved through a single holding in a particular government bond. Diversification becomes an issue as an investor moves away from this "best hedge". Any such move needs to be made efficiently, which will call for diversification of avoidable risks.

The short-term asset allocation models that were given earlier are rooted in the intellectual breakthroughs of the 1950s, and given the flood of advances in finance since then could be described as "antediluvian". They provide an easy short cut to thinking about managing the risk of losing money. They assume that markets are "well behaved" (which they are not), they deal with a single period (which is an unusual focus for an investor), and they assume that wealth is a goal in itself and not a means to an end.

So what does a long-term investment plan look like, and how should it be structured? First, it is not a wealth plan – it is a long-term income or spending power plan. An income plan needs to take account of your financial and other assets, your likely earnings, your financial obligations and your spending plans. The first step will be to establish a base case to see if you are able to "hedge out" your obligations and plans, given your current resources and current levels of interest rates. To do this, financial advisers need to be able to access quite sophisticated modelling tools that enable investors to match up the profile of their investments with the likely schedule of their payment obligations in a way that highlights the low risk (but perhaps high expense) of following a "fully hedged" investment strategy. It should show how the expected cost may fall (with an accompanying danger of accumulating a shortfall from financial objectives) as strategy moves away from the fully hedged position.

A flavour for the differences in strategy from the short-term models indicated previously is shown in Table 4.6 and Figure 4.2. The focus is now on the risk of shortfalls from the fully hedged strategy instead of the risk of negative returns. So instead of showing the expected return and its trade-off with the volatility of that return, the focus is on the expected surplus or deficit in meeting objectives, as compared with the minimum-risk strategy of full hedging investment strategy. The "model strategies" for long-term investors are shown in Table 4.6. The risk return chart is shown in Figure 4.2 on page 58.

Table 4.6 **Stylised model long-term strategies, with only stocks, bonds and cash**

	Unaggressive ("income protection")	Moderate	Aggressive
Equities	25	60	80
Long-term conventional government bonds	50	40	20
Cash	0	0	0
Inflation-linked government bonds	25	0	0
Expected surplus (% per year)	1.4	2.9	3.7
Volatility of surplus	4.3	10.1	13.8

Source: Author's calculations

Inflation, again

There is no role for cash in these long-term models. This is because cash is volatile relative to the safe haven (inflation-linked bonds) and it offers no performance advantage. At the same time, the future relationship between inflation-linked bonds and conventional government bonds is sensitive to views on inflation, the risks to those views and the risk appetite of investors. It should be assumed that these inflation risks cannot be properly reflected in any set of modelling assumptions, and that it will be necessary to rely heavily on judgmental opinions and the tolerance for different uncertainties of different investors. Furthermore, the judgments of "experts" should probably not count for more than the views and experiences of informed investors on issues such as inflation expectations. However, the apparent views of the financial markets on the break-even rate of inflation should always be used as a point of comparison.

The investment decisions of long-term investors often reflect either a conscious or a subconscious view on inflation prospects. Consider the case of a long-term investor (such as a pensioner or an endowment or a pension fund) who has distant financial commitments linked to the cost of living. By following an investment strategy that is anchored on conventional government bonds, this investor (as explained in Chapter 3) is implicitly expressing the view that future inflation will be less than the break-even rate implied by the difference between inflation-linked government bond yields and conventional government bond yields. A market is rapidly evolving in inflation swaps, enabling, for example, companies with inflation-linked revenue streams to lay off their inflation risk and investors to switch conventional debt exposures to inflation-protected (but with corporate credit risk) investments. The embedded

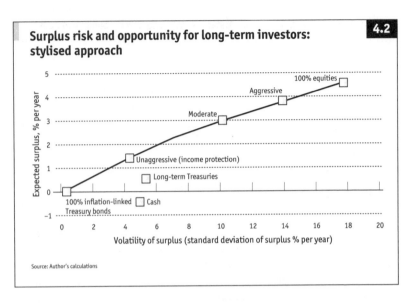

Surplus risk and opportunity for long-term investors: stylised approach `4.2`

Source: Author's calculations

fees may make this uncompetitive for retail investors, although the process of commoditisation means that this is worth monitoring for all investors. Views on expected inflation and the uncertainty about future inflation should be reviewed, probably annually, with the help of some simple "what-if" illustrations for the price level at different dates in the future. In the stylised model for long-term investors shown in Table 4.6, the key decision will be the extent to which the holdings of government bonds should be in the form of inflation-linked or conventional bonds.

Laddered government bonds: a useful safety-first portfolio
A bond ladder is a portfolio of bonds with staggered maturity dates. It secures a stream of income for years ahead, and it reduces the risk of sudden changes in that income resulting from interest rate changes. As each bond matures, it will need to be reinvested at prevailing interest rates and this exposes the income from the ladder to a margin of uncertainty. But this reinvestment risk applies only to an individual rung of the ladder as it matures. It therefore largely takes judgment out of timing movements in long-term interest rates and reduces uncertainty in a pensioner's future income. In principle each step on the ladder might represent one year's income, but spreading maturities within each year allows more reinvestment opportunities and less exposure to regret at the terms with which

any particular bond was reinvested. A greater number of bond issues also enables effective management of different types of risk exposure (see below).

The danger of having to reinvest at lower interest rates than prevailed when the maturing bond was purchased could have been avoided if a life annuity had been purchased instead of a bond ladder (though complicated tax issues arise if the annuity is purchased with taxable savings). However, the laddered approach is more appealing to many investors than a life annuity as it gives greater control over their wealth and avoids the need to lock in a single long-term rate of interest on the day they choose to purchase the life annuity. Although a ladder does involve reinvestment risk, it also offers reinvestment opportunity, namely the chance to reinvest at more favourable interest rates at a later date.

This can even provide an important element of inflation protection to retirement income. If individuals did decide to buy a fixed-income life annuity rather than invest in a bond ladder, they would be wholly exposed to any unexpected increase in inflation for the rest of their lives. However, if an increase in inflation was expected to persist, bond yields would be higher, and the rungs on a fixed-income bond ladder would be reinvested at the new higher rate of interest.

This reinvestment opportunity provides some element of inflation compensation. This protection would be less effective than could be offered by inflation-linked government bonds, and reinvesting a maturing bond will always, if there has been any inflation, support a lower standard of living than when it was first purchased. Nevertheless, this partial element of inflation compensation in a bond ladder, in conjunction with the flexibility and discretion that it leaves the investor, will be an appealing feature to many investors.

However, no sensible person would climb a ladder unless they had confidence that each rung would support their weight. Likewise with a bond ladder: where a pensioner's standard of living depends on income from the bond ladder, the individual rungs have to be of high quality. For this reason, bond ladders should be constructed from high-quality bonds of successive maturities.

A bond ladder is designed to mitigate interest rate risk and it should encourage a proper understanding of the distinction between good and bad volatility. This is because an investor will find it easier to respond to a fall in government bond prices as an opportunity to lock in higher income when the next rung on the ladder matures. However, if the cause of the decline in investment values was a downgrade in the credit quality of a component rung, the result is likely to be, at the least, a worried investor until the bond matures.

Ladders, in particular for cautious investors, should be constructed from government (including high-quality municipal) bonds. With good-quality longer-term corporate bonds there is always the risk of deterioration in credit quality, and this risk obviously increases with longer maturity bonds. When constructing a long-term bond ladder designed to provide dependable income, it is safest to assume that there is no such thing as a blue-chip, safe-as-houses corporate credit risk. (See Chapter 8 for how corporate credit risk evolves over time.) An investor who wishes to take advantage of the higher yields available from assuming credit risk should follow a professionally managed approach to investing in credit risk, and forgo the concept of a bond ladder. Investors can easily see sample portfolios (for example, mutual fund portfolios) of the most highly respected fixed-income portfolio managers. These will show that credit risk is well diversified with modest exposures to individual names. A bond ladder gives much less opportunity for such diversification.

In practice, constructing a bond ladder involves a series of choices (which may be more limited than would be wished) and trade-offs between what is desirable for a buy-and-hold approach to investing and what is available. Bond ladders need to be constructed with care, taking account of the tax status of different issues, as well as credit risk and the existence of call options that enable the issuer to repay the bond early.

Bond ladders, tax and creditworthiness: the case of US municipal bonds

In any jurisdiction investors need to be aware of tax rules which alter the terms on which investments are bought and sold. The $1.9 trillion US municipal bond market is attractive to taxable investors because interest on municipal bonds is exempt from federal income tax and state and local tax in the issuing state, whereas interest on US Treasury and government agency bonds is subject to federal income tax (but exempt from state income taxes). This difference in tax treatment leads taxable investors to bid up the price of municipal bonds compared with similar Treasury bonds.

Rules of thumb are normally used to compare municipal and Treasury bonds, such as a comparison of the difference in yields with the investor's tax rate. (Inaccuracies with this approach arise because of interest coupon reinvestment risk and the tax that has to be paid on the coupon of the taxable bond. The solution is not a comparison of yields, but a comparison of holding period returns.) Nevertheless, a key indicator is the ratio of the yield on highest quality municipal bonds to that on US Treasuries of similar maturity and a comparison of that ratio with the investor's tax rate. In practice, there are a range of factors that need to be compared:

- Whether the municipal bond issue has call provisions which enable the issuer to repay the bond at par (or a specified premium to par) early. Whether the issuer chooses to exercise this option will depend on whether this would reduce the debt interest burden. Call provisions will undermine the usefulness of a bond as part of a ladder intended to secure future income, because the bond will be called when it suits the issuer, not the investor. Call provisions always undermine the interests of investors and provide a valuable option for the issuer, so a callable bond should offer investors a higher yield than a non-callable bond.
- The creditworthiness of the municipal bond issue, as any issue which is less creditworthy than the US government should offer a premium yield on a strictly like-for-like comparison. There is a difference in the creditworthiness of the two main types of municipal bonds: general obligation bonds and revenue bonds. General obligation bonds are backed by the full faith and credit of the issuer and are usually supported by the issuer's tax-raising powers. By contrast, revenue bonds are serviced from specific projects which have been funded by the bonds. If the project fails to generate sufficient income to service the debt, the bondholders have no access to other sources of revenue of the issuing authority. In practice this has led to the spread of insured municipal bonds, whereby an insurance company promises to pay if an issuer does not do so. This is of considerable benefit to less known issuers. By 2004, over 50% of all new municipal bond issues were insured.

  The expansion of insurance has increased the range of issues available for inclusion in high-quality bond ladders. Other highest quality municipal bonds include those where the original issue is "refunded" or collateralised, for example with US Treasury securities. These are usually paid down at the first callable date after the refunding, though some are backed by collateral that matches the original maturity schedule of the issue. These are called "escrowed-to-maturity" bonds (though the existence of earlier call provisions still needs to checked).
- Liquidity, and the ease of selling a bond in the market. For Treasury

securities this will not be an issue, but for many municipal bond issues, the transaction costs can be considerable.

These factors help to explain why the municipal bond market has often traded at higher yields than might be expected by simply making a comparison with the US Treasury market and prevailing tax rates. This difference has been most marked for longer maturity municipal bonds. As a result, the term structure of the municipal bond market has often been steeper than that for US Treasuries. This is a most attractive feature for a laddered, buy-and-hold approach to investing in municipal bonds.

A further possible influence on the attraction of yields in the municipal and Treasury markets is the scale of borrowing by federal compared with state governments. This explanation relies on the fact that tax-paying investors naturally gravitate towards the tax-exempt municipal market, whereas tax-exempt investors naturally avoid the municipal bond market, and so differences in the scale of borrowing by federal or state and local government could, within limits, affect yields in one market more than in the other. In any event, investors should check that they are comfortable with the yield on offer from municipal bonds when compared with the after-tax yield offered on US Treasuries of similar maturity, after allowing for differences in liquidity and credit risk and for any provisions that might lead to the early redemption of a bond.

The Orange County saga: what is a good-quality municipal bond?

In December 1994, Orange County in California filed for bankruptcy following a $1.7 billion loss on a highly leveraged investment portfolio, which through extensive use of sophisticated derivative instruments transformed $7.6 billion of investments into $20.6 billion of market exposure. Ahead of this sudden announcement, there would have been little basis for questioning the creditworthiness of the local authority of such an affluent district. The Orange County crisis was therefore different from the more drawn out, and well trailed, financial difficulties faced by New York City in the 1970s, and so reveals much about risks that could in extraordinary circumstances be incurred in the municipal bond market.

- Many of Orange County's bonds were insured and were revenue bonds, and this reduced investors' exposure to Orange County risk.
- The experience showed that if a state or local authority ever defaults, investors might be more secure with revenue bonds, which are tied to particular projects,

than with general obligation bonds, which are supported by the "full faith and credit" of the issuer. The general rule, though, is that general obligation bonds are less risky than uninsured revenue bonds.

◪ Although the viability of Orange County finances was restored through the successful issue of "recovery bonds" in 1996, which permitted the County's exit from bankruptcy, any episode like this incurs significant costs in terms of anxiety to investors in the securities. It also imposes higher borrowing costs on the defaulter going forward.

What's the catch in following a long-term strategy?

There is a catch for the unprepared, particularly for unprepared cautious long-term investors, in agreeing to adopt a long-term strategy. Cautious long-term investors should be concerned to hedge or stabilise the purchasing power of their wealth. This is very different from stabilising the market value of that wealth. When real interest rates increase the market value of the hedging investment (inflation-linked bonds) will fall. But their ability to match future inflation-linked obligations remains unchanged, despite their decline in price. The hedged portfolio for the most cautious long-term investor (which could be fully invested in long-dated inflation-linked government bonds) will have been chosen as the best means to minimise uncertainty in meeting financial objectives. But its market value may be volatile, and a cautious long-term investor needs to understand this as well as the distinction between good and bad volatility. Furthermore, faced with a forecast rise in interest rates, and thus a fall in bond prices, some advisers might be tempted to recommend selling the most "vulnerable" long-dated bonds, staying in cash and waiting until market yields look more attractive. This might or might not prove to be profitable advice, but it is clear that such a move would represent a substantial increase in risk-taking because, if the forecast is wrong and it was acted upon, the pensioner would probably be locked into a lower income stream and a lower standard of living in retirement. If the forecast seems credible, the investor may want to put some element of future income at risk to back the investment view, but probably not much.

Before the beginning of 2006, the "worst" month for the young US Treasury TIPS market had been July 2003. In that month the yield on the 25-year TIP (3.625% of 2028) increased by 50 basis points to 2.94%, and its price fell by 8.2%. For an investor funding a pension plan from regular cash contributions into inflation-linked government bonds, such an increase in yield and reduction in price is clearly good news as it enables each contribution at the lower price to purchase more pension entitlement. This is at the heart of the distinction between good and bad volatility. For long-term pension investors who were continuing to contribute to their savings plan, the July 2003 increase in real yields and fall in bond prices should not have been a concern to cautious investors, even though with hindsight they may regret not postponing purchases until the higher yields were on offer. But it is normally wishful thinking to believe that they might have been able to succeed at such market timing.

One easy and intuitive way for investors to appreciate these issues is to look at time series information on the long-dated nominal or inflation-linked government bond interest income that could, in principle, be purchased with the market value of an investor's total portfolio. It is the volatility of this potential income stream that should be of particular concern to long-term investors.

But the most important feature of short-term and long-term models is that there is a fundamental difference in strategy design for cautious long-term investors and for cautious short-term investors. These are not small differences that can be ignored: there is an essential difference between stabilising the purchasing power of an investor's wealth, the objective for a cautious long-term investor, and stabilising the value of that wealth, the objective for a cautious short-term investor.

Lifestyle investing: income from employment often helps to diversify investment risk

Much of the value in a young private business is the anticipated contribution of the principals of the business over the years ahead. The same applies to employees who allow for the value of their future earnings potential in making financial decisions (for example, in taking out a mortgage): prospective earnings reduce financial risk for any individual. This will have more value for someone who is young than for someone who is old, or for someone who is healthy than for someone whose future earnings are constrained by ill health. It has been recognised for some time that investment strategy should take account of the flexibility provided by future earnings from employment. In effect, these future earnings can be thought of as a holding of a "wage-linked bond" whose risk characteristics will vary from person to person and should reflect the riskiness of an individual's earnings. These implicitly risky bond holdings can be taken into account in setting strategy.

For example, individuals at the start of their career may be confident that employment (with whichever employer) will provide a means of financing savings over the years ahead. As the years pass, the value of this future stream of earnings becomes less. This justifies a gradual "lifestyle" phasing of investment strategy for many individual investors, whatever their risk tolerance. So even cautious, risk-averse investors might have their financial investments dominated by risky assets when they are young and move to a more obviously "conservative" mix, for example of bonds and some stocks, as they grow older. This approach is warranted because of the financial cushion and flexibility that individuals gain from the prospect of future earnings, not because over a long period equity risk diminishes.

This traditional "life-cycle" phasing of investment strategy is not appropriate for all individuals. It should work comfortably for the pension savings of government employees, who will not have any natural equity market exposure from their employment. It probably would not be appropriate for entrepreneurs whose own business is best thought of as a private equity exposure. For this type of investor portfolio balance may require from the outset a significant allocation within accumulated savings to high-quality bonds.

Long-term strategy: "imperfect information changes everything"

In finance it is possible to imagine scenarios where virtually nothing is certain. In practice it is conventional to assume that governments of developed countries will honour their domestic currency obligations and to treat almost everything else as shrouded in some degree of doubt. But wealth planning and risk modelling exercises generally proceed as if we can precisely quantify uncertainty. This is procedurally convenient; it is also misleading.

We know that we should expect a risk premium for investing in equities, but we do not know how much premium. We know that equities are risky, and more risky at some times than others, but we do not know precisely how to model how risky they will be. Chapter 3 discussed recent research which indicates that equities are less risky over long periods than would be suggested by simple extrapolation of their short-term volatility. But we do not have a good feel for how big a reduction in volatility this will be, or even what the base level is from which the reduction should be measured. If this does not sound comforting to a cautious investor, it is not supposed to. This still leaves equities as risky assets for all investors, while government securities, particularly inflation-linked government bonds, are the low-risk, safe investments.

The strength of the mean reversion story – that good times predictably follow bad times in equity markets – and its implications for setting strategy are still controversial. At a minimum, the "parameters" of the process – the extent and timing of its occurrences, and the catalysts which precipitate reversals of previous trends – are uncertain. This should be regarded as one of those subjects on which received wisdom may change in the years ahead, and strategy needs to reflect this uncertainty by diluting any suggestion of leaning towards extreme positions in risky assets.

If an investor is persuaded by the mean reversion story, this would be an argument for increasing long-term allocations to equities. In turn, that investor should also believe that it is possible to identify whether the period ahead is likely to be one of above-average or below-average equity returns. However, the important issue for long-term investors is how equities are expected to perform relative to their safe-haven investment, typically inflation-linked government bonds. Accordingly, the mean reversion story that should matter would be a predictable pattern of superior, and then inferior, returns from equities relative to inflation-linked government bonds. To date, this has not been a focus of research, partly because this new asset class has only a short track record, and partly because of the margins of error that accompany attempts to create synthetic histories.

If investors wish to exploit the mean reversion phenomenon by tactically varying their allocation to risky or safe-haven investments, they should do it with great care, conscious of the length of time that might be required before such a strategy is successful in adding value or avoiding losses. Such investors could consider allocating some funds to a tactical asset allocation manager whose value orientation and time scale seems likely to have a good chance of exploiting the mean reversion phenomenon. But so long as the manager stays true to his or her investment philosophy, they should also be prepared to be patient. For many investors this degree of tenacity is a tall order, particularly when they can be sure that others will be trying to persuade them that their tenacity is in fact stubbornness that flies in the face of the convincing evidence that has persuaded almost all others to go with the flow of recent market developments. Tenacity is a difficult virtue to sustain in the face of uncertainty.

Some "keep-it-simple" concluding messages

The model allocations described in this chapter are simplified and will often need tailoring to suit an individual investor's needs. Compared with the short-term stylised models, the long-term models have a modest extra allocation to equities, which can be thought of as reflecting a degree of extra flexibility offered by a long time horizon. But this might not be appropriate for all long-term investors. The illustrative long-term models take no account of how investors need to take decisions over time, or of how their circumstances and the risks and opportunities in the market change. But they give a flavour of what strategy might look like if the available investments comprised only cash, domestic conventional government bonds, domestic inflation-linked government bonds and equities. In many cases, appropriate "keep-it-simple" strategies, consisting only of these investment classes, can be constructed for the financial needs of most investors.

In practice, most investors will spend much more time focusing on the detail of implementation, which involves departures from this keep-it-simple approach. How much should go in hedge funds? Isn't finding the right manager more important than the right hedge fund strategy? Surely value will outperform growth? Is high yield too risky? What about emerging markets? And so on.

Despite the time that most investors spend on these issues, the most important one is the extent to which obligations or spending plans are hedged. In the case of the subsistence farmer, how much of next year's food requirement has been secured, and what is the scale of the risk of a shortfall and the opportunity of surplus generation offered by the mismatch? The keep-it-simple framework is more than adequate to address these fundamental issues. What is often thought be the more exciting material about the different asset classes is covered in the second part of this book.

5 Implementing "keep-it-simple" strategies

Market timing: an unavoidable risk

Implementing and changing strategy is a game that is fraught with risk for investors. But it has to be played. There is little advice available to investors on how to decide when to change strategy. For larger institutional investors, investment managers and consultants provide much advice on how to insure against bad outcomes and how to manage transactions costs once an investor has decided when to change strategy. However, there is little profit for an adviser in answering the key question: "When?" But for all investors this is a crucial issue in managing investments.

Implementing strategy change involves unavoidable market timing. You know you have to get from A to B, but how to get there, and particularly when to get there, requires judgments about market timing. These have to be balanced against the knowledge that your investment risk profile is not what you want it to be (which is why you want to change strategy).

A simple rule to follow is that if investors decide that their risk profile is too aggressive, they should move to the new, more cautious strategy promptly, perhaps allowing some small amount of time for trying to be cute about market movements, but with little confidence that this will add much value. Such investors should not let seeming confidence in short-term market forecasts extend the period during which their risk profile is inappropriate. This is easily stated and probably more easily applied in the case of an institution's wealth than for an individual or a family. This is because discussions about risk tolerance are rarely separated from views on market prospects in discussions with families.

However, for all investors critical market timing decisions are a fact of life. Since personal and corporate circumstances change, long-term investment strategy and tolerance for investment risk for almost all investors change, and will continue to change, considerably before the "long term" is reached. These changes will involve decisions on how to adjust long-term strategy, by how much and when. Within each four- or five-year period there is a significant chance for any investor that circumstances may force such a change or adjustment of direction. The obvious group of investors for whom this might not apply is well-resourced "perpetual" endowments (such as some university foundations), which have a clearly articulated and accepted approach to strategic risk management.

Adjustments to strategy involve taking views on markets and, typically, a significant degree of regret risk. As explained in Chapter 2, this can involve two distinct emotions:

- ◪ Outcome risk. This is the potential for feeling regret at having made a well-justified move (for example, to scale back excessive risk-taking) at a date which – with the benefit of hindsight – proves to have been less profitable than later dates would have been.
- ◪ "Self-blame" risk. This might arise if inappropriate risk-taking, although analysed and identified, was not corrected sufficiently expeditiously. Market timing always involves risk, which is why it should always be undertaken with care and with an eye on the consequences of being wrong-footed by markets at substantial financial and emotional cost to investors.

The real issue is not that market timing cannot be undertaken skilfully or profitably: it can. There are a few investment managers whose skill in market timing has manifested itself over time. But these track records are not built by one-off "bet the ranch" decisions on the timing of corrections to inappropriate risk profiles. They are carefully managed and, within limits, diversified. Changing strategy is different. There is normally no way to diversify the investment decision or to give meaningful time to profit from the correction of perceived market anomalies. No good investment manager would wish their skill in reading markets to be judged against such an unforgiving benchmark.

It is often suggested that phasing implementation of a change in investment strategy from one asset class to another is the best way to proceed if an investor has to change strategy. The investor is likely to feel more comfortable with this approach because, on average, spreading implementation over several tranches avoids the hindsight risk of having chosen one particularly unfavourable date to make the switch. But the strong argument in favour of immediate implementation of change is that having decided that the current investment strategy is inappropriate, any delay extends unnecessary risk-taking. When faced with the need to make such a decision, there are always reasons why now is not the best time to act. But managing investments is a risk business, and decisions are often neither comfortable nor easy and market calls have to be made. If an investor's risk profile is recognised as inappropriate, it is inexcusable to wait until adverse market circumstances highlight what had previously been recognised as an inappropriate risk profile, and then to worry about how to implement a change in strategy.

Strongly held market views and the safe haven: the 1990s equity boom

Stockmarket bubbles and manias happen. We all know this. It is easy to say how investors should respond if they see speculative excess in a market. They should divert from their long-term strategy in that market and either buy protection for that exposure or directly scale back their exposure to that market to guard their wealth and spending power. Anything deliberately left exposed to speculative excesses should be no more than a margin which the investor is prepared to risk substantially losing (from the top potential layer of a behaviourist risk and asset allocation pyramid). An investor's "crown jewels", which are required to meet essential financial objectives, should be well protected from speculation. In these circumstances, investors should either look elsewhere or significantly increase the allocation to their safe-haven investments – cash for short-term investors, government bonds for long-term investors.

Bubbles

There is no agreement on what constitutes a "bubble", and there is a clear division between the starting points of those who look for rational explanations of market phenomena and those who emphasise the scope for irrational behaviour to influence markets. The usual interpretation of a "bubble" is a market which appreciates strongly beyond values that would be validated by "fundamentals" and then rapidly deflates. Charles Kindelberger, in his classic book *Manias, Panics and Crashes*, describes the phenomenon as follows:

> *What happens, basically, is that some event changes the economic outlook. New opportunities for profit are seized, and overdone, in ways so closely resembling irrationality as to constitute a mania.*

But it is easy to use this, together with a liberal dose of hindsight, in a way which underestimates how difficult it is to assess the extent to which the value of companies, and so the level of stock prices, should change when new technologies are introduced. This has been explored by Allan Meltzer, professor of political economy at Carnegie Mellon University, in "Rational and Irrational Bubbles" (an address to a World Bank Conference on asset price bubbles in 2002), who emphasises that there are three levels of uncertainty:

- ◪ Does the new technology really represent a one-off "blip" in profits for the affected companies, which is not already discounted by market prices? Or:
- ◪ Does the new technology represent a step change in the future sustained level of profits for the firms concerned? Or:
- ◪ Does the new technology really represent a step change in the future growth rate of profits?

Answers to these questions will emerge only after a considerable period of time (by when they may be "obvious"), but in the meantime the stockmarket will reflect the prevailing weight of market opinion and these uncertainties will be associated with a marked increase in stockmarket volatility. It is crucial that all investors take a view on when rational enthusiasm fostered by the uncertain impact of new technologies trips over into the irrational manias and speculative excesses that Kindelberger describes.

Advice to avoid speculative excess is easier to give than to implement successfully. We know that it is difficult to add value through market timing and that investors are human. Robert Shiller brilliantly timed the top of the 1990s technology bubble with the publication of his book *Irrational Exuberance* in March 2000. He explains later in *The New Financial Order* that he was strongly encouraged to drop other work to complete the book by his friend and colleague, Jeremy Siegel. But as Siegel explains in his magnum opus, *Stocks for the Long Run*, Shiller, together with John Campbell, a Harvard economist, produced research for the Federal Reserve Board in late 1996 suggesting that the stockmarket was already significantly overvalued. These concerns were preoccupying Alan Greenspan, the Federal Reserve's chairman, when he used the phrase "irrational exuberance" to discuss recent appreciation in equities in a speech given on December 5th 1996. The Dow Jones index was then at 6,437. It subsequently peaked, over 80% higher, at 11,700 in January 2000. The lowest point it reached during the subsequent bear market was 7,286 in June 2002, some 13% higher than when the "exuberance" call was made.

Greenspan used those words in the context of asking this question:

> But how do we know when irrational exuberance has unduly
> escalated asset values, which then become subject to unexpected
> and prolonged contractions as they have in Japan over the past
> decade?

The answer is "only with very great difficulty", especially when discussing the market as a whole and not individual sectors or stocks within it. The Fed itself has shared this view. This is what Greenspan had to say in August 2002:

> As events evolved, we recognised that, despite our suspicions, it
> was very difficult to definitively identify a bubble until after the
> fact – that is, when its bursting confirmed its existence.

He added:

> Moreover, it was far from obvious that bubbles, even if identified
> early, could be pre-empted short of the central bank inducing a
> substantial contraction in economic activity – the very outcome
> we would be seeking to avoid.

The perspective of the Federal Reserve is financial stability, which is different from an investor's perspective of wealth management, but Greenspan's comments should encourage people to have some modesty about their ability to call markets successfully. Success in this context would not have involved shifting from equities to cash in 1996 (when the Fed's concerns were first expressed) and when "value" managers were already expressing concern about the value of the US market.

This sense of modesty in the ability to call markets encourages some to argue that long-term investors should buy and hold equities through thick and thin. The reasoning behind this recommendation is that market timing is hazardous and, for some advisers, equities are less risky for long-term investors. Campbell and others agree that equities seem to be less risky over long time horizons than is suggested by their short-run volatility because equities "mean revert". If this is correct, Campbell argues that investors should overweight equities when they are expected to perform better than average and underweight them when they are expected to do worse than average. Many consultants would say that this is "easier said than done, except after the event".

The difficulty with such market timing can be illustrated by the Fed's

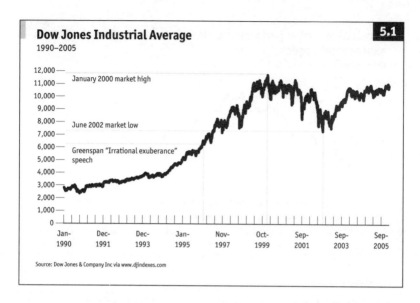

Dow Jones Industrial Average
1990–2005

5.1

- January 2000 market high
- June 2002 market low
- Greenspan "Irrational exuberance" speech

| | Jan-1990 | Dec-1991 | Dec-1993 | Jan-1995 | Nov-1997 | Oct-1999 | Sep-2001 | Sep-2003 | Sep-2005 |

Source: Dow Jones & Company Inc via www.djindexes.com

"irrational exuberance" example of seeming to call the existence of a bubble. This is instructive because it was very public and official. Figure 5.1 gives the level of the Dow Jones Industrial Average index of leading US stocks before and after the "exuberance" call.

More tellingly, consider the cumulative performance (including dividends and interest, but excluding fees) of a broadly based investment in US equities, US government bonds or cash from the end of November 1996 (that is, just days before Greenspan's speech). Since 1996 it has clearly been more profitable to be in equities rather than cash. Sophisticated long-term investors who considered government bonds as the alternative to equities would have performed well (at lower volatility) by investing, and staying, in bonds. But the likelihood is that many (perhaps almost all) investors who had made such a change would subsequently have switched back to equities before the peak in the market, missing out on much of the subsequent rally and then suffering the fall after early 2000. These investors would be much worse off than investors who had, and maintained, a broadly diversified exposure to the equity market throughout the period after the Greenspan exuberance speech.

Common sense is helpful here. Speculative excess is typically focused on individual stocks or sectors rather than the entire equity market. This means that diversification is a first line of defence. In turn, investors need to have the self-discipline to avoid undiversifying their strategies in

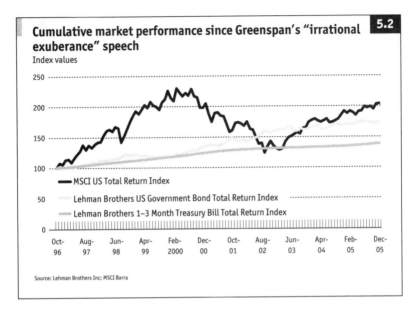

Cumulative market performance since Greenspan's "irrational exuberance" speech   `5.2`

Index values

- ■ MSCI US Total Return Index
- Lehman Brothers US Government Bond Total Return Index
- Lehman Brothers 1–3 Month Treasury Bill Total Return Index

Source: Lehman Brothers Inc; MSCI Barra

pursuit of the latest hot investment fashion. It is a serious error to confuse the risk of an undiversified part of the overall equity market (for example, the NASDAQ market) with that of the market as a whole. A second tier of self-defence is to use investment managers who are intrinsically conscious of market manias as a "hardy perennial" in markets which are known to be particularly subject to waves of euphoria and depression.

Should long-term investors hold more equities?

The existence of stockmarket bubbles brings us back to the time diversification of equity market risk because if booms and busts in the stockmarket predictably follow each other, it may be possible to profit from this pattern. However, if we doubt our ability to time markets, even though we believe in market cycles, then this predictable cyclical nature of equity returns will reinforce the case for a somewhat higher allocation to equities for long-term investors.

A number of studies, notably by Siegel in *Stocks for the Long Run*, have suggested that over long holding periods (for example, 30 years or more) an investor might be more sure, or at least less uncertain, of the after-inflation performance to expect from equities than from conventional government bonds. This builds on the experience of the 20th century, when the impact of unanticipated inflation made cash and bonds much riskier for holding wealth over long periods than shorter-term experience would suggest. The evidence that Siegel uses to support this comes primarily from the United States, but it also appears to be supported, almost without exception, by international data. Taken together, these would suggest skewing, at least to some extent, the investment strategy allocation for long-term investors towards equities and away from bonds for cautious as well as aggressive investors. This leads Siegel to suggest that "an ultra conservative" investor with a 30-year holding period might have a strategy allocation to equities of 71%.

However, he makes clear that although this model does reflect the effect that unanticipated 20th century inflation had on the investments in conventional government bonds and cash of cautious investors, it does not incorporate the potential role of the recent innovation of the TIPS market in the United States.

The introduction of inflation-linked government bonds has changed the ground rules for long-term investment strategy in the 21st century. Long-term investors may have little difficulty in acknowledging that they may also have medium-term objectives (even if they are not articulated today). As a result, investors have no difficulty grasping the importance of measuring the risk of losses or shortfalls at all points in time, as well as the insights of behavioural finance into loss aversion. Taken together, this suggests that it is now neither necessary nor desirable to recommend high equity allocations for long-term cautious investors. However, if long-term cautious investors have confidence in the equity mean reversion story, especially if they have access to other sources of income, they might reasonably hold more equities than would be recommended for cautious investors with a short time horizon.

PART 2
IMPLEMENTING MORE COMPLICATED STRATEGIES

6 Setting the scene

A health warning: liquidity risk

The "keep-it-simple" strategies described in previous chapters should be liquid as well as simple. Almost always, when investment strategy gets more complicated it starts to embrace more liquidity risk. Liquidity is a dimension of risk which is not captured by the off-the-shelf risk models that are routinely used in managing investments. This is because it is difficult to model, not because it does not matter. Dan Borge, a former chief risk manager at Bankers Trust, describes illiquidity as "the most dangerous and least understood financial risk".

Liquid markets give investors the option to buy or sell an investment at modest transaction cost at any time of their choosing at prevailing market prices; illiquid markets do not give them this option. Like any option, this is valuable, though some investors will value it more highly than others. Furthermore, the value that investors put on it varies substantially over time. Investors who value liquidity will need to be offered a premium rate of return before investing in illiquid assets. Correspondingly, investors should pay less for an illiquid investment than for an otherwise identical liquid investment.

Liquid investments should provide the natural habitat for short-term investors, even for aggressive short-term investors. This is because they may need to realise investments at short notice (which is why they are short-term investors). Long-term investors can more easily accommodate illiquidity and with skill may profit from it.

The liquidity of an investment often varies according to the size of the holding. It will normally be possible to buy or sell a marginal holding of any quoted investment at or close to its published price. But the holdings of large investment funds often represent a significant part of the available capitalisation of a security. Any attempt to establish or to realise such holdings requires skill and time so as to manage the adverse "market impact" on the price of the transaction. These are circumstances in which large investors can be heavily penalised or well rewarded for demanding liquidity from or supplying liquidity to the market. For substantial investors in many markets liquidity is at best an illusion, as the published prices provide a reliable guide to realisable transactions for only a small part of their holdings in individual stocks. This means that substantial short-term investors who really do have a short time horizon must maintain a high degree of liquidity in their investments.

Some markets that are usually liquid can become illiquid surprisingly quickly. When you want to sell, which is the same as saying when you want to demand or pay for liquidity, you may be forced to delay transacting and so accept risks that you would prefer to avoid, or you may be forced to concede damaging prices that you do not wish to accept. If the intentions of large investors seeking to unwind or establish substantial positions in a short period become known to others in the market, they will always become victims of predatory behaviour by other market participants. The market never behaves as if it is a benevolent mechanism in these circumstances.

But variable liquidity is both a risk and an opportunity. An alternative definition of a short-term investor is an investor who may need to demand liquidity at short notice. Short-term investors should review and limit the allocation of their portfolio to markets that might be subject to marked fluctuations in liquidity because in these markets the price of liquidity can become prohibitively high in a very short period. This is a clear threat to the achievement of short-term financial goals.

These risks may not be evident from the historical data on price volatility. In some markets, the historical track record for prices may be smoothed because no market transactions occurred at times of crisis in many of the securities that make up the market.

Long-term investors can profit from these swings in liquidity, so long as they are able to employ professional dealers who are skilled at "selling" liquidity. Often, though, the best outcome will be to ride out the occasional liquidity crises without having to accept penal terms for buying liquidity when it is most expensive. By being conscious of the price of liquidity or the cost of "immediacy", long-term investors may be able to exploit the occasional liquidity crises which spread across markets. It is not only at times of crisis that these principles apply. Differences in equity transaction costs between trading desks of different investment houses reflect whether the money managers or traders demand and pay for immediate execution, which raises their "execution" costs, or whether they are content to bide their time, at the risk of missing out on the potential advantages of rapid execution. If they do this, they are able to await opportunities that are presented to them to offer, or provide, rather than to demand, liquidity. In effect, investors get paid for providing liquidity, but pay for demanding liquidity. "Value" equity managers will normally pride themselves on their ability to provide rather than demand liquidity. The opposite will be true of momentum managers, who seek to profit from market trends.

Long-term managers with a clear sense of investment philosophy and discipline, who, at the required time, have the asset allocation flexibility, will be able to exploit the occasional extreme price paid for liquidity. But for waverers, hesitation will always be reinforced by the certainty that there will be highly reputable commentators who argue that prospects have changed for the worse and that what appears inexpensive is at best fairly priced. For "natural habitat" private investors, who have the good fortune (or foresight, or both) to have significant resources awaiting investment at the moment of crisis, these events can present a once-in-a-lifetime opportunity to lay the foundations of a substantial fortune.

Behavioural finance, market efficiency and arbitrage opportunities
Illiquidity indicates a breakdown of market efficiency. Any discussion of market efficiency should start by addressing a widespread heresy, a variation of which Robert Shiller has described as "one of the most remarkable errors in the history of economic thought". This is the notion that the very existence of inefficiency in markets is a sufficient reason to expect outperformance from skilful managers. However, it does not follow that there must be easy rewards for skilled investors just because markets are inefficient, because evident inefficiencies can be difficult to arbitrage. Correspondingly, if there seem to be no easy rewards for active managers, this is not necessarily evidence of markets being efficient. The converse, though, does apply: if markets are efficient, the scope for skilled managers to add value will definitely be limited. The rule of thumb is that if the existence of a market anomaly can easily be demonstrated, the safest conclusion is that there must be some difficulty in profiting from the anomaly. Markets may be inefficient, but this does not mean that there are readily available free lunches available for investors.

To illustrate this, consider the example of an apparent arbitrage opportunity shown in Figure 6.1 overleaf, published by the Bank of England in 2002. It shows the UK's nominal and inflation-linked government bond forward yield curves in December 1999. This shows the pattern of one-year nominal and real interest rates and inflation rates, which were implied by UK government bond prices in late 1999, stretching out into the future. (The inflation rate is the "break-even" rate of inflation.) The implied path for inflation is conspicuous. The initial increase is consistent with tax effects, but there was no obvious reason to expect a pick-up in inflation between years 15 and 25. As Cedric Scholtes of the

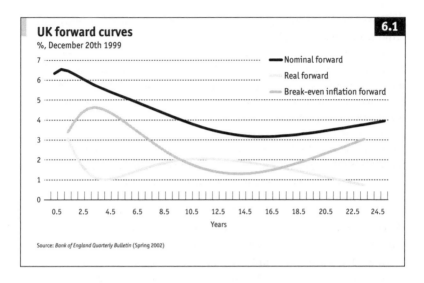

UK forward curves
%, December 20th 1999

6.1

Legend:
- Nominal forward
- Real forward
- Break-even inflation forward

Years

Source: *Bank of England Quarterly Bulletin* (Spring 2002)

Bank of England wrote, this projection was "difficult to reconcile with investor rationality".

In theory there would appear to have been clear opportunities for government bond investors to exploit and to correct this anomaly. These unusual yield patterns in the UK government bond market arose because of regulatory pressure on insurance companies and pension funds to reduce the mismatch between their assets and liabilities. This had a differential impact on the conventional and inflation-linked market at different maturities. The insurance companies needed to buy 15-year conventional government bonds, and the pension funds needed to buy over 20-year maturity inflation-linked government bonds. At the same time, the small size of the government deficit meant that new issues of government debt were scarce. The next section explores the barriers, which for a time can prevent such anomalies from being arbitraged away.

Another widely quoted example of evident arbitrage opportunity is the significant differential that existed historically between the share prices of Royal Dutch (traded principally in Amsterdam and New York) and Shell Transport & Trading (traded principally in London). Shares in both companies gave strictly comparable ownership rights in the same company, but Royal Dutch traded historically as much as 35% underpriced and as much as 15% overpriced compared with Shell Transport & Trading.

Barriers to arbitrage

The Shell share price anomaly did not provide an easy profit opportunity because the anomaly could get worse. This position was resolved only after Shell announced in late 2004 that the two share classes would finally merge in 2005. The corporate announcement provided some assurance of a profitable exit within a specified time period. Often there exists no such exit strategy from a perceived anomaly, which explains why it may persist.

The key to the potential persistence of these "anomalies" lies in the impediments to arbitrage which can prevent instances of irrational pricing translating into easy profit opportunities. These barriers are generally considered to be of three types.

Fundamental risk and arbitrage

The first barrier is the common danger (not present in the Shell example) that fundamental risk may undermine any effort to arbitrage away an anomaly. An example would be where one company in an industry is thought to be expensive and a similar one to be more sensibly priced. A hedge fund manager might sell the former and buy the latter, but the size of these positions will be limited because the arbitrageur will know that unexpected events could cause the expensive stock to appreciate in price and the cheap stock to decline, causing losses to both sides of the "hedge". A graphic illustration of an apparently good hedge resulting in large losses was provided in May 2005 when in the space of two days Kirk Kerkorian, an American billionaire investor, announced his intention to increase his holding in General Motors (GM) stock (which increased in price) and Standard & Poor's (see Chapter 8) downgraded the debt of both GM and Ford from investment grade to sub-investment grade, which fell in price. The problem was that a number of hedge funds thought they were "hedging" GM equity (which they had sold) with GM debt (which they believed to be cheap, and so had bought). The result was substantial losses for a number of hedge funds on both sides of the hedge whose prices, unusually, moved in opposite directions. The simple lesson is to make sure the hedge is a good hedge. The more substantive one is that even the best hedges may fail and the risk of this happening puts a limit on the scale of the arbitrage position that will be applied to correct apparent market anomalies.

To risk money on an arbitrage position, the investor must consider the time horizon for the position. A hedge fund that correctly identified in the late 1990s that "new economy" (technology, media, telecom) sectors of the stockmarket were overpriced relative to so-called "old economy" sectors could easily have bankrupted itself before the validity of its analysis was demonstrated by the collapse of "new economy" stock prices. This illustrates that some types of market anomaly, whose identification will always be subject to margins of uncertainty, may require such long time horizons that the investors best suited to try to exploit them will be long-term investment funds, not hedge funds. In a hedge fund, the balance of long and short positions, which require daily marking to market of profits and losses, will not be able to support large long-term positions. It follows that hedge funds are not ideally suited to correct all pricing anomalies.

Herd behaviour and arbitrage

In fact, hedge funds may exacerbate anomalies in the short run. The second barrier to arbitrage is that "noise trader risk" may undermine arbitrage efforts by making an apparent anomaly even more extreme. A hedge fund, or any other short-term speculator, understanding that investors may behave as if recent past performance will continue, may be more likely to follow and reinforce the anomaly than to hold out against it. This is an application of the "greater fool" theory, namely a confidence that profits can be made out of "hot" overpriced investments by selling them at a higher price on a later date to a greater fool. Recent studies have documented the successful pursuit of this type of behaviour by some hedge funds during the dotcom bubble. Other research has identified evidence of similar investment behaviour by market professionals during the South Sea bubble of 1720.

These patterns of investing will exacerbate irrational market trends. Success in this kind of anomaly exacerbating behaviour, like a policy of dancing by the doorway when you know the music hall may burn down, requires the ability to identify, and respond more quickly than others, to events which may act as a catalyst to burst a speculative bubble. On average for all investors this is a doomed strategy, but wishful thinking about their own nimbleness encourages many to stay on and enjoy the party while it lasts. A few always get out in time thanks to a mixture of skill and luck. The random element of luck is normally downplayed, leading many to conclude that they may have the skill required to play the game next time. The one predictable result is that the market process of correcting anomalies is undermined and, for a while, made less effective.

In these circumstances it can be dangerous to bet against some apparent anomalies with more than a modest investment position. Furthermore, investors' preferred habitat may drive prices away from fundamentals, as the regulation and solvency driven example from the UK government bond market shows. Such anomalies can persist for a long time, reflecting the inability of short-term arbitrageurs (such as hedge funds) to remove the mispricing.

The role of crowd behaviour in driving investment prices away from their fundamental value requires a particular collective role for what are sometimes known as "noise traders". This needs a wide interpretation, because it does not just include the actions of uninformed investors. As well as professional investors who try to exploit momentum trends in crowds of uninformed investors, there are professional investors who feel forced to implement investment decisions which they view with deep scepticism. Such investments should be regarded as generating "noise", in the sense that there may be little fundamental investment justification for the decision. Occasionally, it is a result of spuriously precise definitions of "prudential" regulations. More common, though, may be the impact of peer group pressure generating herding behaviour among investors. This may be purely informal commercial risk management, where a money-management firm determines that its biggest risk is to be different from other firms. Or it may be imposed by formal or informal rules which dictate the margin of difference from the market or from other investors (this is often called relative risk or tracking error) that an investment fund may run. Where funds or managers are assessed relative to an index or relative to competitors this pressure will be present. It may exert most influence in larger, historically successful money-management firms where the pressure to conserve the existing business may be strongest.

The herd mentality is probably reinforced by the legal backing to the "prudent person" rule, which is the benchmark for the assessment of the reasonableness of the actions of fiduciaries in many countries. The 1974 Employee Retirement Income Security Act (ERISA) in the United States defines the obligations of a fiduciary as being to use "the care, skill, prudence, and diligence, under the circumstances then prevailing, that a prudent man acting in a like capacity and familiar with such matters would use in the conduct of an enterprise of a like character and with like aims".

As Shiller points out, this definition tests the reasonableness of a fiduciary's decision against the standard of how a peer might behave. In other words:

> *The prudent person standard refers to someone who does what most of us think is sensible. Ultimately, it must refer to conventional wisdom.*

It is not clear how this standard might be improved, but the inevitable consequence is that it validates the reasonableness of crowd behaviour. As a result, the impact of this standard of care is more likely to reinforce than to correct any tendency toward market mispricing. It will encourage trades that follow and support market trends as managers control their differences from the market or the peer group of other reasonable investors, who are behaving in exactly the same way. The behaviour of pension funds, responding to this pressure, has in the past been likened to a parade of circus elephants following each other round in a circle, joined from trunk to tail. The honest conclusion is that institutional investors never completely break from this circle. Their fiduciaries are, rightly, always looking over their shoulder and comparing themselves with comparable funds. For private wealth there is more flexibility, which brings both more opportunity and more danger.

Implementation costs, market evolution and arbitrage

The third potential barrier to arbitrage activities is that "implementation costs" can be prohibitive. Typically, an arbitrageur needs to sell short an investment. To be able to do this, a hedge fund needs to borrow the stock from another investor so as to deliver it to the investor who has bought it. This works smoothly in the textbooks and in liquid markets. In illiquid markets it can be a nightmare. This is because it is a process that is subject to administrative interruptions that can threaten investment positions. For example, if a stock lender wants the stock returned, the hedge fund's broker needs to find another investor from whom to borrow the stock. If it cannot, the hedge fund manager will be forced to buy the stock back before the anomaly has corrected (or, even worse, when it has become more entrenched). A further potential cost that always lurks in the background is that at times of crisis, hedge funds can be squeezed by cash demands (margin calls) from their prime brokers as they have to make daily cash payments on positions that move against them. The 1998 Long Term Capital Management crisis (see Chapter 9) provides vivid testimony to the reality that hedge funds cannot always afford to maintain large positions that may endure for a long period.

These influences mean that there is no inevitable tendency for markets to become progressively more efficient. The cycles of market liquidity show that market efficiency is itself also cyclical. Nevertheless, the pressures to arbitrage away anomalies will always be a powerful force in any market. If a particular market arrangement is a barrier to efficiency, you can be sure that there will be great pressure to remove that impediment because there will be arbitrage profits available to those who help remove it. Today's barrier to arbitrage may not exist tomorrow, as institutional and market arrangements and instruments are continuously evolving to overcome obstacles and to exploit opportunities to make money. Tomorrow there may be other anomalies, and old ones may reappear, but it would be a great mistake to underestimate what Robert Merton, the John and Natty McArthur University Professor at Harvard Business School, and Zvi Bodie refer to as "the financial innovation spiral" that works to chip away at anomalies and inefficiencies.

Institutional wealth and private wealth: taxation

The three principal differences between private and institutional wealth management are:

- the role of taxation in private wealth;
- the role of committees of fiduciaries in the management of institutional wealth; and
- the contrast between the flexible spending objectives of family wealth and the precise purposes of institutional wealth.

However, these are generalisations. Not all private wealth is subject to taxation and not all institutional wealth is exempt from taxation. Investment committees are found in the management of both private and institutional wealth. Some institutions have flexible objectives, whereas family philanthropic foundations have closely defined purposes and mark the boundary at which private wealth becomes institutional. Yet the broad generalisations remain valid, together with the further observation that the amounts of money represented by private wealth are normally much smaller than those of institutional investment funds.

Some advisers make far-reaching proposals for investment strategy to accommodate tax structures. Others emphasise that the benefits from many tax devices are in practice modest. Investors should be aware that given the same facts, conflicting advice may be offered. A number of things are clear, however. First, the tax authorities are generally well informed about the income of companies and individuals, and a low tax payment, as many good stock analysts will advise, is often a sign of low income. So, for taxable investors, minimising the overall tax bill often makes little sense. What does make sense is to try to maximise post-tax income, given your tolerance for risk, even if it means paying more tax. Any tax-management scheme should be assessed in this light: if it is

Table 6.1 **The impact of taxation on taxable investment returns and wealth accumulation**

Average tax rate (%)	0	20	40
Expected returns (% per year)			
Equities	8	6.4	4.8
Bonds	4	3.2	2.4
$100 becomes after ten years[a]			
Equities	$216	$186	$160
Bonds	$148	$137	$127
$100 becomes after ten years (today's prices assuming 2% per year inflation[a])			
Equities	$179	$154	$132
Bonds	$122	$113	$104
$100 becomes after 20 years (today's prices assuming 2% per year inflation[a])			
Equities	$321	$237	$174
Bonds	$149	$127	$108

a Assuming actual return equals expected return and that tax rate applies to annual total return with no allowances or tax shelters.

not expected to improve post-tax income, after allowing for tax advisory fees and for any special elements of risk introduced by the proposal, it probably should not be pursued. It is worth paying more tax if it is associated with even more income.

Tax does make an enormous difference, however, by constraining the evolution of private wealth. Table 6.1 illustrates its potential impact.

The picture is much more complicated than this. Table 6.1 assumes that capital gains and income are taxed at the same rate, which they are not. It assumes that each individual stock earns the same return, and it ignores any tax allowances that would reduce a headline tax rate to a lower effective rate. But the simple story remains true, that income and capital gains taxes seriously undermine the rate of accumulation of private wealth and the premium offered for taking risk. In practice, the impact on risk-taking varies as income tax particularly affects low-risk assets (bonds and cash) whereas capital gains tax particularly affects equities.

Individual taxpayers have tax-exempt accounts (for example, retirement accounts, which accumulate free of tax but on which withdrawals are treated as taxable income) as well as taxable accounts, and depending upon the jurisdiction an investor may have some tax-exempt accounts (accounts from which the investor can withdraw funds without incurring a tax penalty). Investment strategy and wealth management should take account of the different tax status of different accounts. This starts with any assessment of the sufficiency of wealth to meet future objectives. For example, a dollar in a tax-deferred pension savings account will be worth less than a dollar in a tax-exempt account. At the same time, investment strategy needs to take account of the totality of an investor's wealth in each different account or "location", and the allocation of investments to different locations needs to allow for the differences in the impact of tax on different types of investment.

The impact of taxation on risk-taking needs to be kept in mind when considering the uncertainty surrounding future equity returns. But uncertainty also surrounds future tax rates and allowances. This needs to be acknowledged in the degree to which the details of today's tax rules are allowed to influence the medium- or long-term investment strategy for an investor's taxable investments. If in doubt, keep it simple (but always take advice).

For a taxable investor, investment strategy never starts from a blank sheet of paper. There is always a legacy tax position that exists whenever an investor changes investment manager or adviser. This can have implications for:

- the choice between different styles of investment management;
- whether to have fewer or more managers;
- the desired average holding periods for investments;
- whether to have a bias towards low turnover accounts (though the relationship between turnover and taxation will not be straightforward);
- whether to have a bias against strategies that involve "top slicing" of all positions to rebalance or implement asset allocation decisions.

Investors should consider whether rebalancing between managers leads to needless generation of tax obligation, for example as stocks are reclassified between "small cap" and "large cap" or "mid cap", or between value and growth. An "all cap" flexible strategy, where the managers select stocks from across the whole equity market, may have advantages for a taxable investor, though this should not be assumed to be the case.

To address these issues, taxable investors should consult a tax-literate investment adviser (who may be better placed to advise on strategies to optimise after-tax investment returns) as well as a tax specialist (who may have a bias towards minimising tax payments). However, in responding to tax advice, investors should always retain an overall picture of their tax status as well as their investment strategy. This is particularly important if the investor divides savings and wealth between different objectives, different risk profiles, and a mix of taxed and tax-advantaged accounts. Finally, be cautious before prolonging any excessive investment risk (such as a concentrated stock position) simply because of concern about the tax consequences of selling down a position which represents a substantial capital gain. It is better to make a gain on which you pay tax than not to make a gain.

7 Equities

Concentrated stock positions in private portfolios

The analysis so far has assumed that any equity exposure shares the risk characteristics of the equity market. This is not the case for many investors. This is illustrated by the pattern of risk-taking shown by participants in US defined contribution (DC) pension plans – typically, 401(k) plans. A report written for the US Congress, following the financial losses suffered by participants in the DC pension scheme of Enron Corporation, which collapsed in 2001, showed that 38% of the assets of the major DC pension schemes surveyed were invested in the shares of the companies that employed the DC scheme participants. From the perspective of traditional finance, this shows a peculiar and unnecessarily risky pattern of investing for the individual employee participants in these schemes. For these investors in aggregate the same expected performance could be obtained at less risk by diversifying away from their employers' company stock. The avoidable extra volatility of these holdings in retirement savings accounts represents a major threat to the level of retirement income of many thousands of employees. This danger has been borne out not only by the well-publicised failures of some companies and the stories of impoverishment of individuals who were heavily reliant on stocks of failed companies, but also by the impact on retirement savings of sharp declines in the stock prices of many companies during the 2000–02 bear market.

The Congressional report found that investment in employer stock was greatest when employers made matching contributions into retirement accounts and when the company's stock price had outperformed the market over the previous three years. Anecdotal evidence suggests that company stock is frequently the only individual stock (rather than mutual fund) on many sponsoring companies' roster of investment opportunities for their 401(k) investment programmes. But the explanation is probably also behavioural, for example in extrapolating past performance, in being unduly influenced by how alternatives are presented, and perhaps by extrapolating familiarity with a person's "own" company into a confident assessment of the prospects for the company's stock price and a subjective assessment of a low risk of corporate failure.

Nevertheless, in terms of the prudent management of retirement savings, the message of this book is clear: these investors are incurring unnecessary risk which, on average, will not be rewarded and they should diversify. However, the insights in Chapter 2 indicate that if investors do this, some will be pleased (because their company stock underperforms) and others, whose stock subsequently performs well, will regret having been so cautious and will know (especially with hindsight) that it was obvious that their company would do better than average. Since any such comparison can be made at any time, and will not normally be made with accuracy, it is not clear whether as many who diversify would be pleased with the decision as would regret it. The prescriptions of traditional finance are clear on this issue, but the best way to proceed is probably to consult a trusted adviser and then to implement an agreed strategy.

Corporate executive remuneration programmes

These concentrated holdings within defined contribution pension accounts are separate from the concentrated stock positions that executives accumulate as a reward for success through corporate remuneration schemes. The pension plan holdings reflect a deliberate decision by the individual to acquire, or to retain, the stock. This is different from compensation awards where the executive is the recipient of a grant with conditions attached. Executives' concentrated stock holdings reflect involvement in business through employment or entrepreneurship. The exposure was acquired to align the interests of that individual with those of the company. This is quite different from the savings intention in a retirement savings plan. In an executive stock compensation scheme, if the company and the individual have been successful, significant wealth may have been accumulated. At that stage issues of wealth and risk management become relevant. They are not relevant at the outset of the process. For this reason, concern about how best to manage an executive's concentrated stock position is an "enviable dilemma".

An executive's stock position is often subject to formal or informal selling restrictions. When a restricted holding represents a substantial part of the investor's wealth, a financial adviser may recommend borrowing against the security of that holding to allow investing elsewhere. If the concentrated position is unhedged, the borrowing will not reduce risk-taking. It will increase the potential for wealth accumulation by gearing the investor's overall portfolio, but at the cost of even greater volatility of that wealth. The likelihood of a sudden diminution of wealth is increased, not reduced, by borrowing against an unprotected concentrated stock holding and investing the proceeds of that borrowing in a diversified stockmarket exposure.

Assisting in the management of concentrated stock positions is an important role for many financial advisers. Such positions represent concentrated risk-taking, and this needs to be taken into account when allocating other financial investments. Often this will mean that the appropriate additional financial investments for investors whose financial wealth is dominated by a concentrated stock position will be holdings in high-quality or "safe-haven" bonds to anchor at least part of their wealth over the time horizon that suits them. The same applies whether the company-specific investment risk is a quoted equity or an unquoted family business. It is likely that supplementary financial investments will, taken in isolation, have a cautious investment profile, whether or not the tolerance for investment risk of the owners is cautious. This is because their total wealth is dominated by their volatile exposure to the equity of their own business.

For business executives, holdings of company stock have frequently been accompanied by holdings of long-dated options on that stock. Since options have a fundamental value that is increased by both the volatility of the stock and the time period to expiry of the option, it is often appropriate to scale back exposure to the sponsor company by first selling stock that can be sold. "Sell the stock and keep the options" (at least until close to expiry) is a simplified version of this advice. But where executive options represent a large proportion of an individual's wealth and where that individual is risk averse, it can be appropriate to take advantage of opportunities to exercise significantly in-the-money options even if considerable time remains until expiry of the options. However, the position is usually complicated by taxation and rules on forfeiture of unexercised options and unvested stock on changing employment. Not surprisingly, the safest recommendation is again to discuss all the issues, including those of investment portfolio balance, with trusted financial and tax advisers before deciding on any course of action.

The restless shape of the equity market

At the start of the 20th century, railroad stocks represented 63% of the US equity market and just 0.2% a century later. Russia, India and Austria-Hungary together represented 25% of the global equity market in 1899 and less than 1% a century later. The scale of these changes is a powerful challenge to anyone suggesting that investors should passively accept whatever changes may occur in the market. More recently, the rise then decline of the weight of technology stocks and before that of Japan in market indices suggests the same. An autopilot approach to investing in either domestic or global equities over long periods is not credible. All investors need to be responsive to changes in the structure, risk and opportunities of the market place.

Stockmarket anomalies and the fundamental insight of the capital asset pricing model

Despite these extraordinary changes, an annually rebalanced, passive approach to investing in US equities, if it had been available, could have performed very well in the 20th century (see Chapter 3). However, the belief that it should be possible to do "better" than to reflect the pattern of the stockmarket as a whole is supported by a wide body of research. This has focused on extensive analysis of stockmarket "anomalies", which are well-established patterns of stockmarket performance that do not conform with the predictions of the original simplified theory called the capital asset pricing model (CAPM).

In its original form, the CAPM said that the performance of any stock should be expected to reflect two things: the extent to which the stock is a geared or a diluted "play" on the market as a whole; and a considerable amount of company specific volatility. The first represents a stock's exposure to systematic risk (measured by its "beta") for which investors should expect to be compensated. An example of a stock which would be a "geared play" on the stockmarket, or a "high beta" stock would be the stock of an equity money manager whose fee income, reflecting assets under management, would rise and fall in line with the stockmarket and whose profitability would be highly geared to this influence. Systematic risk cannot be diversified away in an equity portfolio. The second is "noise", or idiosyncratic or diversifiable risk. This should cancel out in a well-diversified portfolio but it reflects the scope for an individual stock, or a portfolio of stocks, to perform differently from the market (or, more precisely, from the beta-adjusted market return).

There have been numerous refinements to the CAPM to reflect research indicating that there are a number of sources of risk for a particular share price in the stockmarket which can help to explain share price performance. These include interest rate and foreign exchange exposure, corporate balance-sheet data, income and dividend information, as well as company capitalisation, industry and geographical location. An understanding of these sources of risk can help in the construction of equity portfolios, particularly if an investor has a view that a particular source of risk-taking is likely to produce good results in the period ahead.

However, the fundamental insight of the CAPM – the division of portfolio risk into undiversifiable, systematic market risk and diversifiable, idiosyncratic risk – has stood the test of time. It provides an invaluable framework for understanding how the activities of portfolio managers alter a portfolio's systematic and idiosyncratic risk exposures and so affect the performance and risk of that portfolio. An understanding of this insight, as well as its strengths and weaknesses, is an important aspect of the interface between finance theory and practical investment.

Among the weaknesses of CAPM is that it is now accepted that the original simplified theory does not fully explain the pattern of performance between different stocks. Low beta stocks, with supposedly diluted exposure to the market, do not systematically underperform the stockmarket as the original theory suggested that they should. Furthermore, stocks with smaller market capitalisation and certain measures of "value" stocks have shown an apparent persistence of superior performance that is inconsistent with the simplest versions of the theory.

There are two possible explanations:

◪ These patterns reflect the impact on market prices of irrational investor behaviour such as investor fads, fashions and concerns to own shares in "good" companies and to avoid "dogs" (for example, historic stockmarket underperformers). If so, the anomalies would disappear only if sufficient weight of long-term investor money recognised the irrational behaviour of other investors, leading the "rational investors" to reorganise their portfolios to profit from these anomalies. This would bid up the prices that had been expected to outperform and depress the prices of expected laggards. If enough investors responded in this way, the anomalies would disappear. But if they persist, "informed" investors who are aware of the anomalies should adjust their portfolios to profit from them.

◪ The old measures of risk-taking may be wrong. If this is correct, then those who seek to exploit the anomalies may simply be gearing up their risk-taking. For example, small cap (see overleaf) and some categories of "value" stocks may be riskier than they appear to be. If so, it may be rational that they should trade at a discounted price to leave room, on average, for superior performance to reflect the extra margin of risk.

If the first explanation is correct (that these groups of stocks tend to be under-priced), cautious long-term investors might reasonably increase their exposure to these groups of stocks. But if the second explanation is correct, this would be inappropriate. Investors need to know that there is no agreement among finance experts on this and that when faced with uncertainty, it is reasonable for cautious investors to err on the side of caution.

John Campbell of Harvard University and Tuomo Vuolteenaho of the National Bureau of Economic Research have argued that the traditional measure of market risk exposure, beta, is clouded by combining two different measures of risk. The first is the responsiveness of a stock to a change in the market's discount rate. As explained in Chapter 4 in the discussion of "good" and "bad" volatility, a fall in price caused by a rise in the market discount rate should be recouped by faster subsequent performance. For a cautious long-term investor this is not a major source of concern. The second element is the response of a stock price to a change in expectations for corporate earnings. This is what has been described as "bad beta", because there is no mechanism for ensuring a recovery of the lost performance in response to a downgrade of earnings growth expectations.

In recent studies of US equity performance, it was found that small stocks and value stocks are more sensitive than the market as a whole to changes in market-wide earnings expectations (bad beta) than growth stocks and large company stocks, which are more sensitive to changes in the market's discount rate (good beta). Any investor should want to receive a premium return for incurring bad beta risk, and it seems that normally such a premium has eventually been paid to value and small cap investors, but it should not be taken for granted.

"Small cap" and "large cap"

In the early 1980s Rolf Banz published research which highlighted the surprising superior performance of smaller companies compared with larger companies. This result has been replicated on numerous occasions since for the United States, the UK and other countries, with a general pattern that the smallest, or micro-companies, have outperformed small companies, which in turn have outperformed large companies. The historic outperformance of smaller companies is the "small cap effect" or the "small cap anomaly", because, although small companies tend to be more volatile than large companies, the degree of outperformance could not be explained by the original simplified CAPM model.

A sense of the small stock "anomaly" is gained by looking at the historical performance of small and large capitalisation companies. Figures 7.1 overleaf and 7.2 on page 99 make use of the comprehensive database maintained by the Center for Research in Security Prices at the University of Chicago. They contrast the performance from 1925 to early 2006 of the largest US companies (represented by the largest 10% of New York Stock Exchange listed domestic companies, as well as companies from the other leading US exchanges which are allocated to the same size bands) with the performance of small companies, indicated by those companies falling within the sixth to eighth decile bands of the same grouping. At the end of January 2006, this small cap band covered US companies with a market capitalisation of between $600m and $1.8 billion. The cumulative outperformance of small cap since 1925 is impressive, with an initial $1 investment in small cap growing (before allowing for inflation, or expenses and taxes) to $7,620 by early 2006, compared with $1,487 for an investment in the group of largest companies. (Over the same period, consumer prices increased a little more than 11-fold.) This translates into an annualised performance of 11.8% per annum for the small cap stocks, compared with 9.6% for the large cap stocks.

A similar pattern is evident from research in the UK by Elroy Dimson and Paul Marsh of the London Business School, although as for the United States the margin of outperformance by small companies depends on the period chosen and the definition of small cap that is used. Their work lies behind the Hoare Govett Smaller Companies Index, which has measured the performance of companies within the bottom 10% of the UK market capitalisation since 1951. Over the 51 years to the end of 2005, this index gave an annualised return (before fees, taxes and other costs) of 16.5%, which is 3.6% per annum above the broad UK market, measured by the FTSE All-Share index.

Figure 7.2 is more sobering, showing a troubling (from an investor's perspective) number of ten-year periods when small cap underperformed large cap in the United States. The most recent period, in the 1990s, coincided with a widespread view that the earlier observed "small cap anomaly" had indeed been corrected by heavy investment in small cap by investors bidding up prices as they tried to exploit the anomaly. In fact, since 1925, US small cap stocks have underperformed large cap stocks (on the definitions used here) during one-third of all rolling ten-year periods. Such relatively frequent periods of underperformance by small stocks are sufficient to caution most long-term investors against holding much more than a significant minority of their equity investments as strategic holdings in small cap stocks.

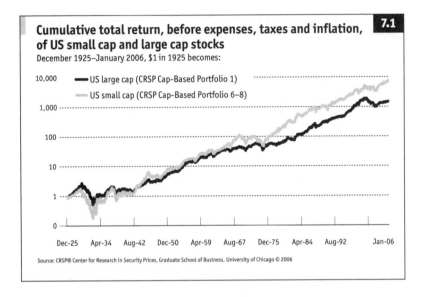

7.1

Cumulative total return, before expenses, taxes and inflation, of US small cap and large cap stocks

December 1925–January 2006, $1 in 1925 becomes:

— US large cap (CRSP Cap-Based Portfolio 1)
— US small cap (CRSP Cap-Based Portfolio 6–8)

Source: CRSP® Center for Research in Security Prices, Graduate School of Business, University of Chicago © 2006

An understanding of what is meant by "small cap" is needed before a decision can be made on allocations. For example, different small cap managers may have different investable universes of stocks. Many money managers would regard stocks in the United States or Europe of less than $2 billion market capitalisation as small cap. In the United States (and globally) such companies represent approximately 10% of market capitalisation. So 10% of total equity investments represents an allocation to small cap that could, if well diversified, constitute a neutral global allocation. Allocations of materially more or less than these amounts should reflect a decision to differ from the market. In the same vein, around 20% of the equity market is represented by companies with a capitalisation of less than $5 billion, and so this can be considered to represent a broadly neutral allocation to the combination of small and mid-sized companies (if defined by these thresholds).

With any equity investment programme, exposure to small cap stocks should be carefully monitored. It is almost always a mistake to approach small cap investing in an ad hoc, piecemeal fashion. This is more likely to be an issue with a private investor than an institutional investor, but the rule should be that exposure to smaller companies should be obtained through dedicated small-company portfolios or funds. In any event, there is a tendency for investment managers to drift into small-company holdings (partly because they may be less well researched by competitors).

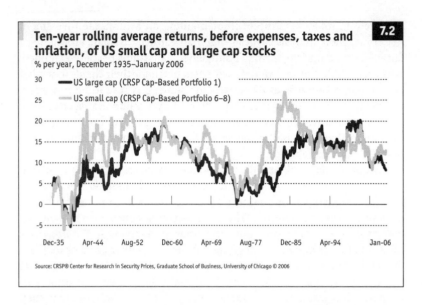

7.2

Ten-year rolling average returns, before expenses, taxes and inflation, of US small cap and large cap stocks
% per year, December 1935–January 2006

— US large cap (CRSP Cap-Based Portfolio 1)
— US small cap (CRSP Cap-Based Portfolio 6–8)

Source: CRSP® Center for Research in Security Prices, Graduate School of Business, University of Chicago © 2006

For this reason, it is not sufficient to aggregate the benchmarks given to different money managers to arrive at a measure of exposure to different segments of the market. Active managers may vary significantly within loosely defined investment remits, and selected passive managers may have been appointed to manage money against index benchmarks that do not reflect the market. Wherever possible, management information should be obtained by aggregating underlying exposures to individual companies and then comparing them with the broadest possible measure of the market (see Appendix 2).

Don't get carried away by your "style"

Equity investment managers have particular investment approaches and philosophies which lead to differences in style of investing. These characteristics are often as ingrained as any personal belief. Investors need to know and understand these differences. They will often find that some approaches are more appealing than others because of the sort of person they happen to be. Investors should be careful not to let these preferences result in unwitting risk biases in their investment strategy.

Philosophically, value and growth managers are quite different. Value managers have in common that they believe that markets repeatedly overreact as investor enthusiasm or alarm becomes detached from investment reality. As a result, value managers are contrarian individuals who are likely to make a virtue of implementing unfashionable investment decisions. Their analysis suggests that market prices oscillate around their fair values and that the turning point, when valuations become extended, is unpredictable. Value managers will try to persuade their clients that what is required is patience, as eventually the strategy is sure to be rewarded. In practice, clients are particularly attracted by a value manager's recent good performance. This is when a value manager would naturally want to caution that such performance cannot be sustained indefinitely and that lean times might lie ahead.

The particular vulnerability for value managers, who believe that "what goes around, comes around", are changes in long-term macroeconomic relationships. For a value investor, according to Sir John Templeton, a notably successful investor, "The four most dangerous words in investing are 'it's different this time'." But sometimes, particularly in the prospects for individual companies, things are different, for either good or ill. From the early 1990s, many international value managers considered that the US equity market was overpriced, many years before it underperformed other international markets after 2000. This was because they failed to understand, and so failed to anticipate, the transformation of the US economy that occurred in the 1990s and the impact of this on the prospects of thousands of US corporations. A growth manager is likely to seize on this as an illustration of the saying "value managers look back, whereas growth managers look forward". For growth managers, analyses of technological and commercial change, and how this can transform the earnings prospects of individual companies (including private companies), are the core element in their pursuit of new investment opportunities and understanding of business prospects. A growth manager's portfolio will consist of a variety of such investment prospects.

A crucial discipline for any manager will be when to sell out of a profitable investment position. This will often be much more instinctive for a value manager than for a growth manager, with the likelihood that a value manager may sell a profitable investment "too early" whereas a growth manager may be more likely to err on the side of selling it too late. This helps to shed light on some of the different risks faced by value and growth managers and their clients.

Value and growth managers

Value managers commonly have an investment process that starts with statistical screening of stockmarket databases for companies whose share price, earnings, dividend and balance-sheet data meet certain characteristics. A value stock will be one that has some combination of:

◪ higher than average dividend yield;
◪ lower than average ratio of the stock price to earnings per share or of the stock price to the book value of the company's assets per share;
◪ lower than average ratio of the company's valuation to sales or of valuation to cash flow.

These are some of the ratios that are used in constructing "value" indices of stockmarket performance. Individual managers will use different combinations of these and other indicators to screen for value in the stockmarket. Apart from purely quantitative managers, this screening process is best seen as a step towards reducing the potential universe of investable companies to a manageable number, which the investment manager can then research qualitatively in detail. This stage, involving management, product and industry research and ad hoc analysis, will often be the most important part of the investment process. But the screens are also important ingredients in describing a manager's investment style, and they will define the universe of stocks that the manager may then research further. As stock prices evolve, managers should be able to relate their actual portfolios back to those screens to demonstrate that the portfolios remain true to the managers' descriptions of their investment style.

Value managers divide into two camps:

◪ "Deep" value managers invest in stocks that meet their qualitative and quantitative criteria irrespective of how unrepresentative the resulting portfolio may be of the market as a whole. In particular, they are happy to have a zero weighting in parts of the stockmarket where the value screens suggest that all stocks offer poor value.
◪ "Relative" value managers manage the risks of their portfolios relative to the market as a whole, and so have disciplines that force the portfolio to hold some less expensive stocks in sectors that the screens suggest are absolutely expensive.

Money manager business leaders (who dislike the instability of assets under management that can be associated with deep value strategies) and investors who are particularly aware of "regret risk" generally feel more comfortable with relative value than with deep value management styles.

Growth managers are particularly concerned to exploit and profit from the relationship between earnings growth and stock price performance. Companies generally do not post unusually strong earnings growth results year after year. But as the market discounts the strong earnings of those companies that are growing rapidly, their stock prices can rise very, very strongly. This puts a premium on primary research into companies that may demonstrate unexpectedly rapid earnings growth in the future. Many growth managers also use statistical screening of databases, but this is generally a less powerful tool than successful qualitative industry or thematic research. But such research is notoriously difficult to undertake successfully and consistently. The statistical screens used by the index compilers to define "growth" stocks are earnings per share growth, sales growth and the ratio of retained earnings to equity capital (the internal rate of growth). Daniel Nordby, a portfolio manager at Alliance Capital Management, makes the important observation that although mean reversion is the value manager's friend, "for growth managers, however, mean reversion is an enemy that stalks them every day".

Should cautious investors overweight value stocks?

Over the longest periods of time, by most measures, value stocks are shown to have outperformed growth stocks (see Figure 7.3). Despite this, by the traditional measure of risk, the volatility of returns, value stocks (in aggregate) have usually appeared to be "safer" or at least "less risky" than growth stocks (see Figure 7.4).

Nevertheless, investors who wish to tilt their investments to profit from this need to be confident of being able to withstand the prolonged periods of underperforming the market and other investors. During the late 1990s growth stocks outperformed value stocks by more than 60% in just over two years, a process that was reversed in the subsequent 18 months (this is reflected in Figure 7.5 on page 104). Few investors have the confidence to withstand being on the wrong side of such swings without making a mistaken reaction that would cost them dearly. As most equity investors now appreciate, maintaining balance is a prerequisite to sleeping easily.

Meanwhile, the possible risk explanations for the outperformance of both value as a style of equity investing and smaller company stocks cast doubt on the suitability of biasing cautious investors' portfolios in favour of value (or small cap). This reinforces the case for a broad market approach to investing. Overweighting value as a style and smaller company stocks then becomes appropriate for more aggressive investors.

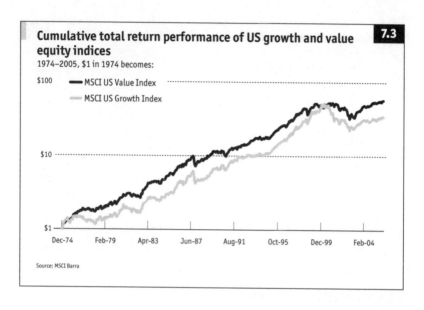

Cumulative total return performance of US growth and value equity indices `7.3`

1974–2005, $1 in 1974 becomes:

— MSCI US Value Index
— MSCI US Growth Index

Source: MSCI Barra

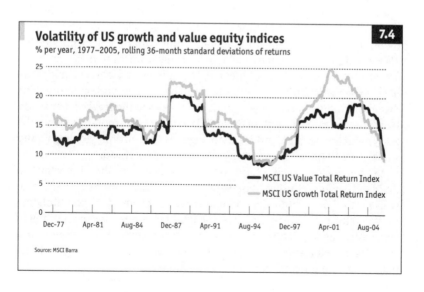

Volatility of US growth and value equity indices `7.4`

% per year, 1977–2005, rolling 36-month standard deviations of returns

— MSCI US Value Total Return Index
— MSCI US Growth Total Return Index

Source: MSCI Barra

103

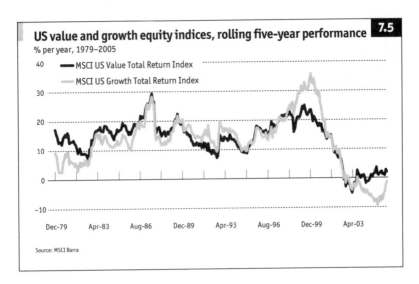

7.5

US value and growth equity indices, rolling five-year performance
% per year, 1979–2005

— MSCI US Value Total Return Index
— MSCI US Growth Total Return Index

Source: MSCI Barra

Equity dividends for cautious investors

Cautious investors should follow cautious strategies. In so far as their caution allows them a margin of equity investments, equity risk should not be magnified by following an undiversified approach to equity investing. A focus on dividend yield can easily result in amplified equity risk. Describing the dangers of "the sin of reaching for yield" in both fixed income and equity markets, Robert Fry, in his book *Non-Profit Investment Policies*, concludes that "typically, the results range from poor to disastrous". The disadvantage of relying on a stock portfolio for essential income is that it will not provide the element of insurance that is available from government bonds. It provides a much less certain source of income. High dividend-yielding equities are likely to be particularly vulnerable to company-specific and economy-wide disappointments in earnings growth and threats to the level of dividends. However, the rapid growth of dividends paid by US corporations since the 2003 reduction in dividend taxation suggests that income-yielding equity strategies will have an important role in the years ahead.

In conclusion, treat sceptically any suggestion that investing in dividend-paying equities represents a sound investment strategy that is likely to deliver both dependable growing income and accumulating capital values. An aggressive investor who has a need for income might emphasise higher-yielding equities and fixed-income investments. For a cautious investor, any such tilt should be modest. Such a strategy is not a magic solution for constrained personal finances.

Home bias: how much international?

Equity investors in almost all countries have a strong bias toward domestic investment. The reasons for this have been debated widely. Any suggestion that domestic equities provide a better "match" for domestic currency obligations has little substance. The appropriate measure of "mismatch" is how well risk assets (such as domestic equities or foreign equities) correlate with the risk-free asset, which for a long-term investor is the domestic inflation-linked government bond. Although domestic equities may correlate better than international equities with domestic government bonds, they do not constitute any sort of "safe-haven" asset for long-term investment. But the reassurance of familiarity and custom, together with misunderstandings about the contribution of currency risk, largely explain the home-country bias.

In most countries, this home-country bias is a significant risk-management issue. However, the size and breadth of the US market means that well-diversified investors in US equities will have already achieved the bulk of the diversification gains that are offered by a global approach to investing. Although US investors can make further diversification gains by investing internationally, the contribution to investment efficiency from these gains is not as large as it is for investors in other countries. (The same may well apply to the pan-European equity market. At the end of 2005, according to Citigroup, the US equity market represented 47% of the global market, while Europe in aggregate represented 27%.) Often, geographical diversification is not the most serious investment strategy design issue that needs addressing. In other words, for investors in most countries international equity diversification matters a lot, but for US investors it matters less. For example, for investors with well-diversified equity exposure that is solely invested in US equities, the possible risk-reducing benefits of international equity diversification would be trivial compared with the potential for inappropriate risk-taking if the maturity of fixed-income investments is not properly aligned with the investor's time horizon.

A recurring theme of this book is that investment strategy should be broadly appropriate for an investor's objectives, risk tolerances and preferences. Except for some cash flow matching bond portfolios, precision in identifying a suitable strategy is a pipedream. International investing is an area where strongly held differences of view on strategy are often indistinguishable within the range of broadly appropriate investment strategies. Despite this, when the performance numbers come in the differences can be very large. This leaves a considerable margin of flexibility for an

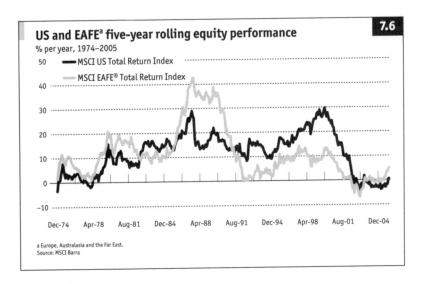

US and EAFE[a] five-year rolling equity performance 7.6

% per year, 1974–2005

— MSCI US Total Return Index
— MSCI EAFE® Total Return Index

a Europe, Australasia and the Far East.
Source: MSCI Barra

investor's gut preferences to influence policy legitimately. It is important for advisers to understand when risk considerations provide clear guidance on what is or is not appropriate for a particular investor and when they do not. In international investing there is a range of appropriate diversified strategies and it would normally be inappropriate to suggest that a particular strategy is expected to be demonstrably superior to all others. For example, the diversification benefits of international investing are always subject to diminishing returns. Doing a little may get an investor a long way towards whatever is reckoned to be an "optimal" strategy.

Figure 7.6 shows (from a US perspective) the scale of the differences that can exist between US and international investing. After 1989, the United States substantially outperformed foreign markets, as much because of the prolonged weakness of the Japanese market after 1989 as the strength of the US market. This pattern should not be assumed to continue, but it gives a reminder of the potential for divergence.

There are two reasons for investing internationally: opportunity and diversification. The natural starting point, from a textbook perspective, is the global market, with consideration being given to the possibility of hedging direct foreign currency risk. Unequivocally, a global approach to investing should be appropriate for all equity investors. But other, domestically oriented approaches can also be appropriate. If adequate diversification (compared with the global investing benchmark) could be obtained from an investor's domestic market, international investing could become a pursuit of opportunity rather than the need to obtain portfolio balance. The perspective on this varies from country to country. The United States comes closest to a case where international investment is a "nice to have" opportunity rather than a requirement for diversification. But even for US investors there are demonstrable diversification benefits to be gained from international equity investing.

The easiest way to assess the benefits from international equity diversification is to examine how it affects the measured risk of equity investing, using the conventional measure of risk: the volatility or standard deviation of returns. (This is technically appropriate only for an aggressive short-term investor who has 100% invested in equities. For all other investors, how the equities correlate with government bonds and with other investments that might be held should be considered.) This is the approach adopted in this chapter. This metric is also used as the guide to the expected gains from international investing, because the prudent (and consistent) assumption is that the same expected rate of return will apply to international and domestic equity investments. The outcome will not (except by chance) be the same, but in setting strategic allocations, it is safest to assume that we do not know in advance which equity market is more likely to do best. In practice, in many asset planning exercises the dice are loaded in favour of emerging markets by assuming that they will deliver a higher rate of return than developed markets. This would be justified if they provided exposure to "higher octane" systematic risk than is provided by the equities of developed markets. Simply being more volatile, which largely reflects their inferior diversification, is not a sufficient reason for such an assumption, nor is a firm expectation that their economies are expected to grow faster. This should already be discounted in share prices.

This sidesteps the issue of whether there are any taxes or additional management costs that apply to international equity investing but not to domestic investors. If these are noticeable they should be taken into account in determining international allocations. In what follows, this concern about incremental fees and taxes is ignored, and the focus is on volatility as the proxy for risk. Figure 7.7 overleaf shows for a number of countries the volatility of the MSCI World Index (shown unhedged for foreign exchange risk) and the volatility of the domestic equity market, both measured in each country's own currency.

The pattern varies with the period that is chosen, but for this 35-year period, the pattern is clear. The smaller the domestic equity market, the more that can be gained, in reducing equity volatility, by following a

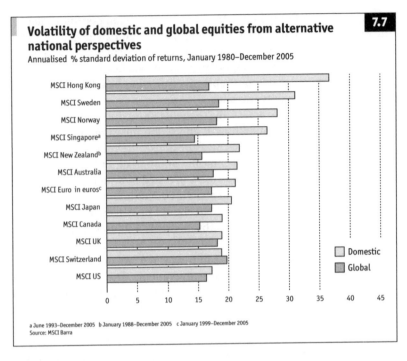

7.7

Volatility of domestic and global equities from alternative national perspectives
Annualised % standard deviation of returns, January 1980–December 2005

a June 1993–December 2005 b January 1988–December 2005 c January 1999–December 2005
Source: MSCI Barra

well-diversified global rather than a purely national approach to equity investing. This is clearly indicated in the cases of Hong Kong and the United States. Not surprisingly, Figure 7.7 suggests that efficient equity management would require substantial international diversification by Hong Kong investors, whereas this is much less clear for US investors.

Repeating this exercise over different periods, the result that consistently emerges is that the US stockmarket provides US investors with a level of equity diversification that is close to that achieved by global diversification. Other smaller national markets have not provided their domestic investors with comparable diversification, except over particular periods, which should not be extrapolated into the future.

Figure 7.8 shows the volatility trade-off between domestic and international equities for the United States, Japan and the UK in more detail. In this case, the comparison is not with global equities (which also includes domestic) but with international equities (that is, world excluding the United States, world excluding Japan and world excluding the UK respectively). The difference in the lines shown for each of the countries tells a story. From a US dollar perspective, investing up to 40% in diversified

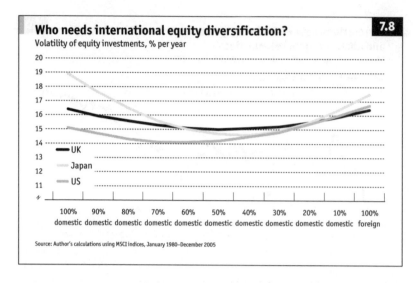

Who needs international equity diversification? `7.8`

Volatility of equity investments, % per year

	UK	Japan	US

Source: Author's calculations using MSCI indices, January 1980–December 2005

unhedged international equities over this period, to reflect the lowest volatility strategy, could have reduced equity volatility by less than one-tenth. These numbers move around with changes in the period examined, but in the context of equity markets whose volatility moves around considerably, this is a noticeable but not a large gain from diversification.

For Japanese investors in particular the historical data show a clear pattern, with equity volatility potentially being reduced by over one-quarter for Japanese investors who make substantial allocations to international equities.

Figure 7.8 reflects the impact of diminishing returns to the process of diversification: the biggest contribution to diversification comes from the initial foray into (diversified) international equities.

The scale of these potential diversification gains from international investing depends on the volatility of the international equities and on how highly their prices correlate with those of domestic equities. The higher the correlation, the less well international equities will diversify domestic equities, and the less will be the scope for reducing overall equity volatility by adding international equities. It should be no surprise that the degree of correlation is unstable as is the level of volatility. Critically, at times of crisis measures of correlation and volatility often "jump" upwards. But just because correlations increase, it does not necessarily follow that the benefits of international diversification are diminished if at the same time volatility increases. This

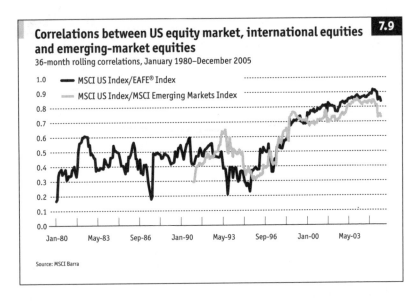

Correlations between US equity market, international equities and emerging-market equities `7.9`
36-month rolling correlations, January 1980–December 2005

— MSCI US Index/EAFE® Index
— MSCI US Index/MSCI Emerging Markets Index

Source: MSCI Barra

will, however, mean that systematic or undiversifiable risk from equity investing has increased.

Figure 7.9 shows movements in correlations of domestic and international equities from the perspective of a US dollar investor. Having been unusually low in the mid-1990s, correlations between domestic and international equities, whether with other developed markets or with emerging markets, have since been unusually high.

To hedge or not to hedge international equities

International investing involves currency risk. But investing in domestic companies with international operations also includes currency risk, although the extent to which this is offset by corporate foreign exchange risk management is always unclear.

There is a big difference between the impact of currency risk on equity and international bond portfolios: foreign exchange movements transform and magnify international bond market risk; currency risk changes the timing profile but generally not the magnitude of international equity market risk. This can be seen in Tables 7.1 and 7.2 from the perspective of a European and a US investor in euro-zone equities and bonds. For almost all the examples examined, the magnitude of equity risk is little changed by currency risk, whereas bond market risk always is.

If the US investor had hedged those international index performances

Table 7.1 **Volatility of stock and bonds, January 1999–December 2005**

	Annualised standard deviation (% per year)
MSCI Euro Equity Index, total return in €	21.2
MSCI Euro Equity Index, total return measured in US$, unhedged	21.7
Citigroup EMU[a] 1+ Yr Government Bond Index, total return in €	3.4
Citigroup EMU 1+ Yr Government Bond Index, total return measured in US$, unhedged	11.8
Exchange rate €/US$	9.6

a European Monetary Union.
Sources: MSCI Barra; Citigroup Index LLC; WM/Reuters

back to the dollar, there would have been a negligible reduction in equity volatility and a substantial reduction in the volatility of euro bonds (see Table 7.2 overleaf).

Investors should normally expect the hedging of international holdings of equities to reduce slightly the volatility of the foreign equities, whereas the hedging of foreign bond holdings dramatically reduces the volatility of such bonds. The normal practice is to leave international equities unhedged and to hedge international bonds. On balance, however, hedging international equities makes sense because it normally slightly reduces volatility. But this line of argument is only valid if the transaction costs of currency hedging (see Chapter 8) are trivial. This should be the case for hedging the principal currencies, but it is not for emerging market currencies, for which hedging costs at times of market stress can be prohibitive. But whether hedged or unhedged, global equities remain a volatile asset class (see Figure 7.10 overleaf).

A decision to hedge or not to hedge international equity holdings can substantially alter the pay-out from an investment strategy, depending on the pattern of movements in currencies. This can be seen in Table 7.3 overleaf, which shows the difference in US dollar terms of Japanese and euro-zone equity performance according to whether the international investments are currency hedged or not.

The practical importance of this is that a decision to hedge international equities, perhaps on risk grounds, can easily result in performance that is either much better or much worse than the majority of investors will achieve. This will have nothing to do with investment manager selection, and everything to do with a single decision on currency

Table 7.2 **Volatility of stock and bonds, January 1999–December 2005**

	Annualised standard deviation (% per year)
Citigroup EMU 1+ yr Government Bond Index, total return in €	3.4
Hedged Citigroup EMU 1+ yr Government Bond Index, total return in US$	3.5
MSCI Euro Equity Index, total return in €	21.2
$ hedged MSCI Euro Equity Index, total return in US$	21.6
Exchange rate €/US$	9.6

Sources: MSCI Barra; Citigroup Index LLC; WM/Reuters

exposure. Nevertheless, if an investor is willing to stand the regret risk of differing so much from the crowd of other investors, hedging is a sensible starting point for investing internationally for most investors. Hedging then gives an additional degree of freedom in managing the investments, by enabling the investor to vary decisions to hedge or partially hedge international equity holdings.

From a risk perspective, this can be an efficient way of implementing medium-term views on future movements in currencies. This is because currency hedging makes little difference to volatility and risk of loss of international equity investing, even though it can have a big impact, positive and negative, on the performance of those international investments. Hedging would have a correspondingly large impact on performance relative to investors who do not normally hedge international equity

Table 7.3 **Currency hedging transforms equity returns but not equity risk (% return per calendar year)**

	MSCI Japan Equity Index total return, unhedged, measured in US$	MSCI Japan Equity Index total return, hedged into US$	MSCI Eurozone Equity Index, total return, unhedged, measured in US$	MSCI Eurozone Equity Index, total return, hedged into US$
Dec 2003	36.0	23.6	42.1	16.0
Dec 2004	16.2	11.5	20.5	9.2
Dec 2005	25.7	50.9	9.5	28.3

Sources: MSCI Barra; WM/Reuters

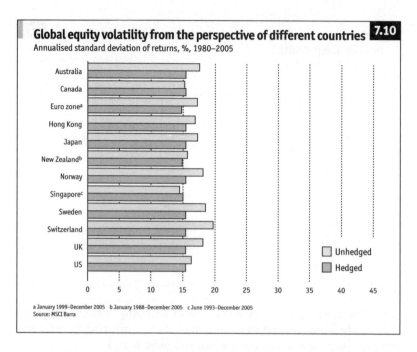

Global equity volatility from the perspective of different countries 7.10
Annualised standard deviation of returns, %, 1980–2005

Australia
Canada
Euro zone[a]
Hong Kong
Japan
New Zealand[b]
Norway
Singapore[c]
Sweden
Switzerland
UK
US

Unhedged
Hedged

0   5   10   15   20   25   30   35   40   45

a January 1999–December 2005   b January 1988–December 2005   c June 1993–December 2005
Source: MSCI Barra

investments. It is likely that investors will experience severe mood swings between elation when they are convinced that they are skilled at reading currency markets and gloom when they lament their bad luck. This is where a currency overlay manager may have a role in implementing currency views alongside an existing investment strategy. However, the scope for regret risk if the manager misjudges currency movements is considerable.

International equities and liquidity risk

In international investing, it is easy for investors to get drawn into the latest "hot" theme. What is "hot" is often potentially illiquid, easy to get into but costly to unravel. In the past, emerging-market equity investments have been sold on a prospect of superior expected returns and diversification from developed market stockmarkets. In recent years, increases in the correlation between emerging-market and developed-market equities have affected the diversification story. This is also illustrated by Figure 7.11 overleaf, which shows the performance of emerging-market equities in months of weakest performance by the US stockmarket. As might be expected, in months of crisis, emerging-market equities perform

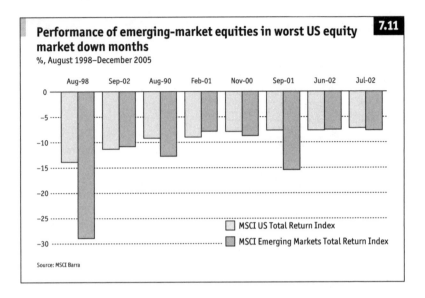

7.11

Performance of emerging-market equities in worst US equity market down months

%, August 1998–December 2005

Source: MSCI Barra

particularly poorly. By all means invest in emerging markets, but make sure you find the prospective performance story convincing, because any diversification may not be there when you most want it.

8 Bonds, debt and credit

Analysis of modern bonds can quickly become off-puttingly complicated. A useful starting point is an elementary review written by John Maynard Keynes in 1925 of a study comparing long-term returns from equities with those from bonds in the United States between 1866 and 1922. The study showed a substantial outperformance of equities over bonds in periods of both deflation and inflation. Keynes found this counterintuitive, his expectation being that a period of deflation would be better for bonds than equities. He suggested a number of reasons for the inferior performance of bonds:

■ The asymmetrical threat of changes in the general price level. While bonds can be eroded by inflation without limit, the scope for the general level of prices to fall (which benefits bond holders, so long as bond issuers have the ability to repay these higher real values), is in practice more constrained.
■ Although a bond may default, no bond ever pays more than the stipulated rate of interest.
■ Company management always sides with equity investors rather than with bond holders and, "in particular, the management will avail themselves of their rights to repay bonds at dates most advantageous to the shareholders and most disadvantageous to the bondholders".
■ Retained earnings provide an element of compound growth, beyond the dividend yield that accrues to the benefit of the stockholder (while making existing obligations to creditors more secure).

Such reasoning, supported by now much more extensive data, underlies the message of a number of advisers and academics that the natural habitat for genuinely long-term investors is the equity market. Or, as one notably successful equity investor expressed it, the natural role for the long-term investor is to be "the proprietor".

Nevertheless, almost all investors do, and indeed should, seek diversification away from equity risk. In Part 1 this was argued from the perspective of investing in government bonds. This chapter provides the background to other types of credit instrument, which introduce new aspects of risk in return for the prospect of new sources of excess performance. An important element in this is the trade-off between credit quality and performance.

Credit quality and the role of credit-rating agencies

Credit-rating agencies originated early in the 20th century to assess the creditworthiness and to publish ratings of securities. In practice, the two related risks that matter are default by a borrower and a deterioration in the assessment of creditworthiness of a borrower who nevertheless continues to meet contractual obligations. The ratings of the leading agencies are widely used to define minimum credit quality eligible for being held by particular portfolios of many institutional investors. (Institutional investors have guidelines for minimum acceptable credit quality in particular portfolios, though they may not have rigid credit quality guidelines that cover all of a fund's investments.) In addition, capital adequacy guidelines for international banks now incorporate a formal role for ratings assigned by the leading rating agencies. This development in the regulation of banks has encouraged the process of securitising bank loans so that risk exposures can be shifted from banks to other investors. This in turn has promoted the development of new credit instruments and markets. Private investors and many institutional investors effectively outsource analysis of credit risk to these rating agencies. The long-term rating classifications used by the three main agencies – Fitch, Moody's and Standard & Poor's – are shown in Table 8.1.

An important break point in Table 8.1 is between investment grade securities and non-investment grade securities. The latter are commonly referred to as speculative or "junk". The ratings are intended to be objective assessments of the creditworthiness of borrowers and are reflected in the spreads that borrowers must pay to compensate creditors for the risk of default (or of a deterioration in credit rating). Table 8.2 demonstrates that the rating agencies perform at least reasonably well in assessing the likelihood of different issuers defaulting. It shows average default rates for periods of up to five years for corporate bonds of differing credit rating based on experience from Fitch over the period 1990–2004. It suggests, for example, that AAA bonds had no experience of default, while junk bonds rated CCC had almost a 25% risk of default over the next 12 months and almost a 33% risk of default over the next five years. These default rates are averages for Fitch rated debt. Data from the rating agencies illus-

Table 8.1 **Long-term rating bands of leading credit-rating agencies**

	Fitch	Moody's	Standard & Poor's
Investment grade			
Highest quality, extremely strong	AAA	Aaa	AAA
Very high quality	AA	Aa	AA
High quality	A	A	A
Moderate to good quality	BBB	Baa	BBB
Speculative grade			
Speculative, marginal or not well secured	BB	Ba	BB
Highly speculative or weak	B	B	B
Poor quality or very weak	CCC	Caa	CCC

Note: precise definitions, which vary between rating agencies, are given on the websites of particular agencies.

trate the cyclical nature of the incidence of high-yield bond defaults. In a review of the high-yield market, *As Good As It Gets*, Fitch reported that in 2004 the high-yield default rate had shrunk to 1.5% by value, compared with a record of 16.4% in 2002. Fitch also reported that the proportion of amounts due on defaulted bonds that is recovered for creditors is also cyclical, rising from 24% of par values in 2001–02 to 42% in 2003–04. Defaults remained unusually low in 2005.

The yield spread over government bonds that corporates must pay on their bonds generally follows the ordering of formal credit rating

Table 8.2 **Corporate bond average cumulative default rates, 1990–2004 (%)**

	Year 1	Year 2	Year 3	Year 4	Year 5
AAA	0.0	0.0	0.0	0.0	0.0
AA	0.0	0.0	0.0	0.0	0.1
A	0.0	0.2	0.4	0.5	0.6
BBB	0.3	1.0	2.0	2.9	3.5
BB	1.5	4.1	6.3	7.6	8.3
B	1.8	4.2	6.4	6.7	5.5
CCC–C	24.3	32.0	32.3	26.1	31.6
Investment grade	0.1	0.4	0.7	1.0	1.1
High yield	3.5	6.4	8.3	8.6	8.9
All corporates	0.6	1.3	1.8	2.1	2.2

Source: Fitch Ratings Global Corporate Finance, 2004 Transition and Default Study

Table 8.3 **US corporate bond yields and yield spreads, January 1987–December 2005**

	Average (%)	Average spread over Treasuries (%)	Average (%)	Average spread over Treasuries (%)
	Under 10 years' maturity		Over 10 years' maturity	
US Treasury debt	5.7	0.0	6.7	0.0
Agency debt	6.1	0.4	7.2	0.4
Aaa corporate debt	6.5	0.8	7.4	0.7
Aa corporate debt	6.6	0.9	7.6	0.9
A corporate debt	6.9	1.2	7.8	1.1
Baa corporate debt	7.5	1.8	8.4	1.6
Corporate high-yield bonds	11.5[a]	5.8	na	na
Ccc corporate high-yield bonds	16.2[a]	10.5	na	na

a All maturities.
Source: Lehman Brothers Inc

assessments, suggesting that the financial markets broadly share the assessments of the rating agencies. A guide to how spreads over US Treasuries have varied with differences in credit rating is shown in Table 8.3.

The spreads shown are averages for January 1987–December 2005, and towards the end of this period spreads were much lower than indicated. Table 8.3 is broken down by maturity band to ensure that comparisons are made with similar maturity bonds. It clearly shows that spreads over Treasury bonds increase as credit quality deteriorates.

Table 8.3 shows average yield spreads offered and does not fully reflect how movements in spreads and defaults affect performance for investors. This is shown in Figure 8.1, which highlights the risks associated with the low-quality end (rated CCC) of speculative grade investments. However, it also shows that a broad cross-section of the speculative grade market in the United States performed on average as well (but by following a more volatile path) as investment grade securities.

The focus of much credit risk analysis is on the scope for changes in creditworthiness or in credit rating. There are indications that formal credit ratings, at least of bonds, are more stable than underlying business conditions would warrant. Part of the reason for this is that investors are believed to want agencies to avoid the risk of short-term reversals of ratings (for example, from investment grade to speculative grade and then back to investment grade). This perceived preference may cause agencies

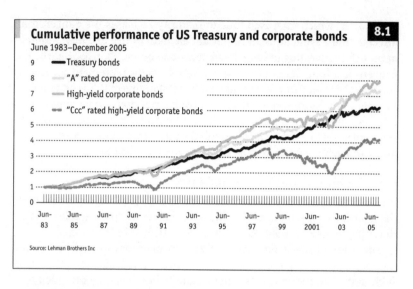

Cumulative performance of US Treasury and corporate bonds 8.1

June 1983–December 2005

- Treasury bonds
- "A" rated corporate debt
- High-yield corporate bonds
- "Ccc" rated high-yield corporate bonds

Source: Lehman Brothers Inc

to delay announcing a change in rating until they are sure that it is unlikely soon to be reversed.

One simple but important feature to note is that a debt instrument with the highest rating, AAA, has no opportunity to improve its credit rating and can only maintain its rating or deteriorate. By contrast, lower-rated debt instruments can improve or deteriorate. Thus highly rated debt instruments should offer a higher spread over Treasury bonds the longer their maturity, because there is greater likelihood that their rating will fall.

Table 8.4 **Total return to US government and corporate bonds, July 1983–December 2005**

	Geometric average (% per year)	Volatility (% per year)
US Treasury debt	8.5	5.4
Agency debt	8.4	4.6
Aaa corporate debt	9.2	6.0
Aa corporate debt	9.2	5.9
A corporate debt	9.2	6.0
Baa corporate debt	9.6	6.1
Corporate high-yield bonds	9.6	8.0
Ccc corporate high-yield bonds	6.6	13.3

Source: Derived from Lehman Brothers Inc data

The way in which increased time to maturity increases the danger of an adverse credit event adds an important element of risk to a buy-and-hold approach to investing in long-dated corporate bonds – a risk of particular concern if a long-dated bond ladder, relied on for retirement income, is constructed from corporate bonds. An understanding of this is essential for long-term investors and the degree of confidence that can be drawn from a favourable rating. In a 2005 article entitled "AAA is a vanishing breed", the *Wall Street Journal Europe* reminded readers that General Motors, Ford and AIG each used to have the highest possible credit rating.

Portfolio diversification and credit risk

The words that rating agencies use to describe sub-investment grade debt, such as "speculative", "highly speculative" or "poor quality", fairly describe the risk of individual issues when treated in isolation.

For a long time it has been evident to investors in well-diversified corporate debt that good performance (with low volatility in comparison with that of an individual speculative grade bond) can be provided by a portfolio of well-diversified high-yield bonds. This means that it is inappropriate to regard a portfolio of high-yield bonds as if it had the risk characteristics of an individual sub-investment grade or junk bond. Equally, the strong language that rating agencies use to describe the risk of individual high-yield bonds should remind investors that the only sensible way to invest in such credit risk is through a well-diversified portfolio, which for all investors will normally mean holding a diversified exposure to US or global high-yield debt. Investment banks have exploited this difference between the high risk of a high-yield security and the lower risk of a portfolio of high-yielding securities by applying financial engineering to create slices or "tranches" which have the highest credit ratings out of portfolios of high-yield debt (see section on collateralised debt obligations, pages 127–30).

Debt issued by sovereign (or corporate) borrowers of emerging markets offers an alternative source of debt based risk-taking. This debt is most commonly denominated in US dollars (but see box on pages 121–3). Such debt performed well in the years after the liquidity crisis of August 1998. In that month, the JP Morgan emerging-market debt index fell by 29%, revealing much about the undiversifiable risk of contagion in the market for emerging-market debt. This risk may, over time, lessen as more emerging markets repay debt, accumulate foreign exchange reserves, acquire investment grade credit ratings and evolve to join the group of developed financial markets. In the years leading to 2006, performance

Table 8.5 **Performance of selected debt markets in months of extreme US equity performance, January 1994–December 2005**

	MSCI US equity Total Return Index	JP Morgan Emerging Market Bond Index plus	Lehman Brothers US corporate high-yield bond index	Lehman Brothers US Government Bond Index
Worst three months for US equities				
Aug 1998	−13.9	−28.7	−5.5	2.6
Sep 2002	−11.3	−3.7	−1.3	2.3
Feb 2001	−8.9	−1.6	1.3	1.1
Best three months for US equities				
Mar 2000	10.0	3.2	−2.1	1.8
Oct 2002	9.1	7.7	−0.9	−0.8
Apr 2003	8.4	6.2	5.9	0.5

Sources: JP Morgan; Lehman Brothers Inc; MSCI Barra

of the market has relied heavily on spread compression and an expectation that this process is under way. History will reveal the extent to which this proves free from major reversals. But the danger of setbacks leaves emerging-market debt exposed to the risk of occasional extreme negative performance, which has historically been a characteristic of the marketplace. This reflects the exposure of the market to political or "country" risk as well as the foreign exchange risks inherent in emerging markets that have borrowed US dollars, often to fund local currency ventures. Not surprisingly, it has suffered from such market contagion to a much greater extent than the US corporate high-yield market. This is illustrated in Table 8.5, which compares the performance of emerging-market debt and US high-yield debt in the months of most extreme performance of the s&p 500 index since 1994.

Between the end of 1993 and December 2005, there were three months when the emerging-market debt index suffered negative returns of more than 10%, whereas the worst monthly performance for the US high-yield market was a decline of 7.4%. The standard statistical measures of extreme returns shows that emerging-market debt is more volatile and has been much more prone to sudden "shocks" than the market in corporate high-yield debt.

Table 8.6 **US corporate high-yield and emerging debt markets summary statistics, January 1994–December 2005**

	Geometric average (%)	Standard deviation (%)	Skewness	Excess kurtosis
JP Morgan Emerging Market Bond Index plus	11.5	18.4	−2.1	10.7
Lehman Brothers US Corporate High-yield Bond Index	6.9	7.5	−0.7	3.6
Lehman Brothers US Government Bond Index	6.1	4.7	−0.5	0.8
MSCI US Equity Total Return Index	10.7	16.6	−0.5	0.4

Sources: JP Morgan; Lehman Brothers Inc; MSCI Barra

Local currency emerging-market debt

Investors in emerging-market debt have mostly invested in debt denominated in US dollars, or in other major currencies such as the yen or the euro. This has suited them because they have not wished to compound the credit risk of investing in emerging-market debt with the currency risk associated with emerging markets. But this can prove to be a superficial reassurance.

The historic inability of most emerging-market governments to borrow for long maturities in their own currencies has been due to a combination of domestic policy failures, underdeveloped domestic markets and probably also some lack of imagination on the part of international investors and international organisations.

The results of this failure have been analysed in depth by Barry Eichengreen, George C. Pardee and Helen N. Pardee professor of economics and political science at the University of California at Berkeley, and Ricardo Hausmann, professor of the practice of economic development at the John F. Kennedy School of Government at Harvard University. Their work shows that there has been an undesirable transfer of risk to emerging-market borrowers (who have been forced to accept currency mismatches). This has led to an increase in risk for international investors, whose comfort in receiving dollar-denominated returns has been undermined by the increase in debtors' credit risk resulting from the currency mismatch that they have been obliged to bear. This in turn has contributed to intermittent currency and foreign debt crises, which have cost international investors dearly (and emerging-market borrowers considerably more).

In the past few years a number of emerging-market governments in Latin America and Asia have issued debt in their own local currency which has been targeted at international investors; and the World Bank and the regional development organisations have facilitated lending by international investors in local currency to corporate borrowers in emerging markets. These steps are responding to a market opportunity that suits both investors and borrowers.

A well-diversified portfolio approach to investing in local currency emerging-market debt can be attractive to a range of investors because:

◪ yields may be more attractive than comparable dollar debt (though this varies between countries);
◪ it enables investors to position strategy to take advantage of a view of the relative performance of the US dollar and emerging-market currencies
◪ it may provide one source of efficient investment diversification for any investor (although the basis for any such calculation needs careful consideration).

Such investments may be particularly attractive to investors from Asia, the Middle East and Latin America who have their investment accounts measured and reported in US dollars, and yet their base currency is to a degree ambiguous (see Chapter 1). The attitude to currency risk of these investors is less clearly defined than it is, for example, for a US resident. For some of these international investors, a portfolio of well-diversified emerging-market debt may offer an attractive way of mitigating some of their exposure to the US dollar.

The available benchmarks for emerging-market debt illustrate that these markets have been very volatile in the past. Although diversification between countries is a major benefit, the impact of the 1997 Asian currency crisis shows how extreme the performance of individual markets can be, and even with a diversified approach, strong negative returns for the market as a whole have been recorded at times of crisis. The JP Morgan local currency emerging-market liquidity index declined in value in US dollar terms by 15.7% between July 1997 and January 1998. Within this, the indices for Thailand and South Korea declined by 60% and 51% respectively. Nevertheless, the financial progress since then of many of these countries (for example, in terms of foreign exchange accumulation) suggests that the risk of a repeat of these experiences has been materially reduced.

Securitisation and modern ways to invest in bond markets

In the last 25 years innovations in securities markets have transformed the ability of banks to manage their credit exposures, which has led to major changes in the composition of investors' bond portfolios. This process has accelerated enormously since the mid-1990s and enables banks to separate their lending decisions from their need to manage the risks of their balance sheets. This is possible because standardised arrangements now exist by which they can offload their risk exposures, either to other banks or to long-term investors, who may be in a better position to bear those risks. This process is known as securitisation, which is best understood as the process which occurs when a bank credit is transformed into a negotiable instrument.

Mortgage-backed securities

The process started and developed in the United States. The major innovation came in 1970 with the introduction of a mortgage-backed security by the Government National Mortgage Association (Ginnie Mae), whose cash payments to investors represented a direct "pass-through" of the cash flows of the underlying household mortgages. Previously, mortgage-backed bonds had represented claims on the issuing bank, with a further claim on the underlying mortgages should the bank default. The principal investment feature of pass-through bonds is that they expose the investor to prepayment risk, because household mortgage holders in the United States can generally prepay fixed-rate mortgages without penalty. Prepayment risk is the main differentiator of mortgage bonds as investments. Individuals prepay for a number of different reasons, some of which, such as when they move home, give rise to turnover that may vary with the state of the economy. But the principal driver is the opportunity to refinance at a lower interest rate and cut monthly mortgage payments, after allowing for the fees involved. So prepayment risk is directly tied to changes in the level of interest rates. Another feature of the US residential mortgage market is that interest and principal payment obligations of pass-through securities issued by the three federally sponsored mortgage agencies are guaranteed by those agencies.

By the mid-1980s the pass-through mortgage market led to the development of the collateralised mortgage obligation (CMO). The CMO arranges for the payments from a pool of mortgages to be split into a series of tranches, which are exposed to different elements of mortgage prepayment risk. These developments in the US mortgage market led to a transformation in the nature of the portfolios of investors in US dollar denominated bonds. Mortgages now routinely represent a substantial part of these investments. At the same time, the introduction of mortgage securities with prepayment risk has increased the degree of complexity in investment portfolios and provided a model for parallel innovations in other areas.

The role of mortgage-backed securities in meeting investment objectives

Mortgages that are subject to prepayment risk represent a peculiar investment, which has become mainstream for many institutional investors. An investor, conscious of the need to meet particular objectives at dates in the future, is unlikely to have thought of an investment with the pay-out profile of a mortgage as a candidate for a core investment to meet those objectives. However, most investors will venture out of their safe-haven, minimum-risk investment strategy in anticipation of a premium yield in return for accepting prepayment risk. The benefits of the mortgage market for issuers is clear. It provides liquidity and has increased access to additional capital, both of which have probably lowered costs to borrowers. The outstanding volume of mortgage-backed securities is of the same order of magnitude as the outstanding volume of publicly held US Treasury securities, which in early 2006 were around $4.8 trillion.

For an investor, replacing government bonds with mortgage bonds, which are subject to prepayment risk, introduces uncertainty to a previously low-risk investment strategy. If long-term interest rates fall, homeowners will refinance their mortgages. This will be reflected in prepayments on a mortgage bond, which will reduce the bond's ability to support a given level of income in the future because the prepaid income has to be reinvested at the lower rate of interest. In this environment, mortgages should be expected to underperform government bonds. By contrast, if long-term interest rates rise above expectations, homeowners will want to retain their current lower level of mortgage payment, and repayments are likely to be lower than expected. In other words, mortgage securities, which are subject to prepayment risk, prepay more when investors want less, and may prepay less when investors want more. They represent a source of dynamic mismatch risk in trying to meet long-term objectives.

In return for these undesirable features, investors in mortgage securities collect an insurance premium, which is the extra yield that mortgage-backed securities offer over conventional bonds (after making appropriate adjustments to ensure fair comparison). This represents the premium that borrowers must pay investors for the option to prepay their mortgages ahead of the maturity date of the loan. This insurance premium represents a source of performance for investors in mortgages.

The phenomenon just described is known as negative convexity and is in general an unattractive characteristic for an investor. However, for long-term investors whose future obligations are subject to uncertain timing (for example, an individual whose retirement date is unclear or a foundation whose expenditure profile is not fixed), introducing an element of negative convexity through investing in mortgages might not increase uncertainty about the ability to meet future objectives, and

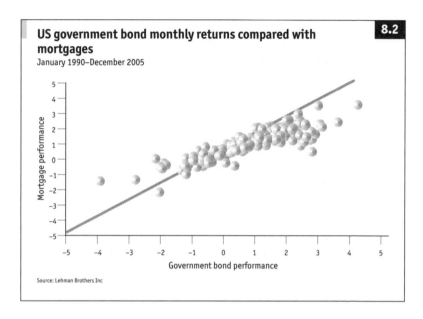

US government bond monthly returns compared with mortgages

January 1990–December 2005

8.2

Source: Lehman Brothers Inc

might, thanks to the additional expected premium income, modestly reduce it.

The performance of mortgages in comparison with government bonds, as reflected in the Lehman Aggregate bond index, is shown in Figure 8.2. A line has been drawn across the chart to indicate equal performance of mortgages and government bonds. Observations above this line indicate mortgage outperfomance; observations below the line indicate months when government bonds outperformed mortgages.

Figure 8.2 indicates that in months of strong government bond performance, mortgage performance has lagged behind. It also indicates that in many months of unexciting performance the mortgage index has outperformed government bonds, as it has done in months of poor government bond performance.

Table 8.7 compares the returns on the major components of the Lehman Aggregate Bond Index since 1990. It shows that over this 16-year period, on average, mortgages did not reward investors with a premium return over other parts of the US bond market but did reward them with a lower absolute volatility.

The position of mortgages in an investor's strategy should depend on analysis of the expected premium return from mortgages, its uncertainty and how it correlates with an investor's other sources of systematic return. Furthermore, since mortgages represent a source of systematic risk-taking and government bonds (of an appropriate maturity) provide a safe-haven investment, the appropriate balance between government bonds and mortgages (as one of a variety of risky

Table 8.7 **Performance and volatility of components of the US Lehman Aggregate Bond Index, January 1990–December 2005**

	Weight in Lehman Aggregate Index December 2005	Geometric average (% per year)	Standard deviation (% per year)
Lehman Brothers Aggregate Bond index	100.0	7.4	4.1
Lehman Brothers Government Bond Index	36.4	7.2	4.7
Lehman Brothers Mortgage Index	34.9	7.2	3.3
Lehman Brothers Credit Index	23.4	7.9	5.2

Source: Lehman Brothers Inc

assets) should be guided by the investor's tolerance for risk-taking rather than the composition of market indices.

Asset-backed securities and collateralised debt obligations

These innovations of the 1980s in the market for mortgages led to parallel innovations in the early 1990s in buying and selling and then securitising a range of financial assets, from credit-card receivables and aircraft leases to bank loans to both corporations and governments of emerging markets. This provided a major advance over early, labour-intensive and time-consuming efforts to buy and sell and "assign" bank loans. "Asset-backed securities" (ABS) is the term used for loans other than residential mortgages that have been securitised. Drawing on developments in the mortgage market, they have grown rapidly since the 1990s. They have transformed risk management for banks and provided new investment instruments for investors. Much of the motivation behind them has been driven by regulatory guidelines on banks' capital adequacy and, for some investors, on the credit quality of the assets that they may hold. In any event, the evolution of these markets provides a rich source of profitable business for investment banks.

This market is full of abbreviations. The basic structure is shown in Table 8.8 overleaf, which provides an illustration of a collateralised debt obligation (CDO).

The arrangement is simple. A pool of assets (such as a portfolio of bank loans to companies) is transferred from the bank's balance sheet to a

Table 8.8 **Illustration of a CDO structure**

Assets			Liabilities					
Type	Size ($m)	Yield	Contractual interest payments	Class	Rating	Size ($m)	Basis point spread over Libor (4.5%)	Interest receipts/ fees ($m)	Yield (%)
Loans	400	8.0	32	Class A	AAA	300	25	14.3	4.8
				Class B	A	30	75	1.6	5.3
				Class C	BBB	30	180	1.9	6.3
				Equity	not rated	40	na	10.3	25.7
				Total/average		400		28.0	7.0
				Memo: fees				4.0	1.0

"special purpose vehicle" or SPV. The liabilities of the SPV are represented by different "tranches", which have claims of differing priority on the cash flows received from the pool of corporate borrowers. The SPV arranges for one of the leading credit-rating agencies to ascribe a credit rating to each of the tranches. The highest-rated tranche, almost certain to be AAA, will have the first priority on cash flows. In each payment period, when obligations to the "senior" AAA tranche have been met, payments are then cascaded down to the mezzanine and then the junior tranches. The most risky "equity" tranche collects residual payments after the entitlements of the other tranches have been met. (Despite its name, the equity tranche of a CDO represents highly leveraged debt, not common stock.)

In this example, if the underlying loans pay 8% a year in interest, management fees are 1% of the total facility, short-term interest rates (London Interbank Offered Rate or LIBOR) are 4.5% and there are no defaults or other payment interruptions, the return to the so-called equity tranche would be 25.7% a year. However, an average shortfall from contractual receipts from the bank loans of more than 2.6% a year would leave the equity tranche with a negative investment return.

These CDOs may also be known as CBOs (collateralised bond obligations) or CLOs (collateralised loan obligations), depending on the type of collateral being used. The corresponding vehicle for residential mortgages in the United States, a residential collateralised mortgage obligation (CMO), would give exposure to mortgage prepayment risk, but not if issued by a US federal agency to credit risk of the underlying homeowner.

A parallel development has been the evolution of the market in credit derivatives, which enables counterparties to buy and sell exposure to particular credit risks and to portfolios or indexes of credit risks. This is a substantial benefit to a bank wishing to manage its credit risk to any particular name, or to any investor (such as a hedge fund) wishing to take an investment position long or short of a particular credit risk.

There are three related generic types of credit derivative:

- Credit default swaps (CDSs). In a CDS, the counterparty seeking protection pays a regular premium. In the event of a default (the detail of the definition of default is critical), the other counterparty (the insurer) pays the agreed amount (for example, making good the value of the insured credit).
- Total return (TR) swaps. In a TR swap, one counterparty pays the return of a specified investment and the other makes a payment of some reference interest rate such as LIBOR.
- Credit options. A credit option is just that, an option. The option buyer pays a fixed premium to the option seller, and in return the buyer has the right to purchase (if the option is a call option) from the seller, or the right to sell (if the option is a put option) the specified credit at a previously agreed strike price.

The growth in credit derivatives has been enormous. One breakthrough that facilitated the development of a liquid market was agreement on a degree of standardised documentation for transactions in 1999. In mid-2004 the market was estimated to have reached $4.5 trillion.

It did not take long for the market to innovate further. Synthetic CDOs were created from these derivatives and made available on market indices as well as individual names. Synthetic CDOs share the characteristics (such as AAA rated senior tranches and a residual equity tranche) of traditional CDOs, which have an SPV holding the underlying assets. But the synthetic CDOs do not physically own the underlying assets, gaining their exposures instead through derivatives. These are then repackaged in the synthetic CDO's different tranches.

Who should invest in CDOs?

No one needs to invest in CDOs, and no one should invest in any instrument unless they are sure that they, or a trusted adviser, understand and can monitor the risks and potential rewards involved. This means that they need to understand the complex issues involved in pricing CDOs and, in particular, different tranches of a CDO.

The difference in the exposure to risk of the different tranches of a

CDO means that a generalised statement about the risk of a CDO will be misplaced. Risk managers emphasise that expected risk is focused on the equity tranches and that unexpected risk and the danger of surprising developments is most concentrated on the lower-yielding, senior tranches, which will have been designed to meet rating agencies' presumed or actual criteria. When unexpected risk materialises, it commonly results in a downgrade of agencies' credit ratings of CDO tranches. Investors who have used CDO tranches as a means of getting around a prohibition on investing in sub-investment grade assets need to assess the likelihood of such a downgrade, and all investors need to be satisfied that these disappointment risks are sufficiently reflected in the investment return that the CDO tranche offers.

Investors should have answers to some standard questions before entrusting money to a CDO manager. As with any investment management arrangement, they need to understand the manager's track record and experience in managing a pool of assets such as a CDO. They should understand the risks of the underlying assets, whether these risks might change, and the leverage introduced into the different tranches by the structure of the CDO. They should also understand the process for redemptions, how the underlying assets are valued and the sources of liquidity or illiquidity. One of the attractions of synthetic CDOs is the great liquidity of the market in credit derivatives. CDO managers are able to reflect this in the terms offered to investors in synthetic CDOs.

Investors should also satisfy themselves that the operational aspects of the CDO appear to be well established. The credit derivative markets have historically experienced severe delays in settling transactions. Investors should make sure that this is not a potential source of disruption for their manager.

International bonds and currency hedging

For all investors, foreign government bonds represent a way of diversifying yield curve risk and of seeking opportunities to add value beyond a domestic government bond benchmark. These opportunities involve foreign currency, which need not be a problem so long as the currency risk is properly managed. Otherwise whatever the rationale for making a particular investment may be overwhelmed by the impact of currency fluctuations.

Currency risk is manageable risk. It is also a big risk, which incorrectly handled can lead to windfall losses (or gains) of 20% or more over a 12-month period. Currency hedging is the way to manage this risk in international investments. The intuitive way of understanding currency hedging is to remember that it is equivalent to placing cash on deposit in the investor's home currency (for example, US dollars) and borrowing the equivalent amount in a foreign currency (for example, euros) to finance a foreign investment. In this way, fluctuations in the exchange rate will wash out, having an equal and opposite effect on the foreign investment and the foreign debt. The investor's investment return will be the performance of the foreign investment in foreign currency, plus the interest rate on dollars (the domestic currency deposit), less the interest rate on euros (the foreign currency debt).

The more conventional way to describe this is to say that foreign currency risk can be neutralised through foreign exchange "hedging", where an investor contracts to sell foreign currency at a date in the future (or "forward") at the current exchange rate. The contract allows for differences in interest rates between the two countries. Typically, the contracts are for one or three months. They are then rolled forward and adjusted as needed to reflect any changes in value of the underlying investment, to ensure that it and any capital appreciation (or decline) remain fully hedged.

What does it achieve?

Currency hedging is interesting because it enables management of currency risk and, for many investments, a marked reduction in volatility of international investments. Figures 8.3, 8.4 and 8.5 overleaf show this from the perspective of investors in euro government bonds. Figure 8.3 shows the pattern of euro government bond monthly performance in euros. Figure 8.4 shows the same investment performance translated into US dollars, with no attempt to hedge the foreign exchange risk. It is demonstrably much more volatile than the pattern of returns in euros. Figure 8.5 shows the same return series, again in US dollars, but this time hedged for foreign currency risk. The profile in Figure 8.5 is a very close approximation to Figure 8.3. The same pattern of a marked reduction in volatility is evident for hedging highest quality investment grade bonds from whichever market over whichever period where there are liquid forward currency markets. For investments of moderate volatility, such as well-diversified high-yield bond funds or many hedge fund strategies, the arguments in favour of hedging currency risk remain strong. For more volatile markets, such as equities, currency hedging alters the profile of investment returns but has a much more modest effect on volatility (see Chapter 7).

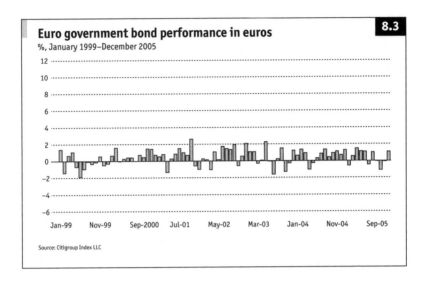

Euro government bond performance in euros 8.3

%, January 1999–December 2005

Source: Citigroup Index LLC

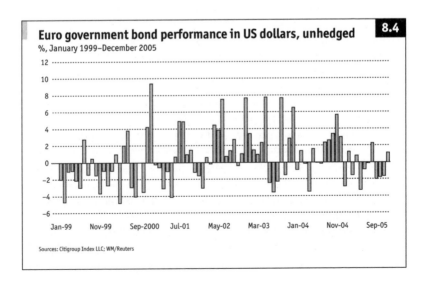

Euro government bond performance in US dollars, unhedged 8.4

%, January 1999–December 2005

Sources: Citigroup Index LLC; WM/Reuters

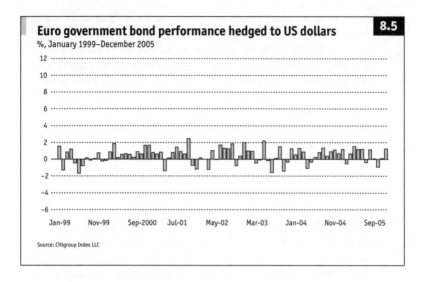

Euro government bond performance hedged to US dollars `8.5`
%, January 1999–December 2005

Source: Citigroup Index LLC

What does it cost?

Three types of costs may be incurred in foreign currency hedging:

- **Transaction costs.** Foreign exchange markets are among the most liquid markets in the world, and the transaction costs of putting in place and particularly of rolling forward hedges in the principal currencies are tiny – a small number of basis points each year. But it is important to check whether there are any supplementary transaction costs which over time could materially reduce the attractiveness of hedging. For currencies that are subject to occasional liquidity crises, the "spread" levied in the foreign exchange market between forward purchases and sales – which would be expected to reflect the difference in short-term interest rates – can widen sharply at times of market crisis. This will dramatically increase the cost of hedging in those currencies. For this reason, an investor should not normally hedge investments denominated in currencies which may, at a time of crisis, become illiquid. However, euro investors in dollar denominated emerging-market debt may treat the position as a US dollar exposure that needs hedging back to euros.
- **Cash flow costs.** There are regular cash flows associated with currency hedging. These represent the currency gains and losses on the hedge which should be offset, perfectly with a perfect

hedge, with currency losses and gains on the hedged investment. In an investment account, the gains and losses of the hedge will normally be painfully evident, while the foreign exchange gains and losses on the foreign investment will be less obvious. Where the investment is illiquid – for example, if a US investor is hedging a European private equity investment back to dollars and the US dollar depreciates against the euro – the scale of the depreciation will be felt as a cash outflow associated with the hedge as the dollar depreciates. (See Chapter 11 for a discussion of foreign currency risk and illiquid investments.) Foreign currency hedging is best suited to highly liquid investments, such as government bonds. The cash flows associated with hedging can be both embarrassing and, for illiquid investments, painful.

- ◾ **Opportunity cost.** This is closely tied to regret risk, that is, the risk that the decision to hedge an international investment will be regretted because subsequent currency movements would have made it more profitable not to have hedged. In this case, the investor's accounts will show the cash flow impact of the hedge and encourage statements such as "this hedge has cost me ...". Investors need to reflect on the reasons for the hedged investment when making these statements.

Sometimes, as with international equity investing, hedging decisions are finely balanced (see Chapter 7). Frequently, though, the appropriate rule of thumb is that certain types of international investment should not be made unless they are to be hedged. The obvious examples are investments in foreign bonds. In addition, most hedge fund strategies should be either managed or hedged to the investor's base currency. This is because exposing bond and hedge funds to unmanaged currency risk transforms the performance pattern that should be expected from the investment and this will often undermine the role that the investment is supposed to have in an investment strategy. If an investor likes the foreign bond market and likes the currency, a critic might ask: why hedge? The answer is that since currency volatility will contribute much more to the risk of losing money than bond-market volatility, the position should be seen as a foreign currency view and not a bond-market view.

How easy is foreign exchange forecasting?
Central banks, which ought to be well informed about the nature of currency markets, sometimes admit that they do not know how to forecast

exchange rates. With hindsight it may appear that a particular exchange rate was "bound" to trend in a particular direction. With foresight it is never that easy. One of the most dangerous things an investor can do is to take unstructured foreign currency bets. These almost always degenerate into "bet the ranch" gambles which make a nonsense of any considered risk-taking that might until then have characterised investment strategy. This is because foreign exchange is a source of significant volatility with, on average, no expected pay-off. Nevertheless, carefully managed foreign exchange risk can have a role in any strategy where an investor uses a team that has both insights and a track record, and where the risk-management process reassures the investor that the downside risk for when things go wrong – which is inevitable from time to time – is acceptable.

9 Hedge funds: try to keep it simple

There has been an explosion in money managed by hedge funds in the past decade. In the early 1990s they were fringe investment vehicles, managing money for some enterprising private investors as well as the hedge-fund managers themselves. Since then they have become increasingly popular with endowments, innovative pension funds and insurance companies. Over $1 trillion is now managed directly by hedge funds. Over the past 15 years, there has been a flow of talented individuals from the proprietary trading desks of investment banks and from established money managers to join or to set up hedge funds. Every investment bank and virtually every established money manager will have suffered from this exodus of talented staff, and over this period hedge funds have become leading players in a global process of shifting elements of risk-bearing from the banking sector to investment institutions.

This chapter examines this modern phenomenon and explores how different types of hedge fund strategy can contribute to achieving an investor's goals.

What are hedge funds?

The Managed Funds Association defines a hedge fund as "a privately offered, pooled investment vehicle that is not widely available to the public and the assets of which are managed by a professional investment management firm". But hedge funds are best understood as entrepreneurial investment companies that operate with few constraints. Their investment strategies differ substantially from each other, though they can be sorted into generic types. They have so far been lightly regulated, if at all, though this position is changing. All hedge funds have in common remuneration structures that are exceptionally favourable to the hedge fund managers when their fund performance is good. Three other characteristics are the investment of a substantial part of the managers' net worth in their own fund; their ability to have short positions in investment portfolios; and the secrecy that often surrounds their underlying investment positions. They are also distinguished in being managed to generate positive returns, rather than to beat or match a stock or bond market index. The illiquidity of the underlying investments means that many hedge fund strategies are not suitable for short-term investors.

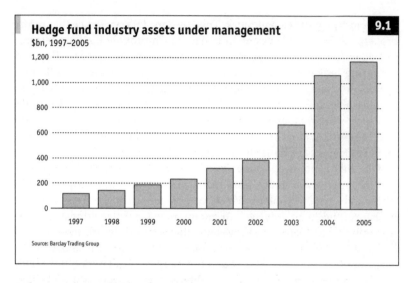

Hedge fund industry assets under management 9.1
$bn, 1997–2005

Source: Barclay Trading Group

What motivates hedge fund managers?

The remuneration of hedge fund managers is important in understanding what to expect, and what to demand, from hedge fund arrangements and for judging whether enough value is likely to be left over for external investors. Hedge fund remuneration is an attempt by hedge fund managers to ensure that they personally retain as much as is sustainable of the investment return that comes from their scarce financial skills.

The skill of a hedge fund manager is subject to uncertainty. This puts some constraint on the fees that the most skilled hedge fund managers can charge, as they have to share their investment return with the owners of the capital that they put to work. At the same time, the extraordinary potential income of hedge fund managers and the difficulties in assessing skill has encouraged a rush of wannabe hedge fund managers, who see the hedge fund industry as offering a free call option on great wealth. The penalty for lack of success is seen as quite modest, while the difficulty of identifying skill might suggest that luck may offer better prospects for good financial rewards than skill alone would suggest. Money managers who have recently been successful will naturally attribute this achievement to their own innate ability. They will, unsurprisingly, be confident of extending and even improving on that record by evolving into a hedge fund manager. It will be investors' money that is used to discover the difference between skill and luck, even though in some instances skill will be obscured by bad luck, and in others lack of skill will continue to be obscured by extended good luck. There is anecdotal evidence that prime brokers (divisions of investment banks which provide banking services to hedge funds) encourage start-up hedge funds (which are clients of the prime brokers) to pursue volatile investment strategies. A collection of volatile strategies from different young hedge funds is more likely to produce at least some commercially eye-catching short-term track records, and so more rapid growth of funds under management in aggregate (and so more business for the prime broker) than a collection of stable investment strategies with duller track records.

This highlights a disconnection between the interests of investors and the interests of hedge fund managers and is another aspect of the "principal–agent" problem which complicates relationships between investors and their advisers in many investment relationships (see Appendix 2). In hedge fund investing, the extent to which investor and hedge fund manager interests are aligned will change if and when a particular fund starts to prosper and the manager's call option on wealth moves "in-the-money". In this case, hedge fund managers are likely to be much more concerned to preserve and grow rather than put at risk their own wealth, which is invested in the fund. This can lead to a subtle shift in hedge fund business strategy from the pursuit of performance to a greater focus on asset gathering, on the basis of the past performance record. At this stage, some hedge funds diversify their business and wealth risk by adding new strategies; others, who continue to manage a single strategy, may respond by reducing risk-taking. Investors should be alert to this possibility and decide what the impact would be on their own appetite for hedge fund risk-taking.

Are hedge fund fees too high?

Many hedge fund managers would say that this is like asking whether sports or movie stars are paid too much. But while luck can play some part in any successful career, investment management is unique in the way in which luck can masquerade as skill. The problem with luck getting large financial rewards is that it gives a misleading signal to investors and leads to a misallocation of investment capital.

Hedge fund fees need to be kept at the forefront of investors' minds. The standard fee payable on an individual hedge fund is "1 and 20", "1.5 and 20" or "2 and 20". In other words, 1%, 1.5% or 2% a year of the value invested is levied as a base fee and 20% of the return earned each year is retained as a performance fee, so long as the return is positive and exceeds the previous "high watermark" or maximum level of performance. It is notable that there is normally no hurdle rate of return before performance fees are paid, other than the high watermark. In other words, a "2 and 20" fee can be payable on a performance no higher than a Treasury bill return. Although it is bizarre to offer to pay a performance fee on a return that is less than the Treasury bill return, such an agreement is made in expectation that a premium return will be earned. Anecdotal evidence indicates that some hedge funds which are normally closed to new business do selectively accept new business for a performance fee of as high as 50% of future positive returns.

The fee structure places great pressure on hedge fund managers to generate positive returns. There have been numerous examples of hedge funds that have incurred significant negative returns closing, not just because existing investors lose confidence and withdraw funds, but also because the managers have difficulty motivating staff (and themselves) when there is little immediate prospect of a performance fee being earned. In these circumstances, they would rather start a new fund than have to wait to recoup past performance losses before earning a performance fee. This becomes a self-fulfilling prophecy as investors come to expect managers to respond to poor performance in this way. Industry anecdotes also point to instances of the opposite response, with some hedge fund managers appearing to increase risk-taking in response to poor performance, a dangerous game of "double or quits". Continuing vigilance by investors for signs of changes in risk-taking by hedge funds never ceases to be important.

The existing fee structure is already sufficiently rich to weaken the case for investing in hedge funds. As stated in Chapter 4, a reasonable magnitude for the equity risk premium is 4% a year over ten-year Treasury bonds, and a normal relationship might be for Treasury bonds to offer a yield premium of around 1% a year over cash. A "2 and 20" fee schedule means that if investors expect to receive an after-fee return from hedge funds that is comparable to the after-fee return from a passive equity strategy, they need to be willing to pay to hedge fund managers around 50% of the pre-fee excess return over Treasury bills. This is a generous take by any reckoning.

Before getting carried away with indignation at seemingly exorbitant hedge fund fees, it is instructive to compare them with the fees routinely paid for traditional active money management. Active long-only investment management arrangements universally charge a higher base fee than passive strategies that can provide a minimal cost exposure to market returns. This higher fee is paid in anticipation of superior performance, whether or not it is justified by actual performance. For institutional portfolios, performance fees are sometimes also paid when long-only managers outperform their market index benchmarks by some agreed threshold. A fair comparison of the trade-off between different fee arrangements can most easily be made when there is a policy norm for investment strategy, expressed in terms of stocks, bonds and cash. This can easily be replicated with low-cost passive investment strategies. If, as some have suggested, an investor's hedge fund strategy can be replicated in a similar way, a basis for comparing the fees paid and the plausibility of the expected returns under the two strategies can be devised.

The importance of skill in hedge fund returns

By far the longest chapter in Charles Mackay's highly regarded book, *Extraordinary Popular Delusions and the Madness of Crowds*, is devoted to "the alchymists". For centuries they gripped the popular imagination of Europeans in their search for and false claims to have discovered the secrets of the philosopher's stone, which was to create an abundance of wealth by turning base metals into gold. Hope springs eternal, and the alchemists' claims would stand comparison with some hedge fund marketing material.

An example is given in Figure 9.2. It shows a positive impact of adding hedge funds to the menu of investment choices for investors by suggesting that superior risk-adjusted returns might be available for all levels of risk-taking, including no risk-taking.

Plenty of such examples have been shown to potential investors to illustrate the supposed benefits of adding hedge funds to a strategy previously based only on stocks, bonds and cash. It is nonsense to suggest that the minimum risk safe-haven investment return can be increased, except by leaving the safe haven and taking risk. However, diversification gains can increase expected returns for efficient risky portfolios when hedge funds are added. An optimistic illustration of how adding hedge funds might improve the efficient frontier is shown in Figure 9.3. This assumes that hedge fund returns are not correlated with equity and bond markets (but they are) and that all investment returns follow a well-behaved normal distribution, which is less true of many hedge fund strategies than of equity and bond returns. Nevertheless, diversification gains are a principal attraction of hedge funds. In practice, for a well-constructed hedge fund strategy, which succeeds in mostly offsetting risks of extreme returns and in achieving notable diversification gains, the pattern may look like that shown in Figure 9.3.

There is an abundance of research and practical experience that testifies

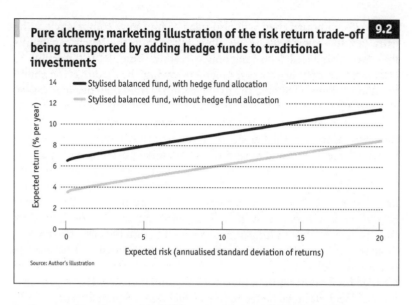

Pure alchemy: marketing illustration of the risk return trade-off being transported by adding hedge funds to traditional investments 9.2

Source: Author's illustration

to the scarcity of unusual skill in managing traditional investment portfolios. This is demonstrated by the difficulty of identifying managers who are likely to outperform in the future.

However, hedge funds give skilled managers greater scope to implement

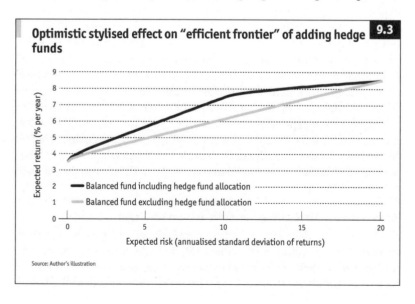

Optimistic stylised effect on "efficient frontier" of adding hedge funds 9.3

Source: Author's illustration

their skills, although they will also need to find new competencies. The extra latitude offered by hedge funds arises from the fewer constraints they face (compared with long-only investing). The first is the ability to establish leveraged positions through borrowing; the second is the ability to establish short positions, and to make money from their negative investment views (long-only managers have to pass up such opportunities to make money for their clients). Long-only managers who become hedge fund managers are quickly struck by the contrast between the way in which a large investment position in a traditional portfolio, which underperforms because its price falls, becomes a smaller, less risky position, whereas a short position in a hedge fund which underperforms, because its price increases, becomes a larger, more risky position. Often these opportunities are exploited through the more flexible use of derivatives than is permitted with long-only investment mandates. These extra flexibilities require additional investment risk management and back-office operational skills. However, they do not make it easier to assess the skill of a hedge fund manager than that of a long-only manager. This is probably more difficult because hedge fund strategies are less transparent.

It is a mistake to think that unusual manager skill is the only element of performance that should attract investors to hedge funds. Hedge fund performance is a reflection of manager skill and market returns. Sometimes the exposure to market returns generated by hedge funds represents exposure to equity or credit market returns that can be obtained at much lower cost by investing passively in equity or credit markets. There is no need to pay hedge fund fees to access such returns. However, there are other types of market returns that cannot be accessed efficiently through traditional investment manager mandates and which represent investment performance paid for providing valuable services. In an article in the *Journal of Portfolio Management* (autumn 2004), "An Alternative Future Part II: an exploration of the role of hedge funds", Clifford Asness, a hedge fund manager and a perceptive analyst of the industry, said that hedge funds "allow liquidity to be provided by those who have it to those who need it, and allow risk to be transferred from those who do not want it to those who do".

Alternative sources of systematic return and risk

Chapter 8 covered the investment characteristics of mortgage-backed securities which incorporate prepayment risk and explained why these offer a source of systematic investment performance and risk which should be a source of added value to long-term investors. It also described other asset-backed securities, including collateralised debt obligations (CDOs), which enable investors to access different tranches of systematic risk and return previously to be found only on the balance sheets of commercial banks. The systematic risk and return that is packaged within CDOs reflects aspects of credit that can also be found in corporate and emerging-market bond markets. But CDOs also give exposure to sources of credit risk that are not represented in conventional bond portfolios, so if they are appropriately structured, they can be seen as a complement to an investor's existing exposure to credit risk.

Hedge funds offer further aspects of systematic risk and return, some of which cannot be accessed in a suitably risk-managed format in long-only stock and bond portfolios. One, which is spread across different hedge fund strategies, is the ability to treat market volatility as an investment to be bought and sold and to exploit clear trends in its pricing. There is no long-only equivalent to this, and the technical skill and market timing involved in such strategies provide a source of risk and return that has no parallel outside hedge funds.

Others include a number of market efficiency raising arbitrage strategies, including merger arbitrage, statistical arbitrage (exploiting short-term momentum in markets), fixed-income and convertible arbitrage. Each of these represents a potential source of systematic return, although the hedge fund industry's casual use of the word "arbitrage" must not be taken to mean that these strategies are low risk (see below). Correspondingly, macro and commodity trading advisers (CTAs, also known as managed futures funds) are other strategies that have no long-only parallel, and in the case of CTA strategies represent an indirect way of profiting from the systematic return that appears to be offered to long-term investors who supply liquidity to the commodity markets.

In these and other areas, hedge funds provide a risk transfer and liquidity service which in previous times was either not systematically provided or provided by commercial banks. The banks are often eager to pass on, or "lay off", these risks to hedge funds as this facilitates the banks' management of their capital adequacy and adherence to new statutory standards. Hedge funds need considerable skill in providing these services, but the return that investors should expect from these services derives primarily from the market return to such risk-taking. These are the alternative sources of systematic investment return and risk that are increasingly understood to explain the performance of various hedge fund strategies and to provide a justification for investing in hedge funds.

Does the hedge fund industry face a capacity constraint?

My first involvement as an investor with a hedge fund was in the early 1990s, when I persuaded the trustees of the large pension fund for which I worked to make what was (for that pension fund) a modest allocation to a promising, tightly risk-managed arbitrage strategy that focused on exploiting anomalies in the pricing of UK equity derivatives. The strategy had earned a respectable return with a modest volume of assets under management. Our allocation, which substantially increased the size of the hedge fund, coincided with the disappearance of those anomalies, significantly reducing the profitability of the strategy. We drew the obvious conclusion: that an opportunity, having been identified, attracted a sufficient weight of money from a variety of sources to remove the anomaly and therefore the profitability of the strategy. Where hedge fund strategies are exploiting technical anomalies which can relatively easily be translated into profits, flows of money in search of profit will overwhelm any such anomalies.

This is something that must be taken seriously in arbitrage hedge fund strategies. There are other areas where administrative factors, for example in establishing short positions, limit the scale of hedge fund strategies. As a result, short-selling managers may find it difficult to manage very large funds. This constraint also applies to equity long/short managers, who in practice, and for a variety of reasons, often make use of exchange traded funds and equity futures contracts to reduce their market exposure. By contrast, some of the skills-based strategies (such as global macro), as well as strategies that are intended to provide systematic exposure to credit markets, have no obvious market-imposed capacity constraint. In these strategies it makes no more sense to suggest that these hedge fund strategies are capacity constrained than to suggest that bond or equity markets face similar constraints.

"Do hedge funds hedge?"

During the equity bear market of 2000–02, aggregate hedge fund indices comfortably outperformed equity market indices. At this time many private investors profitably moved money out of direct investment in equities into hedge fund strategies. For many of them hedge funds did provide a good hedge against the equity bear market. But how dependable is the hedge that hedge funds provided at that time?

The answer is provided in a comment that a private investor made to me in 2003, when explaining how pleased he was that his financial adviser had persuaded him "to keep his equities in the form of hedge

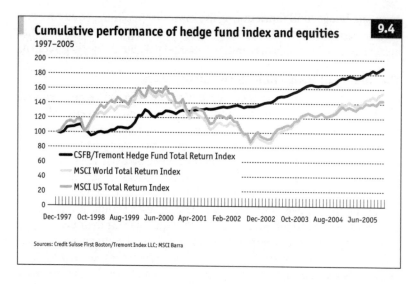

Cumulative performance of hedge fund index and equities `9.4`

1997–2005

- CSFB/Tremont Hedge Fund Total Return Index
- MSCI World Total Return Index
- MSCI US Total Return Index

Dec-1997 Oct-1998 Aug-1999 Jun-2000 Apr-2001 Feb-2002 Dec-2002 Oct-2003 Aug-2004 Jun-2005

Sources: Credit Suisse First Boston/Tremont Index LLC; MSCI Barra

funds". This investor had exactly the right impression of what he had done with his strategy.

Many equity hedge fund managers adjust their exposure to what they see as trends in markets, raising exposure after market rises and cutting after market falls. The 2000–02 equity bear market was unusual in being long and drawn out. It is therefore likely that that experience may mislead investors about the ability of hedge funds to hedge in the event of sharp, sudden equity market reversals. Table 9.1 shows the performance of an

Table 9.1 **Hedge fund and fixed-income performance during months of equity market crisis since 1994 (% total return)**

	MSCI US Index	MSCI World Index	MSCI Emerging Markets Index	Lehman Bros Intermediate Term US Government Bond Index	Lehman Bros Long Term US Government Bond Index	CSFB/ Tremont Hedge Fund Index
Aug 1998	−13.9	−13.3	−28.9	1.9	4.4	−7.6
Sep 2002	−11.3	−11.0	−10.8	1.7	4.1	0.1
Feb 2001	−8.9	−8.4	−7.8	0.9	1.6	−0.6
Nov 2000	−7.9	−6.1	−8.7	1.5	3.1	−1.6
Sep 2001	−7.6	−8.8	−15.5	2.1	0.8	−0.8

Sources: Credit Suisse First Boston/Tremont Index LLC; MSCI Barra; Lehman Brothers Inc

aggregate hedge fund index during the most disappointing equity market months since it started in January 1994. These figures emphasise that investing in hedge funds may mitigate market risk, but it does not avoid it.

The quality of hedge fund performance data

Figure 9.4 on the previous page, comparing the cumulative performance of a hedge fund index with the performance of equity markets, will raise concerns about the reliability of the hedge fund data. This is a subject which arouses considerable debate and on which many research papers have been written. The hedge fund performance data used in this chapter come from the CSFB Tremont database. The indices are asset weighted to show the performance of the average dollar invested in the CSFB Tremont sample for that strategy. Other index providers use a simple average of the returns of each fund (of whatever size) that qualifies for their index.

The focus of much commentary on hedge fund performance is that published indices overstate the actual experience of investors. One example is given in Table 9.6 on page 154, which shows the performance of fixed-income arbitrage funds in months of stockmarket crisis. This reports the average dollar invested in this strategy as measured by CSFB Tremont showing a return of -1.5% in August 1998, the month that Long Term Capital Management (LTCM), the largest hedge fund that would be described as following this strategy, imploded. During that month LTCM experienced a loss of 44.8% of its capital. This is not reflected in the hedge fund industry performance numbers because from the outset LTCM, a highly secretive organisation, did not wish to share its performance numbers with anyone apart from its investors. In other words, participation in databases of hedge fund performance is in part voluntary and the indices are not comprehensive. This incomplete coverage may particularly affect successful funds which are closed to new investors.

The August 1998 example is a dramatic illustration of incomplete reporting distorting the performance of hedge fund indices. However, consistent non-reporting by individual funds is not an obvious reason for the index numbers to overstate performance. The opposite may be true as consistent non-reporters may typically be among the group of successful, historically well-performing funds. Other data issues might more obviously bias the numbers. One is that new hedge funds are able to "backfill" their performance numbers in databases of hedge fund perform-ance after they decide to start reporting performance (the disappointing "incubator" results may not get reported at all). However, reporting data to a database says nothing about the rules for eligibility for inclusion in an index, which are generally designed to exclude backfill bias by ignoring data for months before the date the data are first reported.

Nevertheless, the consensus is that hedge fund indices do suffer from some element of survivor bias, which causes reported performance to be higher than the average experience of hedge fund investors. Furthermore, the track records that investors are shown ahead of new investment decisions are almost always (apart from those from purely passive strategies and some convincing contrarian sellers) subject to upward bias – investors do not invite the poor performers to make new business presentations. However, investors should not take investment decisions on either a type of investment, or a particular investment manager, on the basis of past performance alone. The key is always the expected future performance (and its source), how this relates to the pattern of performance expected from the investor's other assets, and whether the investor can access that source of performance and risk from anywhere else. An understanding of these issues should be much more important than historical reported performance numbers in informing investors' decisions.

Types of hedge fund strategy

With market developments evolving rapidly, recognised categorisation of hedge fund strategies can become obsolete. One traditional broad classification of hedge funds draws a distinction between "directional" and "non-directional" strategies. Directional strategies deliberately seek to make opportunistic profit from movements in the level of the market. They include macro, short selling and emerging market, most equity long/ short and distressed debt strategies (see below).

By contrast, "non-directional" strategies deliberately seek to profit from anomalies in the pricing of securities that should, in principle, be comparable. These are called arbitrage or relative value strategies. A narrow definition of the word "arbitrage" refers to the exploitation of different prices for the same security, or the same risk exposure, in different markets. However, as pointed out in Chapter 6, there can be barriers that prevent low-risk, profitable arbitrage, even between two securities which give directly comparable ownership rights.

Arbitrage is often used more loosely in hedge fund investing to describe offsetting positions which a hedge fund manager judges to be similar and speculates ought to provide a reasonable hedge for each other, most of the time. In practice, there are almost always strong elements of risk that can undermine many so-called arbitrage hedge fund strategies, so use of the word arbitrage should not be interpreted as meaning that a strategy is

Table 9.2 **Hedge fund industry: assets under management, 2005[a]**

	$bn	%
Hedge fund industry[b]	1,141	
Fund of funds industry	651	
Sectors		
Convertible arbitrage	50	4.4
Distressed securities	81	7.1
Emerging Markets	125	11.0
Equity long bias	157	13.8
Equity long/short	175	15.4
Equity long-only	28	2.4
Equity market neutral	41	3.6
Event driven	107	9.4
Fixed income	124	10.9
Macro	54	4.7
Merger arbitrage	20	1.8
Multi-strategy	97	8.5
Other[c]	18	1.6
Sector specific[d]	63	5.6
Total	**1,141**	**100.0**

a Third quarter.
b Excludes fund of funds assets. c Includes funds categorised as regulation D, equity short bias, option strategies, mutual fund timing, statistical arbitrage, closed-end funds and without a category. d Includes sector funds categorised as technology, energy, bio-tech, finance, real estate, metals and mining, and miscellaneous.
Source: Barclay Trading Group

low risk. Other strategies, often called event-driven strategies, can involve a combination of arbitrage and directional strategies. It is recognised that virtually all hedge fund strategies involve exposure to greater or lesser combinations of market risk.

The size of the hedge fund market

Table 9.2 shows the weight of money directly invested in the different types of hedge funds. Approximately one-third of the $1.8 trillion estimated to have been invested in hedge funds in September 2005 was invested through fund of hedge fund arrangements, where fund of fund managers are responsible for selecting individual hedge fund managers and for the risk management of the hedge fund arrangement. The balance of $1.1 trillion was directly invested in hedge funds by investors. Also in

September 2005 a further $131 billion was invested in managed futures programmes with CTAs, which are not generally classified as hedge funds but are directly comparable (see below).

Table 9.2 shows that of the total amount allocated directly by investors to hedge funds, 35% was placed with equity hedge funds and around 9% each with event-driven and multi-strategy funds; emerging markets accounted for 11% and fixed-income and distressed debt strategies for 18%. Historic data indicate that compared with late 2003, the significant changes have been relative declines in allocations to convertible arbitrage and to a lesser extent multi-strategy funds, offset by increased allocations to event-driven strategies. Even longer-run data indicate that there has been a major decline in the formerly pre-eminent position of global macro hedge funds and funds managed by CTAs, although in the last few years there has been a recovery of interest in CTA funds.

Directional strategies
Global macro. In the early 1990s macro funds were the dominant type of hedge fund. Their importance has diminished in the past 15 years as the range of other hedge fund strategies has grown.

A macro fund may use leverage to exploit a diverse range of opportunities, investing in individual companies, equity or bond markets, commodities or currencies. The instruments a macro fund uses range from long and short positions in highly liquid (and potentially highly leveraged) currency or futures markets through quoted securities to illiquid investments in private equity or direct loans to companies. Investment banks can replicate this range of opportunistic investing, but no other investment vehicle can come close to a macro hedge fund for the diversity of its entrepreneurial risk-taking. Performance comes from manager decisions: the changes in their market exposures means that there may be no persistence of such exposures. This does not mean, however, that a macro fund diversifies equity or bond market risk. Sometimes it will and sometimes it will amplify it, and the macro fund's investor probably will not know until after the event how the fund was positioned during turbulent market conditions.

Equity hedge, equity long/short and equity market neutral. The hedge fund business is traditionally considered to have started with the partnership set up by Alfred Jones in the late 1940s. It would be recognised today as an "equity long/short" or "equity hedge" fund. It incorporated short selling of overvalued stocks alongside holdings of undervalued stocks. In

Table 9.3 **Hedge fund performance during months of equity market crisis since 1994 (% total return)**

	MSCI US Index	HEDG Global Macro Index
Aug 1998	−13.9	−4.8
Sep 2002	−11.3	0.8
Feb 2001	−8.9	1.0
Nov 2000	−7.9	3.6
Sep 2001	−7.6	1.2

Sources: Credit Suisse First Boston/Tremont Index LLC; MSCI Barra

this way its exposure to market movements was reduced and its exposure to manager skills was emphasised.

Equity long/short funds normally have some positive exposure to equity markets and are considered to be directional funds. Furthermore, the pattern of returns generated by these funds indicates that the stocks that they "short", or sell, tend to be easy-to-borrow liquid large cap stocks or even index futures contracts, whereas the stocks that they purchase (or go long) tend to be less liquid, smaller company stocks. This pattern introduces a distinctive element of systematic risk into many of these hedge funds, which often have a leveraged exposure to the performance of small companies relative to large companies.

Equity/long short hedge funds typically have much less diversified portfolios than conventional long-only portfolios. Some of these funds seek to neutralise market risk exposures and to offer an investment return that, as near as possible, reflects only the investment manager's stock-picking skills. These, called equity market neutral, form a minority of the equity hedge funds.

Short-selling or short-biased managers. Short-selling managers sell stocks that they expect to decline in value in the expectation of being able to buy them back at a later date at a lower price. These directional funds should perform particularly well when the stockmarket declines. How well a short-selling fund provides this insurance will depend upon how well it is diversified. In practice, the average performance of the short-selling strategy in months of equity setback has been strongly positive. The August 1998 performance (22.7%) is particularly striking. It shows that the evolving crisis at that time – it was the month that Long Term Capital Management unravelled – gave the short-selling managers sufficient time

Table 9.4 **Equity hedge fund performance during months of equity market crisis since 1994 (% total return)**

	MSCI US Index	MSCI US Small Cap Index	HEDG Dedicated Short Index	HEDG Equity Mkt Neutral Index	HEDG Long/Short Equity Index
Aug 1998	−13.9	−20.7[a]	22.7	−0.9	−11.4
Sep 2002	−11.3	−7.4	8.1	0.0	−0.5
Feb 2001	−8.9	−4.1	8.3	0.9	−2.4
Nov 2000	−7.9	−10.2	13.8	0.3	−3.8
Sep 2001	−7.6	−13.5	2.9	−0.1	−1.6

a Price change only.
Sources: Credit Suisse First Boston/Tremont Index LLC; MSCI Barra

to leverage their negative bets on the stockmarket. The unusual nature of the returns that month is shown in Figure 9.5 overleaf (August 1998 is circled).

The long bull market of the 1990s proved an inhospitable environment for pure short-selling funds and this category of hedge funds is now dominated by short-biased managers, in other words funds which maintain a combination of long and short positions, but a bias towards short positions. Short-selling funds are particularly used by fund of hedge fund managers to reduce the overall equity market exposure of their portfolios of hedge funds. In practice, the money managed by short-selling funds is normally modest.

Long-only equity hedge funds. These exist. They do not hedge, but they call themselves hedge funds and they are becoming increasingly common, in particular as hedge fund managers branch out into new strategies making use of their existing skills. Long-only hedge funds are constituted as partnerships. The principals own a significant equity stake and typically they invest opportunistically in smaller quoted and perhaps some unquoted private companies. The fee arrangements are much more attractive to the managers of these funds than the fee arrangements for their close relative, the small cap mutual fund. Furthermore, they are given a greater degree of investment flexibility by being in a stronger position (than a mutual fund) to manage the terms on which clients can exit from the fund.

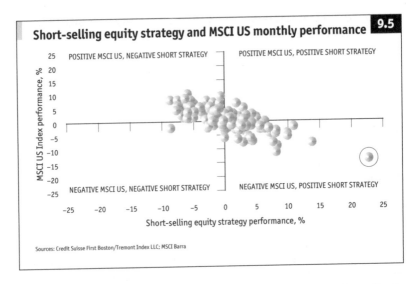

Short-selling equity strategy and MSCI US monthly performance `9.5`

Sources: Credit Suisse First Boston/Tremont Index LLC; MSCI Barra

Emerging-market hedge funds. As the name suggests, these funds exploit opportunities in emerging markets. They are directional funds which invest in both equities and bonds. In the past it has been difficult to borrow stock in many of these markets, although in recent years this has become easier. One means of altering market exposure is by leveraging the entire portfolio through borrowing, or by scaling back exposure through building up holdings of cash. Anecdotal comments by hedge fund managers suggests that risk management of hedge fund portfolios can, from time to time, be extremely challenging in these illiquid markets.

Fixed-income hedge funds: diversified fixed-income. Hedge funds have been at the forefront of developing markets in new credit risk instruments in recent years (see Chapter 8). These instruments, in the form of CDOs and credit derivatives, enable investors to buy or sell different types of exposure to diversified groups of borrowers or to individual named borrowers. They allow hedge funds to exploit any anomalies in the pricing of the different types of loans or credit derivatives, and they provide hedge funds with an efficient means to implement views on the direction of credit markets. They also enable hedge funds to act as intermediaries, creating synthetic CDOs and then selling tranches of credit exposure to investors. Diversified fixed-income hedge funds represent an important step towards building a long-term franchise for a hedge fund. This reflects the process, described in Chapter 8, whereby risk transfer activities previously undertaken by banks

Table 9.5 **Emerging market hedge fund performance during months of equity market crisis since 1994 (% total return)**

	MSCI World Index	MSCI Emerging Markets Equity Index	JP Morgan Emerging Market Bond Index plus	HEDG Emerging Markets Index
Aug 1998	−13.3	−28.9	-28.7	−23.0
Sep 2002	−11.0	−10.8	-3.7	−2.0
Sep 2001	−8.8	−15.5	-3.7	−4.4
Feb 2001	−8.4	−7.8	-1.6	−2.9
Nov 2000	−6.1	−8.7	-0.5	−3.6

Sources: J P Morgan; Credit Suisse First Boston/Tremont Index LLC; MSCI Barra

are now being channelled through hedge funds. This process focuses on securitising the financial risks associated with bank loans (by transforming loans into negotiable securities), and the fixed-income strategies of hedge funds are at the centre of it.

Some of the largest hedge funds are fixed-income hedge specialists which provide their investors with assorted combinations of exposure to credit risk. Sometimes they are classified as "distressed-debt" and sometimes as "diversified fixed-income" hedge funds. But a great attraction is that these hedge funds offer access to systematic returns from various credit markets in a form that is often not available from traditional markets.

Fixed-income hedge funds: distressed debt. "Distressed debt" conjures up images of the obligations of companies that are close to bankruptcy. This is the traditional fishing pond for hedge funds specialising in distressed debt. This group of hedge funds also includes some significant hedge funds which can resemble "private debt funds". The largest of these have much in common with large private equity conglomerates (see Chapter 10). For an investor, there is likely to be a close overlap in terms of risk exposures with the much less expensive, well-diversified, high-yield corporate debt fund. But the distressed-debt fund has some advantages compared with the high-yield mutual fund. First, the hedge fund managers may be the bankers extending loans to their investee companies. They will have a much more direct sense of ownership for their holdings, and greater scope to influence corporate management, than the best informed high-yield manager. Second, the hedge fund can impose disciplined lock-up periods

Table 9.6 **Fixed income hedge fund performance during months of equity market crisis since 1994 (% total return)**

	MSCI US Index	Lehman Bros Intermediate Term US Government Bond Index	Lehman Bros Long Term US Government Bond Index	HEDG Distressed Index	HEDG Fixed Income Arb Index
Aug 1998	–13.9	1.9	4.4	–12.5	–1.5
Sep 2002	–11.3	1.7	4.1	–0.3	–1.1
Feb 2001	–8.9	0.9	1.6	1.9	0.5
Nov 2000	–7.9	1.5	3.1	–1.1	0.7
Sep 2001	–7.6	2.1	0.8	–0.8	0.2

Note: See comments in text on August 1998 fixed-income arbitrage reported performance.
Sources: Credit Suisse First Boston/Tremont Index LLC; MSCI Barra; Lehman Brothers Inc

on investors and so can gain the advantage of time and be in better control of flows of liquidity into and out of the fund. This provides a significant investment advantage to a distressed-debt hedge fund compared with a high-yield bond mutual fund. The hedge fund is then better able to provide liquidity when borrowers are willing to pay most for it.

Arbitrage strategies
Fixed-income arbitrage. Fixed-income arbitrage strategies exploit anomalies in the pricing of fixed-income instruments while minimising exposure to interest rate risk. Fixed-income arbitrage funds establish long and short positions in closely related fixed-income markets or securities. Where the offsetting positions are close substitutes, high leverage may be used. Short positions are generally highly liquid and long positions may be less liquid. These strategies will often be positively affected by a narrowing of credit spreads and vice versa, although the hedge funds can equally easily bet on credit spreads widening as narrowing.

Merger arbitrage. Merger arbitrage (sometimes simply called "risk arbitrage") funds provide an insurance which previously was left as unsought risk by long-only equity managers. When an intended merger or takeover is announced, the share price of the target company moves close to the announced takeover terms. Its new share price is normally (unless a higher bid is anticipated) less than a cash bid price. The amount of the discount will reflect the probability that the bid will succeed, as well as

Table 9.7 **Arbitrage hedge fund performance during months of equity market crisis since 1994 (% total return)**

	MSCI US Index	HEDG Convertible Arbitrage Index	HEDG Risk Arbitrage Index	HEDG Event Driven Index	HEDG Fixed Income Arb Index
Aug 1998	−13.9	−4.6	−6.2	−11.8	−1.5
Sep 2002	−11.3	1.4	−0.6	−0.2	−1.1
Feb 2001	−8.9	2.1	1.5	1.6	0.5
Nov 2000	−7.9	−0.5	0.3	−0.8	0.7
Sep 2001	−7.6	0.7	−2.7	−1.5	0.2

Note: See comments in text on August 1998 fixed-income arbitrage reported performance.
Sources: Credit Suisse First Boston/Tremont Index LLC, MSCI Barra

the intervening rate of interest. Merger arbitrage funds provide insurance against the risk that the announced merger might fail, by acquiring the target company and hedging that by selling the acquiring company. This strategy is vulnerable to two risks: company-specific issues could cause the merger to fail; or a severe equity market decline could cause a rene-gotiation of the terms of the deal. In common with other difficult to diversify insurance arrangements, merger arbitrage provides a steady flow of income with the risk of occasional large losses.

Convertible arbitrage. Hedge funds were said in early 2005 to hold around three-quarters of outstanding convertible bonds, such was the popularity of convertible arbitrage strategies. Convertible bonds pay a low coupon (or low yield) because they have the added benefit that they can, at the discretion of the investor, be converted into equity. They thus provide the upside potential of equities and the downside protection of a bond. They provide a natural opportunity for hedge funds seeking to exploit any technical anomalies in the pricing of the debt, convertible bonds, warrants (that is, options on equity) and equity of a particular issuer. In principle, these strategies should be able to deliver steady profits. However, a danger is that market illiquidity for some elements of the hedge can cause anomalies to become more exaggerated before the possible distant date at which the arbitrage profit should be crystal-lised. If the fund is subject to severe redemptions as investors respond to disappointing performance, forced sales can easily have a cumulatively negative impact on performance. Nevertheless, in principle there can be clear arbitrage profits for patient long-term investors, and hedge funds provide the obvious vehicle to exploit such anomalies.

Statistical arbitrage. There are a number of different strategies that are or have been followed by relative value hedge fund managers and which may be found within multi-strategy funds. These include liquidity arbitrage trades to exploit (and correct) the short-term impact on market prices of securities of large market trades. Historically, another type of trade was the observed positive or negative impact on stock prices of companies joining or leaving an index which is widely used as an investment benchmark. This declined in profitability as new money chased the unusual profits which had previously been earned by exploiting these phenomena. Both these types of statistical arbitrage trades show how hedge funds can improve the efficient functioning of markets by reducing the scale of these short-term anomalies. But they also illustrate how anomalies can be eroded by a weight of money, leaving few if any profits for latecomers.

Multi-strategy funds

From the beginning of the hedge fund industry, larger funds have often managed their own risks and their investors' risks by having more than one team of portfolio managers, each dedicated to a different investment strategy. This enables the hedge fund's management to take responsibility for allocating resources as opportunities in the different strategies change. Multi-strategy funds can be expected to provide increasing competition with fund of hedge fund arrangements because of the central ownership of risk management and decision-making, and, critically, lower fees.

The multi-strategy funds include some of the largest hedge funds.

Table 9.8 **Multi-strategy hedge fund performance during months of equity market crisis since 1994 (% total return)**

	MSCI US Index	HEDG Multi-Strategy Index
Aug 1998	−13.9	1.2
Sep 2002	−11.3	0.8
Feb 2001	−8.9	0.2
Nov 2000	−7.9	0.3
Sep 2001	−7.6	−0.5

Sources: Credit Suisse First Boston/Tremont Index LLC; MSCI Barra

A number of these have moved aggressively to develop expertise in corporate finance, enabling them to supplant the traditional roles of investment banks in structuring financial packages for corporate borrowers. It is now common to hear of the involvement of one or more hedge funds in corporate takeovers and even in management buy-outs.

Commodity trading advisers (or managed futures funds)

Commodity trading advisers (CTAs) provide one of the most interesting absolute return strategies. Their investable universe is provided by the world's futures, options and foreign exchange markets. CTA managers may concentrate on trading in agricultural commodities, metals, currencies or other financial futures and options markets. As a result they are highly liquid and easy to value, so there should be no qualifications about their performance and risk statistics. What you see is what you get, whereas with hedge funds it is better to proceed on the basis that what you ultimately receive is what you get. CTA strategies have been subject to extensive statistical analysis, which shows that, on average, they have demonstrated strong diversifying characteristics and a tendency to perform well at times of equity market crisis when other hedge fund strategies often underperform.

The pattern of returns shown by indices of CTA manager performance during months of equity market weakness (see Table 9.9) is immediately different from the corresponding figures for hedge fund performance. With the exception of the dedicated short strategies, the overriding message from the hedge fund data is that hedge funds do not provide short-term insurance against poor equity market performance. On average, CTAs have provided some such hedge. The question

Table 9.9 **Managed futures fund (CTA) performance during months of equity market crisis since 1994 (% total return)**

	MSCI US Index	HEDG Managed Futures Index	CSFB/Tremont Hedge Fund Index
Aug 1998	−13.9	10.0	−7.6
Sep 2002	−11.3	4.1	0.1
Feb 2001	−8.9	0.2	−0.6
Nov 2000	−7.9	6.7	−1.6
Sep 2001	−7.6	3.7	−0.8

Sources: Credit Suisse First Boston/Tremont Index LLC; MSCI Barra; Lehman Brothers Inc

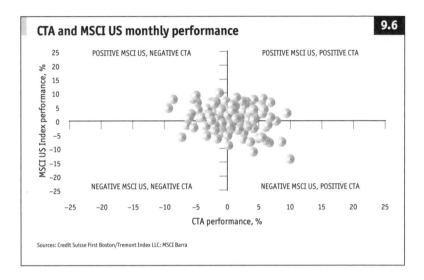

CTA and MSCI US monthly performance `9.6`

Sources: Credit Suisse First Boston/Tremont Index LLC; MSCI Barra

investors must ask is how confident they can be that this pattern will continue in the future.

Figure 9.6 shows this graphically (using monthly data). The statistical research suggests that there are surprisingly few negative returns shown for the index of CTA manager returns in those periods when equity markets show negative returns. (This is the relatively empty area in the lower left-hand quadrant of Figure 9.6.) However, when the stockmarket delivers positive returns, there is essentially no relationship between stockmarket returns and CTA performance.

To decide whether there may be some element of dependable protection in CTA strategies, it is important to understand how CTAs manage money. CTA managers are typically either highly quantitative, using models to generate buy and sell decisions, or they are discretionary, using their own judgment and experience to guide decision-making. The trading strategies of the CTA managers vary considerably, but they have a strong bias towards following trends and identifying changes in trends. They operate in markets in which liquidity is normally high and in which they can easily implement rapid changes in portfolio strategy.

There are a number of possible explanations for the apparent insurance against equity market setbacks that CTA strategies have provided. It may be down to luck that in the relatively small number of months (or quarters) with large negative equity returns the average CTA manager has delivered a somewhat surprisingly strong performance. Or, more likely, it may be that CTAs have been successful in providing insurance against equity market weakness when the setback in equity markets has given CTA managers sufficient time to identify the change in trend and switch positions. Sometimes this will work and sometimes, when markets are affected by a sudden setback, it will not.

Hedge fund risk

A little-regulated environment

Hedge fund risk should feature prominently in any assessment of hedge fund investing. Since the funds have been largely unregulated, investors need to consider how this undermines their level of comfort. There have been several well-publicised examples of hedge fund fraud and apparent fraud, and it is likely that the entrepreneurial, cottage-industry nature of some parts of the hedge fund industry make it more prone to elementary process weaknesses. These should be less likely in well-established, more process conscious, highly regulated but less entrepreneurial parts of the traditional investment management industry. Investors need to be comfortable with this change in environment in moving from a regulated to an unregulated sphere of investment business.

However, regulation is coming: from early 2006 US hedge funds (that is, hedge funds with more than a few US investors) have been required to register as investment advisers with the Securities and Exchange Commission (SEC). Although a minority of hedge funds are known to have avoided the new rules by either closing to new investors or imposing a two-year "lock-up" before investors can withdraw their funds, industry sources estimate that the overwhelming majority of hedge funds belonging to US hedge fund industry associations have registered with the SEC.

Operational risks

The hedge fund industry is rapidly evolving and the flurry of industry reports on hedge fund risks and best practice are indications of both shortcomings and the emergence of an understanding of best practice. These are also signs of a growing maturity and even institutionalisation of the hedge fund industry. Nevertheless, investors cannot take for granted that their hedge funds are managed to a high standard. Operational risk should be a particular focus of a hedge fund due diligence process since it has been highlighted as a prime reason for sudden catastrophic closures of hedge funds. One issue that investors need to consider arises from the difficulties that hedge funds have in developing an enduring franchise, partly because of the incentive effects of the structure of hedge fund performance fees, which has led to a high rate of fund closures. As a result of the potential incentive for hedge funds to close after a period of poor performance, investors in hedge funds or their advisers should always be searching for replacement hedge fund managers – which adds to the cost, at least in time and effort, of hedge fund investing.

Illiquid hedge fund investments and long notice periods
Many hedge funds find promising opportunities in unquoted and illiquid investments. Typical examples include private loans to corporations, which may be investment grade or distressed debt, and unquoted or illiquid equity opportunities. These are precisely the sort of opportunities that an entrepreneurial investment company would be expected to exploit.

However, investors need to be satisfied that what they judge to be a first-rate hedge fund investment process is accompanied by an approach of similar standard to determining the terms on which inflows and outflows from the fund occur. This is a concern because margins of error give rise to windfall transfers of wealth among fund participants. It is important to note that these issues are likely to arise only in hedge fund strategies that involve illiquid or unquoted investments and that give investors access to a regular schedule of dealing dates. For these reasons investors in illiquid hedge fund strategies should not object, indeed should demand, that fellow investors are subject to early redemption penalties (to accrue to the fund) that properly reflect the underlying illiquidity of the hedge fund. Long lock-up periods, seemingly inflexible redemption arrangements or wide bid-offer spreads for hedge funds with illiquid underlying investments can be in the best interests of all investors in those funds.

Lies, damn lies, and some hedge fund risk statistics
There are other problems that arise with illiquid hedge fund investments. Any price for an unquoted investment will be an appraisal price. Appraisal prices unavoidably smooth and lag changes in underlying market prices. This means that if investors have the opportunity to transact at an appraisal price for a fund, trends may be evident that enable them to buy or sell when they reasonably assess that the appraisal price is higher or lower than where the market actually appears to be.

Furthermore, appraisal prices are less volatile than market prices. This means that the volatility of monthly appraisal prices should never be used as a guide to the risk of a strategy that involves a significant element of appraisal prices in its valuations. Where the price data are smoothed, calculations for volatility and for risk-adjusted returns (such as Sharpe ratios, see Appendix 1) will be distorted, with risk looking lower than it is and risk-adjusted performance better. Appraisal prices can provide useful management information, but they must be used with care.

There has been extensive research into the issue of illiquidity and the unavoidable smoothing of hedge fund returns, and the implications of this for measures of hedge fund risk. The results tend to be uniform in establishing the importance of the issue and the way that it is focused on illiquid hedge fund strategies. The affected categories include distressed debt, convertible arbitrage, event-driven and emerging-market strategies. The strategies that are not normally affected by this valuation smoothing phenomenon are the generally liquid strategies: equity long/short, macro, short biased and especially CTA or managed futures funds.

Compiling prices for funds that include large proportions of illiquid and private investments runs the risk of accurately following a procedure to compute valuations, but then using the data to construct performance and especially risk statistics that are more likely to misinform than to inform. In private equity and real estate, where the same issues arise, appraisal valuations of underlying investments provide management information, but not normally dealing prices, and it is understood (at least in private equity) that the only performance that matters is the internal rate of return calculated from the amount of cash originally invested, the cash subsequently paid back to investors and the passage of time in between (see Chapter 10). Subscriptions to private equity funds are designed to be held until realisation, and in so far as there is a secondary market for holdings in private equity funds, these do not set the terms for wholesale exits from a fund. For example, investors in a private equity fund would be surprised if they were shown a pattern of monthly statistics of returns for a venture capital or private equity portfolio from which "risk" statistics, such as standard deviations or Sharpe ratios, were calculated. But in the hedge fund world this sort of thing happens routinely, even for portfolios that include a large element of illiquid investments. More useful as performance indicators that may shed light on risk may be measures such as maximum drawdown, which measure the experience of negative returns in the fund and generally mitigate the problem of smoothed valuations.

Another danger that investors should look out for is where there is a combination of price smoothing and the pursuit of an investment strategy involving the collection of option or insurance premiums which happen not to have been reflected in periodic poor performance, so far. Clifford Asness says:

Combining some lags in marking to market with invisible option writing can produce one heck of a historical Sharpe ratio, but with a potentially toxic combination going forward.

"Perfect storms" and hedge fund risk

It is worth repeating that money managers often attribute unusual poor performance to a highly improbable confluence of events in financial markets. Nowhere is this more true than in hedge fund investing. Events that are described by hedge fund managers as "being expected" to occur only "once in a million years" seem to be so common as to be unremarkable. This reflects above all the weakness of risk models and, as was stressed in Chapter 1, a failure to imagine combinations of events which in themselves are unremarkable. For example, the model-defeating combination of events surrounding the downgrading by rating agencies of General Motors and Ford debt in May 2005 and the almost simultaneous unexpected announcement by a major investor of plans to increase significantly his holding in GM stock (referred to in Chapter 8) was described by one hedge fund as an "eight standard deviation event", which should almost never happen if markets behaved as simple models would suggest they should. However, the apparent frequent occurrence of "bad news" in hedge fund performance reflects a particular characteristic of many hedge fund strategies which investors must understand. Since many hedge fund strategies are comparable to investment insurance-type arrangements, they provide steady returns most of the time, as the insurance premiums are collected, while being exposed to the risk of occasional large losses, when the insurance policy must pay up.

This is illustrated in Figure 9.7, which compares the pattern of monthly returns for a series of multi-strategy hedge funds with a symmetrical normal distribution.

The circled area reflects the entirely predictable disappointing monthly performances of an insurance-type arrangement, which are only surprising if the volatility of monthly returns is taken as a simple guide to the likely range of future performance results. As Bill Sharpe, the Nobel Prize-winning originator of the standard measure of risk adjusted returns, said in an article in August 2005 in the *Wall Street Journal*: "Past average performance may be a terrible predictor of future performance."

This pattern of returns is particularly common in some hedge fund strategies that offer investors the prospect of systematic market returns for bearing this insurance risk. This characteristic pattern of "extreme" returns

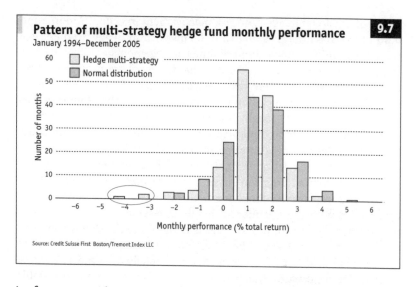

Pattern of multi-strategy hedge fund monthly performance 9.7
January 1994–December 2005

Source: Credit Suisse First Boston/Tremont Index LLC

is often most evident at times of market stress when average past relationships are typically overwhelmed by a flight to quality.

Managing investor risk: the role of hedge funds of funds

Investors should accept the risk of an occasional extreme negative return only if it is judged to be more than outweighed by the prospect of compensating performance over time; even then the risk will need to be offset as far as possible within an overall asset allocation. Most commonly this means combining different hedge fund strategies in a way which manages these risks, and then ensuring that the allocation to hedge funds fits in with the overall risk appetite, or at least comfort level, of the investor. This is where the addition of managed futures funds may mitigate the risk of extreme negative returns that is evident in hedge fund strategies.

The portfolio construction role is commonly undertaken by hedge fund of fund managers, who manage portfolios of hedge funds. Hedge fund of fund managers perform two critical roles: one is portfolio construction and overall investment risk management; the other is hedge fund manager due diligence. At the end of this chapter there is a list of some of the issues that need to be covered in a hedge fund due diligence process. Given the high level of operational and reputational risk involved in hedge fund investing, a hedge fund of funds arrangement is often the most appropriate way for novice hedge fund investors to proceed. Following the work of the hedge fund of funds manager is also an effective way for investors to see professional hedge fund risk management in action. Around one-third of the $1.6 trillion estimated to be invested in hedge fund assets is channelled through hedge fund of funds arrangements.

Investors need to be satisfied that the due diligence process they are using is thorough. But there will always be a risk of a surprising invest-ment performance or operational mishap and of investors saying to their due diligence team: "I thought you were supposed to check on that."

These risks should be mitigated by a hedge fund of funds approach. However, it does come at a price. In particular, it has to overcome the hurdle of imposing an additional level of fees on top of an already expensive structure. This can make attractive the passive "investable" hedge fund index series that have been introduced since 2002 and are constructed with the intention of being representative of the principal categories of hedge fund investing. If hedge fund returns represented only manager skill, it would be difficult to justify a passive approach to investing in a selection of representative available hedge funds. However, since hedge fund performance includes ingredients of both repeatable manager skill (for example, in accessing and risk managing otherwise inaccessible sources of returns) and systematic market returns that cannot easily be accessed elsewhere, a passive approach to hedge fund investing may provide a way of introducing a diversifying source of investment return into an investment strategy.

How much should you allocate to hedge funds?

A common weakness with a fund of funds approach to hedge fund investing is that it is typically structured in ignorance of the investment risks that are present elsewhere in an investor's strategy. A theme of this book is that investors need to search for as many different sources of market performance as possible and then to decide how best to combine their risks, opportunities and interdependencies. With some aspects of hedge fund performance and risk being close substitutes for that available elsewhere and others being unique, asking how much to allocate to hedge funds ceases to be a sensible question. Instead, the investment issue is how much should investors wish to allocate to different types of system-atic risk? Thus there is a strong argument in favour of the approach of some funds of hedge funds managers, which is to offer combinations of funds segregated into different categories or "buckets" of risk-taking. For example, some hedge fund strategies (such as equity hedge funds) offer combinations of equity market risk and manager skill exposures which are obvious alternatives to, or competitors with, the risks and opportunities that investors expose themselves to when they select conventional equity managers. The same principles apply to hedge funds that specialise in, for example, emerging markets or some credit market strategies: the allocation to such managers should be considered at the same time as decisions are made to allocate to emerging-market debt or equity or, for example, sub-investment grade corporate debt (allowing for the different elements of diversification provided by each).

This much is clear, but it is not the process that is usually followed. More interesting is how to decide what to allocate to hedge funds and other investment vehicles which offer sources of investment performance and risk that are different from those found in equity and bond markets. This is the reward offered to hedge fund investors for providing a variety of insurance services, most commonly through the provision of liquidity and intermediation services in different markets. These include the range of "alternative market beta" strategies, loosely described as arbitrage strategies, each of which also has a strong component of manager skill. The process of determining how much to allocate to these strategies should be driven by a view of the risk associated with them and how well it is diversified by other investments, and by an informed opinion on how much reward is expected to be earned from allocating capital to them.

From an investor's perspective this is where difficulties arise because this is still relatively uncharted territory, particularly in respect of return expectations. Nevertheless, several conclusions would be broadly agreed:

- The diversification benefits of a number of these strategies appear well established (although they may not be robust in all periods).
- It is reasonable to assume that the market should reward these services since other market participants are demonstrably willing to pay for them.
- The diversification benefits are such that the required premium return (above the return on safe-haven investments) needed to justify an allocation to these alternative hedge fund strategies is quite modest.

This leads to the two final conclusions:

- The uncertainties involved mean that an allocation to these alternative betas should err on the side of caution by not dominating an investor's strategy.
- For most investors, some such allocation can normally be justified.

Questions to ask

Your hedge fund manager

A good starting point is the guidance provided on the Securities and Exchange Commission's website The background of some individual hedge fund managers licensed by the National Association of Securities Dealers (NASD) can be checked on the NASD website. The questions that follow are too detailed for most hedge fund clients to be able to ask a representative of a hedge fund or even a financial adviser who is recommending hedge fund investments. However, they are the sort of questions that an investor should want to know someone at some stage has asked a hedge fund manager on behalf of investors, and received satisfactory responses.

Performance and investment

- Please provide a monthly track record of the performance of the fund.
- What was the size of assets of the fund at the start of this track record, and what is the most recent size of the fund?
- How has the strategy of the fund changed since the start of the track record?
- Do you manage or have you managed a fund with comparable objectives? If so, what was its performance track record?
- How do you judge the investment success of the fund?
- Please describe the investment decisions that led to your most disappointing monthly performance results and, separately, the best monthly performance results.
- What conclusions did you draw for the future management of the fund?
- How do you expect performance to correlate with equity and fixed-income markets?
- How do you manage the possibility of extreme negative performance results?
- How large could the fund grow and still have the same prospect for success?
- Has your (and your fund's) past success led you to scale back the risk-taking in the fund?
- How do you conduct research?
- How does research affect portfolio construction?

Business, operations and valuation

- What proportion of the fund is valued at month end using third-party pricing sources?
- What proportion of the fund is represented by quoted securities?
- Are any investments valued at book cost?
- Has this proportion changed over time?
- Please describe the unquoted investments and explain how they are valued.
- Do these investments smooth the reported performance of the fund?
- Do you monitor net asset value each day? How do you price unquoted investments for this?
- How frequent are the fund dealing dates, and are there any lock-up periods for new investments?
- To whom does the back office report?
- How often are reports produced for investors?
- How do you manage inflows and redemptions?
- How do you monitor the fund's counterparty exposure?
- Who is your fund administrator? Please describe their role for you.
- Who is your prime broker? Please describe their role for you.
- What credit risks do your clients face vis-à-vis your prime broker?
- What problems do you encounter in short selling?
- Do short-selling difficulties limit your ability to implement investment policy?
- How many failed trades do you have outstanding at present?
- Is this number of failed trades usual or unusual?
- How do you monitor failed trades?
- Is pricing done in-house or by a third party?
- Who are your external auditors?
- Please provide a time line for payments on redemption of units in the fund.
- How do you ensure fairness in pricing illiquid or unquoted investments when making redemption payments?
- How is your personal financial interest aligned with that of your clients?
- Who are the founders or principals of the fund? When are they expected to retire? What succession plan is there?
- Please provide references

Risk

- How do you monitor investment risk?
- Who does this work and to whom do they report?
- How reliable are the risk measurement tools? Please illustrate.
- How do you allow for the weaknesses that are inherent in risk models?
- How do you manage the credit risk of your investments?
- How do you manage the credit risk of your counterparties?
- Have you stress tested your strategy against the market developments of extreme market conditions, such as October 1987, August–September 1998, or September 2001? Has this affected investment policy?
- What is the worst historical drawdown the fund has experienced?
- Has investment policy been altered to reduce the risk of this happening again?
- Are there any elements of investment strategy that make the fund exposed to the low risk of an extreme negative return?
- How does this relate to your investment policy, redemption terms and assessment of extreme events in markets?
- Do you have formal parameters that limit your risk-taking? Please describe.
- What is your leverage policy?
- How do you define leverage? Please contrast this with other definitions used in the hedge fund industry.
- Is it intended that the risk profile of the fund should be predictable or opportunistic? If predictable, please provide a proof statement of practice.
- Do you have a formal set of permissible investments?
- What is the best or worst monthly performance that I should expect to experience?
- How do you allocate risk in constructing the portfolio?
- How do you manage liquidity risk in your investments?
- How do you manage the liquidity of your funding or client redemptions?
- How do you monitor the adequacy of your fund's access to liquidity? How do you monitor the liquidity of the investments of the fund?
- How do liquidity considerations alter your approach to portfolio construction?
- Do you monitor any liquidity risk metrics?

◪ Does illiquidity of your investments cause the measures of risk that you show to investors to be understated?

Your hedge fund adviser

◪ Do you get an introduction fee or any other form of remuneration from the hedge fund if I invest?

◪ If yes, how much and how does it influence your recommendations? Please provide a statement proving your answer.

Your hedge funds of funds manager

◪ How do you manage the investment risk for your recommended or chosen combinations of funds?

◪ Do you receive a fee from funds that you select for your fund of funds?

◪ Do you include any funds which do not pay you fees?

◪ Do you use leverage? If so, why?

◪ How many funds to which you were regularly directing new flows of money have become closed to you in the past 12 months?

◪ What is your biggest administrative headache?

◪ How do you manage cash inflows and outflows?

◪ Can client cash flows alter the investment allocation for all your clients?

10 Private equity: information-based investment returns

The past and prospective investment performance of the private equity market has been analysed in numerous studies. But even if the estimates produced by those studies are reliable, investors cannot take for granted that they will be able to earn them.

Investors should avoid private equity investing unless they believe that they have access to skilled investment managers. The key to unlocking returns in private equity is information, and investors have to believe that their managers have an edge that enables them to deliver at least market returns. Investing in an arrangement that lacks this edge will condemn the strategy to inferior performance.

The appropriate place for private equity in investment strategy is straightforward. Private equity is what it says. It is equity, and so if included in strategy it must form part of an investor's allocation to equity. And it is private, and so unquoted and illiquid and not suitable for short-term investors. All the comments about diversification by style, by size and by geography for investing in quoted equities (see Chapter 7) can be applied to private equity. However, since private equity is only part of an investor's allocation to equity, there is no requirement to include in a private equity portfolio all the diversification that can be obtained from the private equity market, when it can also be obtained inexpensively and with confidence from the quoted equity market. The key for investors is to be driven by a dispassionate assessment of their ability to gain access to skilled managers, and then to make an allocation (or no allocation as appropriate). The next step is to ensure that the total equity allocation (public as well as private) has the degree of diversification with which they are comfortable.

What is private equity?

It is useful to think of the market in two distinct parts. The first is start-up venture capital. The second is the market for leveraged buy-outs of existing businesses. The market is commonly divided further, with venture capital differentiated between seed capital and early-stage venture capital, whereas the later stages of investing differentiate between buy-outs and expansion capital. Another important area for private equity funds is the funding or co-financing of public-sector projects. In the United States these undertakings are known as PIPE (private investment into a public entity) investments; in the UK similar ventures fall under the generic titles of private finance initiative (PFI) and public private partnership.

Expansion capital may take the form of "mezzanine" financing, which is the riskiest form of debt obligations. It will often have options to convert into equity if the firm fails to meet the terms of its debt, which will be priced to deliver a high rate of return. Mezzanine finance is expensive for companies. Management buy-outs occur when an existing management team is supported with external private equity, for example when a family business is sold, or a larger firm decides that an existing division is no longer a core business for the parent company.

The word "leverage" in a leveraged buy-out (LBO) refers to the financing of the deal, when the new private equity owners will have leveraged their equity ownership. This may occur, for example, through the issue of asset-backed loans, the sale of high-yield bonds – or, where bond or loan covenants are weak, by restructuring the company's balance sheet such that existing debt becomes devalued, and so higher yielding. This focus on the use of leverage is the principal reason private equity should, in general, be regarded as more risky than quoted equity.

Since the late 1990s there have been big changes in the private equity market. Mark Anson, who recently moved from being the chief investment officer of Calpers, the largest US pension plan, to being chief executive of Hermes, a London fund manager that invests the assets of the British Telecom Pension Fund and other institutional investors, has analysed how the successful fundraising by private equity groups in recent years led to an overhang of capital waiting to be invested. This has led to intense competition between private equity groups, resulting in higher prices being paid when they acquire firms, which is likely to diminish future performance. The more competitive environment may also have resulted in private equity groups being forced to spend much less time on due diligence before bidding for target companies, as well as encouraging them to explore new areas of investing. These include a renewed emphasis on mid-sized buy-outs, a greater acceptance of purchases and sales of private companies between private equity groups, real estate investing (see Chapter 11) and the sponsoring by private equity groups of their own affiliated hedge funds.

Private equity market risk

In all countries there is a wide variety of private companies, of which most are small but some are large enterprises. In recent years, the development of private equity groups controlling large amounts of investor money has led to the emergence of substantial private industrial and commercial conglomerates controlling private companies across different sectors of the economy throughout the world.

Private companies often look similar to the quoted companies with which they compete. However, this does not mean that the risks for investors are comparable with those of the stockmarket. The first difference is illiquidity, and the much greater difficulty of transferring a part ownership in a private company than one in a public company. The second is that there are systematic biases in the characteristics of private companies compared with quoted companies (for example, private companies will have a bias towards small and medium-sized companies). Nevertheless, it might be thought that the inherent risk or volatility of their aggregate value should be broadly comparable to that of quoted companies.

One perspective on this is given by the volatility of the world's largest quoted company, whose core business is the management of a diversified private equity portfolio. This is the UK-listed 3i Group. In the late 1990s 3i had a volatility that was around half as volatile again as that of the UK stockmarket as a whole. This changed in early 2000 as the equity bear market set in and the volatility of the share price of this diversified private equity portfolio increased to between two and three times the volatility of the UK stockmarket. This will have reflected the experience of many private equity investors, as a bias towards new companies in the volatile technology sectors became a feature of many private equity funds, especially venture capital funds. That this occurred is unsurprising, as a bias towards whatever is the latest "new, new thing" will always be a characteristic feature and risk of early-stage venture capital investing.

The evolution of the volatility of the 3i share price and that of the UK stockmarket, as measured by Riskmetrics' RiskGrade, is shown in Figures 10.1 and 10.2.

Researchers have used a variety of other more or less satisfactory ways of getting a handle on private equity market volatility. These include examining the volatility of returns earned from private equity funds and using indices of smaller company stocks as a proxy for private equity.

Individual venture investments will always be subject to considerable stock-specific risk and, diversifying this risk, venture portfolios tend to

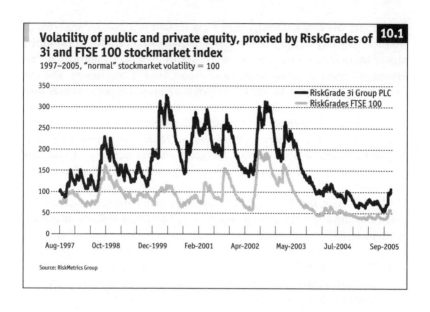

Volatility of public and private equity, proxied by RiskGrades of 3i and FTSE 100 stockmarket index `10.1`

1997–2005, "normal" stockmarket volatility = 100

Source: RiskMetrics Group

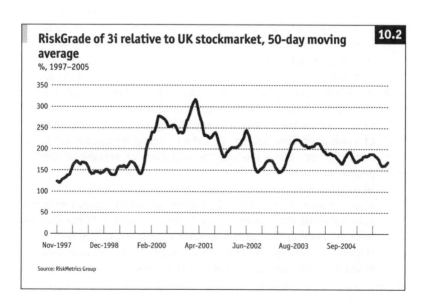

RiskGrade of 3i relative to UK stockmarket, 50-day moving average `10.2`

%, 1997–2005

Source: RiskMetrics Group

173

hold more positions (though they may focus on a particular sector or theme) than buy-out portfolios. The financing structure is critical to the risk of LBO investments. Typically these are, as their name suggests, highly leveraged, more so than otherwise similar quoted businesses. For this reason, the intrinsic volatility of the private equity market, however well diversified, is probably significantly higher than that of the quoted equity market. Investors should not be satisfied with an expected return that does not compensate them for this leverage. Moreover, it makes no sense to pay performance fees simply to leverage an investment portfolio. Any investor can achieve this at minimal cost by buying equity index futures contracts.

Nevertheless, the process of allocating investment capital requires some rules of thumb for the risk of private equity. Here are some suggested guidelines:

- The biggest risk for both investors and managers of private equity portfolios is to act on inferior information. Do nothing in private equity unless you think that you have a credible information advantage.

- A broad-brush fund of funds approach that combines exposure to buy-outs and venture capital, so long as it is well diversified and not excessively leveraged, is likely to avoid sudden loss of a significant part of the allocation to private equity. However, investors need to ask what information advantage the arrangement is likely to have (and fund of funds managers with the most attractive track records – see below – may be closed to most investors).

- An assumption that a well-diversified fund of funds has a volatility approximately twice that of the quoted market is not unreasonable. For a more concentrated approach, an assumption of a volatility three times that of the market might be used, but this might exaggerate the intrinsic volatility unless leverage was particularly high.

- In so far as private equity represents a leveraged version of quoted equity, investors should require a premium return for incurring the additional risk introduced by that leverage, and should benchmark their private equity against a leveraged quoted equity index. However, investors should be aware that the level of leverage, and so the level of risk-taking, in buy-outs is cyclical.

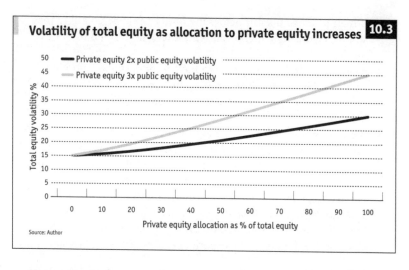

Volatility of total equity as allocation to private equity increases **10.3**

These magnitudes matter because investors need to have a feel for how an allocation to private equity is changing the risk that is already present in their allocation to quoted equity. Figure 10.3 gives an indication of how an allocation to private equity, alongside an allocation to the quoted equity market, may affect the volatility of the combined equity portfolio. The important message is that a diversified allocation to private equity of, say, 10% of an investor's equity allocation will, with the assumptions used here, have a noticeable but not transforming effect on the volatility of the overall equity portfolio.

Private equity portfolios

An old adage in private banking says that you should concentrate investments to get wealthy (at the risk of losing your shirt), but that having become wealthy, you should diversify to maintain the wealth that you have already accumulated. This has parallels with the safety-first and aspirational portfolios described by behavioural finance (see Chapter 2). Private equity is about exploiting information advantages by identifying entrepreneurial skill. It is not about being financially conservative. It may form a component of an efficient diversified approach to investing, but within that it clearly forms part of an aspirational strategy to accumulate wealth.

This leads to several conclusions:

◪ Well-diversified fund of fund arrangements are likely to diversify away precious elements of information advantage.

◪ If high leverage persists across the funds, intrinsic volatility may still be surprisingly high even with a well-diversified fund of funds.

◪ It can be entirely appropriate to have a modest allocation to a small number of funds (even from just one team), so long as the combined allocation to private and quoted equity is reasonably balanced.

◪ A common danger in private equity investing is to fail to diversify private equity over time. Once a preferred arrangement has been selected, it makes sense to maintain a commitment to the market over time, most probably staying with the same team (or teams). Otherwise, risks that were particularly prevalent in the market at a particular point in time (for example, high leverage or exposure to particular themes in venture capital investing) will unduly characterise the investor's experience of investing in private equity.

Private equity returns

Private equity performance data suffer (as do those for private equity risk) from the absence of market indications of the value of private businesses. The need to rely on appraisal estimates for interim valuations smoothes the reported performance included in published calendar year performance results. Appraisal valuations are still useful as they provide important management information for investors on what is "work in progress". However, the only private equity performance data that really matters is the internal rate of return (IRR) earned on investments. This combines the amount invested, the amount received back and the interval of time in between. In substance, these are the only financial magnitudes that the investor knows for certain when investing in private equity (or any private investment). The IRR is the standard rate of return reported for funds and individual investments, but it is important to note that unrealised investments will be included at an appraisal value in reports of fund IRRs.

Industry data often report IRRs for funds started in a particular "vintage" year. This information does not reveal the volatility of the way in which those returns were earned or enable like-for-like comparison with stockmarket performance. Such information is often broken down in marketing material to show the attractive performance of better-performing managers (for example, the top 25%), with the message that it is important to select a manager who will be in the top quartile in the future. It is always desirable to select winners, but the issue is whether the historic relative performance of private equity managers provides any guide to future performance.

In mutual fund investing it is agreed that past performance in league tables is a poor predictor of future league table performance. But in private equity there have long been suggestions that success is repeatable, and there is now increasing evidence from academic research that this may be the case. One of the problems in comparing the performance of private equity managers is the impossibility of obtaining reliable values for private businesses and the difficulty of comparing the performance of a manager, or a private equity fund, with that of the stockmarket.

One way to do this is to compare the IRR that a fund achieved on its private equity investments with the IRR that it would have achieved if the cash had instead been invested, on the same dates, in the stockmarket index, and if the correspondingly equivalent distributions had then been made to investors. Recently published academic research has done this for funds on the Venture Economics database of US venture-capital and buy-out funds. Examining data from 1980 to 2000, researchers found that the average performance of such funds, after fees, was approximately in line with the S&P 500 index. There was a wide dispersion of results among funds as well as strong evidence that good and poor perform-ance persisted in successive launches of funds by particular private equity teams. The researchers also found that new private equity teams are more likely to have disappointing performance.

This research highlights the importance of a number of themes empha-sised earlier in this chapter. First, it seems that investors in private equity have not on average earned a premium reward to compensate them for the extra financial gearing often involved in private equity. Second, the pattern of manager performance persistence is important, as investors need to convince themselves that they can identify better than average managers. Skill is essential. Investors cannot profit from market returns in private equity through a passive, market-matching strategy, so they should not expect to do even averagely well unless they can gain access to skilled managers. Without skilled managers, investors will be condemned to underperform unless, for a period, they happen to get lucky.

Private investments, successful transactions and biases in appraisal valuations

Everyone likes to get a good price in any transaction. One way to increase the likelihood of a successful transaction is to ensure that the criterion by which success is judged is credible but undemanding. In private investments, the immediate benchmark against which a transaction is judged is the most recent appraisal valuation for that investment.

However successful or disappointing an investment might have been, private equity and real estate managers always like to be able to demonstrate the successful terms on which they achieved a sale (such ready benchmarks do not exist when a manager makes a purchase). Evidence to support these assertions relies mostly on anecdotal comments over the years from private equity and real estate managers, as well as an indication that real estate turnover declines in down markets when it becomes much harder to achieve a "successful" price (because the level of the market is more likely to be below the most recent appraisal valuation). The art market, whose pre-auction brochures give appraisal valuations, provides an opportunity to study the existence of such a bias. One such study some years ago (by the author and a colleague) found that of 1,700 items sold at auction, largely over the decade before 1991, 28% failed to reach the auctioneer's low estimate of value, 25% fell between the low and high estimates and 47% exceeded the high estimates. Successful results were so much more common than disappointments (as indicated by the frequency with which the high and low estimates were overshot or undershot) that there is little likelihood of there being no downward bias in these pre-auction estimates. More recent evidence for such a bias in pre-auction appraisal valuations comes from the market for rare stamps. Apex Philatelic Auctions, British stamp auctioneers, reported in its November 2005 catalogue that its preceding £8m of stamp sales "fetched 104.21% of estimate on average", confirming the pattern of realised prices tending to exceed pre-auction estimates.

11 Real estate

Three things condition the experience of investors in real estate investing: the performance of the market; the skill of their advisers; and the degree of leverage involved in whichever vehicle is used to access the market. This, in turn, depends upon the level of interest rates and the ease with which income yielding properties can support debt interest payments. As with all other markets, it is a routine weakness in appraising investment managers to fail to account properly for the impact of leverage on performance and risk.

In recent years, developments in the US public market for real estate investment trusts (REITs), and parallel developments elsewhere in the world, have made the public market for real estate comparable to the rest of the quoted equity market for the ease with which investors can now obtain, at low cost, exposure to market returns and risk. Furthermore, the REIT market has introduced investors to the benefits of leverage at a time when in most countries debt interest costs have been lower than the income received from real estate rents, and the underlying market conditions have been benign.

Investments in real estate equity divide between ownership of properties directly by an individual investor (the direct or private market), through a commingled fund, or through stock exchange listed vehicles, most commonly REITs, a US innovation dating from the early 1970s. These vehicles represent the public or quoted market. REITs have grown substantially in the United States to reach an aggregate value of $366 billion in early 2006. Similar entities have been introduced in a range of jurisdictions including Australia, Brazil, Canada, France, Japan, Netherlands, and Singapore. In the United States, individual REITs specialise by sector of the market, with a minority investing primarily in commercial and residential mortgages.

The principal difference between a REIT and a conventional company, whose business is investing in and managing properties, lies in their tax treatment. Generally, REITs are exempt from profit or corporation tax and, in the United States, have a guideline that at least 90% of their income must be distributed to investors as a taxable dividend. Guidelines vary between countries. The equivalent in Australia is the large, long-established listed property trust market. The UK (where the stockmarket

The four quadrants of real estate investing 11.1

	Private investments	Public or quoted investments
Real estate equity	Direct properties Real estate Commingled funds	Real estate investment trusts (REITs) Real estate operating companies (REOCs) Real estate mutual funds Listed property trusts Other listed property companies
Real estate debt	Individual mortgages "Mezzanine" debt	Commercial mortgage backed securities (CMBS)

Source: Author

has a sizeable property company sector) and Germany are considering legislation to introduce REITs.

The main differences between listed real estate vehicles, such as REITs, and direct investments in property are that the former are securitised, have daily prices and are typically leveraged to some degree through borrowing. They are ideally suited to giving diversified exposure to real estate for modest levels of investment. Since they have daily prices, appraisal valuations of underlying properties help analysts construct estimates for the net asset value of REITs, but they do not set the terms on which investors transact.

What is real estate investing?

It is common to divide segments of a broadly defined real estate market according to the schema shown in Figure 11.1 or a variation of it.

In a number of international markets, private equity funds have become important participants in the real estate market. Private equity funds have a shorter time horizon than traditional institutional investors, commingled funds, or REITs, and they also bring a more aggressive attitude to leverage, with the introduction of high-risk, potentially high-return "mezzanine" debt into real estate transactions. These developments mean that investors now have more ways of gaining access to real estate returns than was previously the case.

The underlying real estate market is divided into the main types of property: retail, office, industrial and residential. (Other categories include

Table 11.1 **Direct real estate investment by type of property (%)**

| | US | | UK |
| | NCREIF | REIT^a | IPD |
	Dec 2005	Jan 2006	Dec 2004
Retail	23	27	53
Office	37	18	28
Industrial	19	10^b	16
Apartments	20	16	0
Other	2	29^c	3
Total	100	100	100
Value ($bn)	189.7	306.3	231.5

a Equity REITs.
b Including mixed use.
c Including diversified, lodging/resorts, healthcare, self-storage, speciality.
Sources: National Council of Real Estate Investment Fiduciaries; National Association of Real Estate Investments Trusts; Investment Property Databank (IPD)

hotels and resorts and mixed category properties.) The REIT market provides access to each segment of the market. Two principal databases for institutional real estate are the National Council for Real Estate Investment Fiduciaries (NCREIF) in the United States and the Investment Property Databank (IPD) in the UK. The US National Association of Real Estate Investment Trusts (NAREIT) is the source for information about US REITs. Table 11.1 gives a breakdown of the types of properties owned by investors in the United States and UK.

Using derivatives to gain real estate market exposure

Since the 1990s it has been possible to buy and sell notes called property index certificates (PICs) on direct commercial property indices in the UK. Transactions have also been executed on residential property indices. These derivatives give investors the opportunity to hedge or gain exposure to the direct UK real estate market.

This derivatives market has been developing quite slowly. In the residential housing sector, part of the problem may be that the indices are provided by market participants. In the commercial property sector, the market has probably been restrained by the characteristics of the direct property market. The word used for "property" in most west European languages is a variant of the word "immobile". In individual properties, immobility, indivisibility and heterogeneity are all barriers to the creation of liquid derivatives markets because they impede and raise the costs of hedging investment positions. This is very different from the situation in the modern markets in credit derivatives, for example, where exposure to an individual credit risk can be bought or sold without such limitations.

A different development is the market for exchange traded funds (ETFs), which give exposure to the market indices in the United States. These derivatives provide daily liquidity and the ability to establish short positions. The liquidity in REITs means that transaction costs in REIT ETFs (and any other derivatives) can be kept to modest margins. This is making the real estate market, as represented by REITs, comparable to that of quoted equities and bonds for the ability to access the market return at modest cost irrespective of the ability of investors to identify skilled managers.

The direct market remains dominated by informational inefficiencies where it is likely that patterns of persistence of outperformance or underperformance by real estate managers are evident. However, it is a mistake to assume that the private and public real estate markets are equivalent: pricing comparisons between the two point to significant inefficiencies and investment opportunities for investors with the size, risk tolerance and time horizon to exploit them.

What are the attractions of investing in real estate?

The traditional reasons for making investments in real estate equity include portfolio diversification; accessing premium and generally secure income yields; and the potential for attractive total returns that should be protected from inflation.

Diversification

Appraisal valuations of properties complicate an assessment of the diversification qualities of real estate. Smoothing of performance results often gives short-term comfort to trustees and especially private investors who do not need to be confronted with the reality of market prices except when they transact. This paucity of reliable price information does not provide a substantive reason for favouring real estate investment. The market for REITs and similar vehicles in other countries gives both a dependable market valuation (although it may represent a premium or discount to property valuations – see below) and a time series of transaction prices, which permits a market-based assessment of the contribution of real estate in an investment portfolio.

Table 11.2 **North American REITs: correlations of returns with other asset classes, January 1990–December 2005**

	North America REIT	MSCI US Index	MSCI EAFE® Index	Lehman Bros Credit Index total return[a]	Lehman Bros Government Bond Index total return[b]
North America REIT	1.00				
MSCI US Index	0.42	1.00			
MSCI EAFE® Index	0.32	0.54	1.00		
Lehman Bros Credit Index total return	0.25	0.23	0.13	1	
Lehman Bros Government Bond Index total return	0.13	0.05	0.01	0.92	1

a Measures the performance of all US publicly issued, fixed-rate, non-convertible investment grade dollar-denominated, SEC-registered corporate debt.
b Measures the performance of bonds issued by the US Treasury and government agencies.
Sources: FTSE EPRA/NAREIT Global Real Estate Index; MSCI Barra; Lehman Brothers Inc

Using US data, the diversification benefits of real estate investing become clear. The historical performance of the US REIT market since 1990 is shown in Table 11.2, together with measures for volatility of returns and the correlation between the different asset classes.

The correlation of 0.4 between the REIT sector of the US stockmarket and the S&P 500, together with a negligible correlation with US treasury bonds over this period, indicates scope for significant diversification benefits from investing in the REIT sector and, by inference, in real estate more generally. The experience of direct investments in real estate generally confirms this pattern of diversification.

The performance experience from investing in REITs compared with the market indices used in Table 11.2 is shown in Table 11.3 overleaf.

Since 1989, investing in the REIT sector of the US stockmarket has been profitable, but there have been periods of acute pain (particularly in the early 1990s). Table 11.3 also shows the volatility of performance and maximum drawdown statistics for the period since 1989. These reveal that the volatility and risk of large decline in values from REITs should be regarded as comparable to that of the stockmarket as a whole.

The conventional view is that the intrinsic volatility of well-diversified direct investments in real estate probably lies somewhere between that of

Table 11.3 **Summary performance experience: REITs and US equity and bond markets, January 1990–December 2005**

	Geometric average (% per year)	Standard deviation (% per year)	Maximum decline (cumulative %)	Peak month	Trough month
North America REIT total return	15.2	16.8	−30.1	Dec 1989	Oct 1990
MSCI US Total Return Index	10.7	16.0	−46.1	Mar 2000	Sep 2002
MSCI EAFE® Index	5.1	17.5	−47.5	Dec 1999	Mar 2003
Lehman Bros Credit Index total return	7.9	5.2	−6.9	Jan 1994	Jun 1994
Lehman Bros Government Bond Index total return	7.2	4.7	−5.4	Jan 1994	Jun 1994

Sources: FTSE EPRA/NAREIT Global Real Estate Index; MSCI Barra; Lehman Brothers Inc

bonds and that of equities. Since REITs are normally leveraged, the underlying volatility of the property portfolios within the REITs will be lower than indicated in Table 11.3. The level of REIT leverage has varied over time, but at the end of 2004 it was around 40%. If maintained throughout this period, this would suggest that the volatility of the underlying markets for unleveraged properties might be just over 11% a year. This provides evidence to support the conventional view of the volatility of the direct real estate market being between that of equities and bonds.

The overall relative performance differential in favour of real estate was strongest during the equity bear market of March 2000–March 2003. During this period the total return on the S&P 500 index was −40.9%, while the REIT sector of the stockmarket showed a positive total return of 45.7%. This is a huge differential in favour of real estate (even if part of the difference is due to leverage).So over this 15-year period REITs performed not only relatively well, but also particularly well when the rest of the quoted equity market was weakest. Not surprisingly, since 2003 the popularity of REITs has grown rapidly. Investors need to decide how far they can rely on past performance patterns to be repeated in the future.

Income yield
A recurring argument in favour of real estate investing is the provision of a dependable income that can be expected to increase in line with inflation. The ability to gain access to seemingly reliable income becomes particularly attractive to investors at times of low nominal interest rates.

Table 11.4 **Income return from REITs, quoted equities and bonds, January 1990–December 2005 (% annual average)**

	North America REIT	MSCI US Index	MSCI EAFE® Index	Lehman Bros Credit Index	Lehman Bros Government Bond Index
1990–94	7.4	3.2	2.0	8.3	7.4
1995–99	7.4	2.1	1.9	7.2	6.4
2000–04	6.1	1.5	2.1	6.5	5.3
2005	4.7	1.8	2.8	5.4	4.3

Sources: FTSE EPRA/NAREIT Global Real Estate Index; MSCI Barra; Lehman Brothers Inc

Over the period, the income return for REITs has been somewhat lower than that on investment grade bonds, which have been subject to much less price risk. The income stream from REITs may appear stable, on average, but the price volatility has been comparable to equities. This means that REITs cannot be regarded as "low-risk" substitutes for a safe-haven high-quality bond portfolio.

Inflation hedge

Real estate investments always have one clear advantage over investments in conventional bonds: whereas bonds are eroded by any unexpected inflation, rents from real estate should always be expected to respond over time to inflation. This does not mean that rents will always keep up with inflation. A market with excess or obsolete capacity should expect to see rents fall, and if monetary policy is tightened to restrain inflation, there is likely to be an adverse impact on rents. Nevertheless, it is reasonable to assume that rents will increase faster the higher is the rate of inflation. This in turn will be reflected in the value put on buildings, which should also respond to inflation. In this way long-term investments in real estate provide an element of insurance against the biggest danger facing long-term investors in conventional bonds: erosion of wealth by inflation.

Styles of real estate investing and opportunities for active management

Entrepreneurial real estate managers have always liked real estate for the same reason that money managers of any asset class do: they see it as an opportunity to use their skills to make money for themselves and their clients. Since the real estate market is such a heterogeneous, lumpy and immobile market, it provides a natural habitat for well-informed, skilled managers to add value (and for other market participants to underperform). This, together with its other advantages such as long-term inflation hedging, helps explain why some investors have focused particularly on developing an expertise and portfolio concentration in real estate investing.

Characterising equity managers by their style of investing is well established, and this is starting to happen with real estate managers. It has the advantage of helping investors understand better what to expect from a particular manager. Broadly, there are two approaches to real estate investing: a core approach, with an emphasis on the generation of steadily growing income from a balanced portfolio of well-let prime properties; and an opportunistic approach, which is more concerned with the prospects for price appreciation through redevelopment and exploiting changes in market trends and fashions. The first should deliver a less volatile, less exciting performance than the second. Real estate managers point to a third category, a distinctive "core-plus" approach for the more entrepreneurial institutional portfolios; the more aggressive, opportunistic approach is likely to be reflected in the real estate activities of, for example, private equity or hedge funds. These have become major players in some parts of the international real estate market since the late 1990s.

What is a property worth and how much return should you expect?

One of the attractions of real estate investing is that it is often easy to analyse individual investments in direct property quantitatively. Although this is no guarantee of investment success, it helps to identify the opportunities that rely on unusually strong assumptions.

The financial appraisal of real estate requires assessment of a number of variables:

- today's government bond yield;
- market supply and demand forecasts as influences on prospects for rental incomes;
- tenant creditworthiness;
- property depreciation or obsolescence.

No real estate investment should be undertaken unless it is expected to perform better than the guaranteed return from government bonds; and any real estate investment should be sold if it is expected to underperform government bonds over some relevant time horizon.

Rental income

The return to be expected from a property is the discounted value of the expected rental income, net of expenses, plus the proceeds from selling the property at some date in the future.

The key variables in this evaluation are the future rate of change in rents (which is almost always assumed to be an increase) and the appropriate rate at which to discount that rental stream back to a present value or fair price for the property.

Just as forecasts of corporate earnings growth drive an analyst's valuation of a company, so in real estate investing the principal driver of valuation is the forecast growth of earnings, or for a property, rent. The raw material for these forecasts is detailed real estate market forecasts or views, focusing on changes in trends in either local or regional markets. When appraising these forecasts, it is often helpful to gauge how the rent forecast relates to a forecast for economy-wide inflation. This is because rents need to be forecast, either implicitly or explicitly, for long periods, if only to provide a basis for estimating the price at which the building might be sold in the future (which will itself be a function of expected rents). This encourages a focus on any implicit strong assumptions.

This focus on rental income is important to avoid two common mistakes. First, the value of a property has little to do with the cost of rebuilding it. It is the value of future rent that determines its value. Given the value of the property, this can be broken down into the cost of rebuilding, proxied by the insurance value put on the property, and a residual, which is the value of the land underneath the building. Second, a property is never expensive because the land underneath it is expensive. It is always the other way round. Land is expensive because rents are high, and because rents are high property is expensive. A third important feature for real estate investing follows from this: the price of land, the residual in property valuation, can be very, very volatile. Consider the simple illustration in Table 11.5 overleaf.

If the value of the property increases by 10%, and if rebuilding costs stay the same, the value of the land will double to $2m. This is important both as an explanation for the speculative nature of development land and as a useful cross-check on valuations. Equally, the importance of the price of land will depend upon the scarcity of land. Where land is abundant and planning restrictions do not impede new construction,

Table 11.5 **A notional property valuation ($m)**

	Initial value	Subsequent value
Property value	10	11
Cost of rebuild	9	9
Land value	1	2

rents will tend towards reimbursing with a "normal" profit, the marginal cost of new building, which may or may not keep pace with the general level of inflation.

So long as this situation persists, land will always be cheap. With technological progress in building, commercial properties risk becoming a commodity, something that individuals or corporations who need to use real estate (for homes, offices, industrial or retail space) must decide whether to own, rent or lease on the same basis as other financial decisions. So although rents, and the cost of land, will move with changes in supply of and demand for properties, there is no inexorable tendency for them to increase faster than inflation. Rents can lag behind inflation for a long time. For example, at the height of a boom in City of London property prices in 1973 rents are reported to have been in the region of £20-30 per square foot. Allowing for inflation since then, rents should now be in the range of £170-250 per sq. ft. In fact, in late 2005 prime rents were around £50 per sq. ft in the City of London which is still high by international standards. There is no assurance that rents will keep pace with inflation, and little reason to expect them to increase in line with the rate of growth of the economy. However, this may be a reasonable assumption for corporate dividends in the long run.

It follows that investors rely on rental income, rather than capital appreciation, as the principal source of investment performance in real estate investing. This also explains why the income return from real estate investing is normally much higher than the income return from mainstream equity investing. Nevertheless, investors should invest in real estate only if they expect to be rewarded for the incremental risk that they would be assuming, within the context of a balanced investment strategy.

It is not clear how much premium return over government bonds should be expected by financial investors in real estate in the long term. This required premium is reduced by the diversification benefits that real estate brings to a balanced investment strategy. It can be influenced by the degree of confidence that investors have in the quality of the investment process that they are able to deploy in investing in real estate markets. Most importantly, as with private equity, direct investors in real estate should not assume that the market return will be accessible unless a demonstrably skilful investment process has been put in place. However, the more skill that is assumed, the easier it will be to justify a large allocation of an investment strategy to real estate. In this case, great caution needs to be exercised in interpreting past performance, in isolating the effects on performance of leverage during a rising market and in differentiating between skill and luck. As was emphasised in Chapter 4, in the presence of uncertainty, the prudent approach is to err on the side of caution.

Government bond yields as the benchmark for real estate investing

Using government bond yields as the benchmark for assessing real estate investments is helpful in several respects. First, it focuses on the only legitimate reason to move away from safe-haven investing: to achieve a superior return which more than compensates for the risk of a disappointing result. The prospects for superior returns will largely be determined by the state of the market in that location and for that type of property. Second, it allows focus on the quality of the contractual income stream to be earned from a property, which will be influenced by the creditworthiness of the tenants (though other factors, such as building depreciation, are also important, see below).

Tenant credit risk

A property with a government agency as a long-term tenant will be directly comparable with government bonds, although some allowance should be made for the illiquidity of the real estate investment as well as the likely existence of options to break the contract. This is most likely to be an issue for institutional investors, who may be too compartmentalised to make such direct comparisons, but all real estate investors should make the effort to analyse opportunities in this way.

More normally, the required spread over government bond yields needs to allow for the credit risk associated with its tenants. This is the risk that the tenant will fail to honour the terms of the lease, and that there will be an interruption to rental payments as well as costs associated with attracting new tenants, and that a new tenant might be attracted at less favourable terms than the existing one. The costs involved will be directly influenced by the state of the market – in a buoyant market replacement tenants can be found more quickly and at less expense than in a depressed market. Corporate credit ratings can provide a guide to the credit risk spread that investors should demand from tenants, but it is unclear whether the spread should apply to the entire rental stream expected from the client.

Property obsolescence
The required yield spread over government bond yields needs to allow for the expected rate of depreciation of the property, which may be a very different cost from the actual outlay on property maintenance. This rate of obsolescence will be a major determinant of the rents that will be earned on the property in the future. Obsolescence is partly a matter of physical deterioration, but it is also accelerated by changes in the pattern of demand for particular types of building or location. Standard depreciation schedules rarely reflect actual experience, which is what matters for market investment values. Obsolescence is always subject to uncertainty, but it is uncertainty of a kind that can affect whole parts of a diversified real estate portfolio. This is why it is appropriate to allow a material risk premium.

Private and public markets for real estate
The parallel private and public markets for real estate invite comparisons of where it is cheaper to buy exposure to real estate – by buying REITs or by directly buying properties. This is the old stockmarket valuation question: are corporate assets valued below or above their replacement value? The ratio of the market value of a company to the replacement cost of its net assets is called Tobin's Q, reflecting the hypothesis that if markets are efficient and without transactions costs, this ratio should tend towards 1. In Figure 11.2 evidence from the United States is shown for the movement in this ratio for the real estate market in recent years, and its average value. Substantial real estate investors in countries with a thriving REIT market have a clear choice between investing in direct property or through REITs, although for most private investors it is not realistic to seek to achieve a diversified portfolio in direct real estate.

The relationship between the two real estate markets in the United States shown in Figure 11.2 illustrates that over the past ten years the price of REITs has, when taken together, ranged from a premium to net asset value of the underlying properties of 33.5% in 1997 to a discount of 20.4% in 2000. Green Street Advisors, a research and consulting firm, whose research is shown in Figure 11.2, says that since the early 1990s bond and equity markets have had a much more direct influence on property

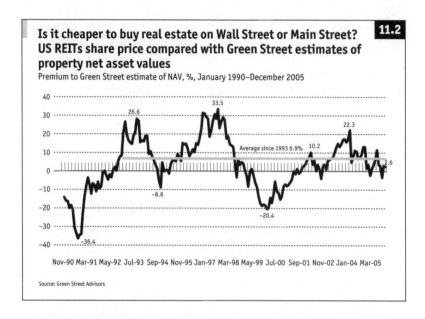

Is it cheaper to buy real estate on Wall Street or Main Street? `11.2`
US REITs share price compared with Green Street estimates of property net asset values
Premium to Green Street estimate of NAV, %, January 1990–December 2005

Source: Green Street Advisors

market developments than previously. This is evident in the seemingly closer correlation between the yield or "cap rate" on direct real estate and movements in investment grade corporate bond yields in recent years, which is also revealed in their market research.

International diversification of real estate investment

With the spread of REIT markets around the world, international diversification of real estate investing has never been easier. The word diversification implies risk reduction. But does international diversification of real estate reduce risk? It turns out that currency risk is a particularly knotty issue for international real estate investing.

Currency risk and international real estate investing

The guidelines on foreign currency exposure and the desirability of foreign currency hedging suggested in this book can be summarised as follows:

- Lower volatility international investments (such as government bonds) need to be hedged for foreign exchange risk otherwise currency fluctuations will transform the risk and return of the underlying investments by markedly increasing their volatility.
- Higher volatility international investments (such as equities) do

not need to be hedged for currency risk because currency hedging will simply alter the pattern of returns, not materially increase or decrease the magnitude of volatility.

∎ It is easy to put in place foreign currency hedges between the major liquid currencies and to hedge liquid investments. It can be expensive and or impractical to hedge the foreign exchange risks which involve one or more less liquid currencies.

∎ Foreign currency hedging involves frequent accounting for cash gains or losses on the hedged investment. These gains and losses are much easier to accommodate in an investment arrangement if the hedged investment is itself highly liquid. In these circumstances, for example, currency gains on an investment can be offset by investment sales to fund offsetting currency losses on the currency hedge. With an illiquid investment this is much more difficult to achieve, and accumulated cash flow losses from a persistent foreign currency appreciation would require additional injections of cash, which can be substantial. Investors should therefore not hedge illiquid and lumpy international investments, such as whole properties, unless they are sure that they can fund the potential liquidity drain from the hedge. (Note that an alternative is to raise a mortgage abroad to fund the foreign investment, and if need be to offset this with a cash deposit at home so as to reduce the scale of leverage. This would reduce the scope for liquidity pressures in managing the investment, and would hedge the greater part of the foreign exchange risk.)

The implications of this for international real estate diversification are as follows:

∎ Private market international real estate investments should not be hedged because the investments are illiquid and the holdings are generally indivisible.

∎ This means that the unhedged investments will be volatile and so should only be made for their opportunistic performance potential and not, for example, for the potential income yield. An exception to this arises if investors genuinely have an exceptionally long time horizon (and do not simply wish that they had). In this case, the investor may be justified in putting faith in an expectation that eventually currency movements will keep track with the relative purchasing power of different countries.

◪ Investments in public market real estate securities (such as REITs) in international markets can easily be hedged. This will be necessary if investors intend to rely on the income from the overseas REIT. However, they should check whether the level of leverage in the REIT causes it to have a volatility that will swamp any cushioning effect from hedging. Nevertheless, hedged or unhedged, investors should expect the price of a REIT that invests in direct real estate equity to be volatile.

Appendix 1 **Glossary**

This glossary does not repeat definitions and explanations of concepts that are provided in the main text, for example in Chapter 2 (terms relating to behavioural finance) and chapters in Part 2 (for terms relating to equity markets, credit markets, hedge funds, private equity and real estate). For references to these, please consult the index.

Active management	Investment strategies of active investment managers who are appointed in the expectation or hope that they will perform better than the market as a whole, after allowing for the extra fees paid for active management. These strategies always involve avoidable turnover (compared with a passive or market matching strategy) and the avoidable risk of underperforming the market. See also **passive management**.
Annualised returns	See **geometric average returns**.
Arithmetic average returns	The simple average over time of investment returns. This is higher than the compounded or geometric average of returns. The difference is easy to illustrate. Suppose a portfolio performance in one period is –50% and in the next is +100%. The arithmetic average performance is +25% [(–50 + 100) ÷ 2]. The geometric average or compound return, however, is 100x(0.5x2.0)–100 or 0%. Standard risk measures such as the standard deviation should be used in conjunction with the arithmetic average. However, the geometric or compound return describes the evolution of wealth over time.
Asset allocation	Allocation of investments among different markets. Contrast with stock selection, which is the allocation of investments within a particular market.

Base currency	Investors' home currency in which their investment objectives are expressed. Their base currency is normally, but not always, unambiguous. See Chapter 1.
Beta	A measure of the extent to which a stock might provide diluted exposure (if the measure of beta is less than 1.0) or leveraged exposure (if the measure of beta is greater than 1.0) to equity market risk. See Chapter 7 for discussion of the fundamental insights, strengths and weaknesses of the capital asset pricing model, in which the concept of "beta" plays a central role.
Bond ladder	A portfolio of high-quality bonds of successive maturities designed to provide a steady stream of investment income. See Chapter 4.
Break-even rate of inflation	This is (approximately) the difference between the redemption yield on conventional government bonds and that on inflation-linked government bonds of the same maturity. If inflation happens to equal the break-even rate, the total return on inflation-linked and conventional government bonds will be approximately identical. See Chapter 3.
Call option	A contract that gives the right to buy a specified investment at a given time in the future for a predetermined price. See also **option** and **put option**.
Capital Asset Pricing Model (CAPM)	See **beta** and Chapter 7.
Conventional bond	A fixed-income bond (which has a predetermined schedule of fixed-interest coupons and a fixed redemption value). The word "conventional" is used to distinguish the bond from inflation-linked or floating-rate bonds. Inflation-linked bonds have coupons and/ or redemption values that are adjusted in line with inflation. Floating-rate bonds have coupons that are reset in line with a specified short-term reference rate of interest, such as the London Interbank Offered Rate (LIBOR).

Convertible bond	Usually a corporate bond that gives investors the option to convert at some stage in the future for a given number of ordinary shares of the issuing company. Convertible bonds generally pay lower coupons than bonds issued by the same company which do not offer the option to convert into equity.
Convexity	A measure of the change in a bond's duration that is a result of a change in interest rates. Allowance for a bond's convexity enables a more accurate assessment of how its price will respond to interest rate changes than can be provided by considering only its duration. This is because the relationship between a change in interest rates and the consequent change in bond prices is generally not linear. Positive convexity is a desirable characteristic and is an attribute of conventional bonds whose duration increases as interest rates fall and decreases as interest rates rise. This is because the present value of future payments increases with lower interest rates and vice versa. Thus these bonds perform better than calculations based only on the bond's duration would suggest when interest rates change. Negative convexity is the opposite, and bonds which display this characteristic tend to underperform when interest rates fall and or rise. Bonds which are exposed to certain types of embedded options, such as mortgage bonds, can display negative convexity. See Chapter 8.
Coefficient of loss aversion	A concept from behavioural finance. The ratio of the sensitivity to losses compared with the sensitivity to gains. A commonly cited result is that the coefficient is around 2, in other words, that investors weigh losses twice as highly as they weigh gains.
Contrarian	An investor, or a strategy, that deliberately seeks to be unfashionable and to go against recent market trends. Typically, this is an adjective that is used to describe value investors, see Chapter 7.

Correlation	The degree of linear association between two variables. In other words, it is a measure of the extent to which the prices of two investments move together (but not necessarily by the same amount). The correlation coefficient, R, can vary between −1 and +1. A correlation coefficient of 0 suggests no relationship between the movements in the prices of the two investments. A positive correlation suggests that the prices of the two investments tend to rise or fall at the same time. A negative correlation suggests that the prices of the two investments tend to move in opposite directions at any particular time. Negative correlations are highly desirable in constructing portfolios of risky assets, because they reduce risk. However, negatively correlated attractive investments are rare.
Derivatives	Derived investment contracts, which are designed to replicate certain aspects of risk that can be obtained from direct investment in markets such as equity or fixed income.
Directional funds	A common categorisation of hedge fund strategies is to divide them between directional and non-directional strategies. Directional strategies are those whose performance is expected to be highly correlated with equity or other market risk.
Disinflation	The process of reducing the rate of inflation – that is, the rate at which prices are increasing. Disinflation should not be confused with deflation, which refers to actual declines in prices.

Duration	The average life of a bond and also a measure of a bond's sensitivity to movements in interest rates. (Slight differences in calculation are reflected in these definitions.) Duration is the weighted average time to the total of scheduled payments, where the weights are determined by the present value of each payment. Duration is shorter than the maturity of a bond, because it takes account of the earlier dates on which interest coupons are paid. The exception is a zero coupon bond, the duration of which is the same as its maturity.
	There are two common but similar technical definitions of duration: Macaulay duration, which is most useful in precisely matching a future stream of payments; and modified duration, which provides a measure of the sensitivity of a bond portfolio to small changes in interest rates.
Efficient frontier	On a graph which plots for different investments (and for portfolios of different investments) the expected return (y-axis) and expected volatility (x-axis) of those investments, the efficient frontier shows the most efficient combinations of risk and return. At any point on the frontier curve for a given level of volatility, expected return is maximised, and for a given level of expected return, expected volatility is minimised. See **fuzzy frontier** and Chapter 4.
ETF	Short for exchange traded fund, an investment product that gives exposure to a particular market. The ETF itself is listed on the stockmarket, and so is highly liquid and generally accessible at modest transaction prices.
Family office	The private office of a wealthy family which is entrusted with the management of the family's financial affairs.
Fat tails	See **kurtosis**.

Forward contract	Similar to a futures contract, except that it may not be standardised (though most probably it will be) and does not benefit from the transparent pricing and support of a formal exchange. As a result forwards are not marked to market each day. This gives rise to larger issues of counterparty risk than exist with futures contracts, which are transacted on a formal exchange.
Futures contract	A standardised contract entered into on a futures exchange to buy or sell a particular investment or basket of investments at a given date in the future. The exchange guarantees payments between members of the exchange (but not their clients). In practice, profit and loss on a futures contract is calculated on a daily basis and reflected in payments of variation margin to and from the exchange's clearing house by both parties to a contract.
Fuzzy frontier	An adaptation of the concept of the efficient frontier which acknowledges that, because investment relationships and investment classifications are to a degree uncertain, there is rarely one most efficient strategy that a particular investor should follow. Instead there is always a range of broadly efficient appropriate strategies. See Chapter 2.
Geometric average returns	Another term for compound or annualised investment returns. For the difference between geometric or compound and arithmetic investment returns, see **arithmetic average returns**.
Hedged	An indication that market risk, for example from the stockmarket or a foreign exchange market, has been neutralised using derivatives or other instruments.
High watermark	This concept is important for the calculation of hedge fund performance fees. It refers to the preceding highest cumulative total return. Hedge fund performance fees are normally payable only if cumulative performance exceeds the preceding "high watermark". See Chapter 9.

Inflation risk premium	An amount by which the break-even rate of inflation exceeds the expected rate of inflation to allow for the risk that inflation may be higher than expected. See Chapter 3.
In-the-money	A call option is said to be "in-the-money" when the market price of underlying investment is above the "strike" price at which the option to buy that investment can be exercised. A put option is in-the-money when the market price is below the strike price at which the option can be exercised. An option can be exercised profitably only if it is in-the-money.
Investment grade	The group of credit ratings given by the principal rating agencies to debt securities whose credit rating is assessed as being at least moderate to good quality. This differentiates investment grade debt from issues which are judged to be at best speculative or not well secured. See **sub-investment grade**, **junk bond** and Chapter 8.
Junk bond	A debt issue which is judged by credit-rating agencies to be at best speculative or not well secured. See also **sub-investment grade, investment grade** and Chapter 8
Kurtosis	Also called excess kurtosis. A measure of whether a series of investment returns has more extreme results than would be suggested by the normal distribution. A distribution with more than expected extreme results is called leptokurtic. This phenomenon is more commonly referred to as "fat tails". A number of hedge fund strategies, and some stockmarket returns, demonstrate pronounced fat tails or excess kurtosis. See Chapter 9.
Large cap	One of the largest companies by stockmarket capitalisation. In the United States a common definition is that a quoted company is large cap if its market capitalisation exceeds $6bn. See Chapter 7.

Leverage	An indication of the extent to which an investment, and thus its performance, is geared through the level of debt embedded in it.
Listed investment	An investment, typically a stock or bond, which is listed on a recognised exchange and provides regular quotations for its price. Contrast with an unlisted or private investment (such as a venture capital investment or a property investment), the price of which, except when it is bought and sold, represents appraisal valuations.
Lognormal distribution	See **normal distribution**.
Long-only strategy	A traditional investment strategy or portfolio consisting only of investments which are owned, not investments which are borrowed or sold short. See also **short position**.
Long position	An investment which is owned, as distinct from an investment which is borrowed. See also **short position**.
Mark-to-market	The process of accounting for the value of investments, and so profits and losses, at their market prices, rather than their book or historic cost.
Market risk premium	The premium return expected for investing outside the secure safe haven and incurring the risks associated with investing in volatile markets that offer systematic investment returns to investors.
Mean reversion	The belief, fundamental to the outlook of value investors, that prices in financial markets tend to overreact, oscillating between overvaluation and undervaluation. Mean reversion refers to an expectation that expensive markets can be relied upon to become cheaper and inexpensive markets can be relied upon to become priced closer to "fair value". See Chapters 3 and 7.

Mental accounting	A concept from behavioural finance. The set of cognitive operations used by individuals and households to organise, evaluate and keep track of financial activities.
Mezzanine debt	Often the most junior – that is, the most risky – category of debt in a borrower's balance sheet. Typically it will be accompanied by options to convert into equity. It is best considered as sharing the risk characteristics of equity rather than debt.
Natural habitat	The natural investment home for a particular investor, such as long-dated Treasury bonds for a pension fund.
Negative convexity	See **convexity**.
Noise	Meaningless apparent market signals which make it more difficult to interpret market developments. Noise is both a cause and a reflection of uncertainty. One cause of noise is the impact on markets of the transactions of investors who lack insight or who transact for reasons other than in response to market signals (for example, investors who have an impact on markets because, for whatever reason, they need to sell). See Chapter 6.
Normal distribution	The normal and lognormal distributions are the two most commonly used statistical models in finance. A normal distribution is symmetrical, with a bell-shaped curve and one peak; a lognormal distribution is skewed to the right. Return series that are lognormally distributed lead to geometric, or logarithmic, returns that are themselves normally distributed. The popularity of the normal and lognormal distributions reflects their comparative ease of use in analysis and the evidence that it provides a plausible approximation to many market performance data series. Much effort has been invested in examining when the normal, or lognormal, distribution fails to describe how markets behave. See, for example, Chapters 3, 5 and 7.

Option	A contract that gives the purchaser the right, but not the obligation, to buy (call option) or sell (put option) a particular investment at a given price on (if a European option) or before (if an American option) the given expiry date for the contract.
Passive strategies	Market-matching investment strategies which involve minimal turnover and expense. Turnover typically occurs only to accommodate inflows or outflows of investor funds and to improve the market-matching features of the investment portfolio.
Prepayment risk	The risk that a bond, particularly a mortgage bond, will experience faster than scheduled repayments of principal because residential mortgage holders, particularly in the United States, can exercise the right to repay mortgages earlier than specified in a repayment schedule. This reduces the term of a mortgage bond and is most likely to happen when interest rates fall (or when mortgage providers compete aggressively for new business), giving profitable opportunities for borrowers to remortgage property at more attractive interest rates. See Chapter 8.
Price/earnings ratio	The ratio of the share price of a company to its earnings divided by the number of shares it has issued. A high price/earnings (P/E) ratio indicates that the stockmarket expects the company's earnings to grow fast, and vice versa.
Price performance	The performance of an investment that makes no allowance for its income or dividend yield. Contrast with total return, which includes the price performance and the income return.
Prime broker	A department of an investment bank which provides banking services to hedge funds
Private investment	An unlisted or unquoted investment for which price quotations are generally not readily available.

Prospect theory	A key part of behavioural finance. It is based on experiments that indicate that people are more motivated by losses than by gains (see coefficient of loss aversion) and so will try hard to avoid realising losses. See Chapter 2.
Public investment	A listed or quoted investment for which prices are regularly quoted on a formal exchange at which, or close to which, transactions can be effected.
Pure discount bond	See **zero coupon bond**.
Put option	A contract that gives the right to sell a specified investment at a given time in the future for a predetermined price. See also **option** and **call option**.
Quoted investment	A public investment.
R^2	The square of the correlation coefficient. This measures the percentage of variation (that is, variance) in the price of one investment that is "explained" by a change in the price of another.
Real interest rate	The rate of interest after allowing for inflation.
Redemption yield	See **yield to maturity**.
Relative risk	Typically, the risk of an actively managed portfolio relative to that of the market or the investor's benchmark or neutral investment policy.
Risk premium	See Chapter 3.
Safe haven	An investor's minimum risk strategy. See Chapter 3.

Sharpe ratio	A measure of risk adjusted performance. For an investment portfolio or strategy, the Sharpe ratio is the ratio of performance in excess of the risk-free investment (generally Treasury bills) to the volatility of performance relative to the risk-free rate. Performance and volatility are generally calculated as annualised rates. Investors should be aware that illiquid investment strategies distort measurement of Sharpe ratios since the apparent volatility of those strategies will be artificially reduced by markets that rely on appraisal valuations of underlying investments. Furthermore, Sharpe ratios are only meaningful if the distribution of performance of the underlying investments approximately resembles a normal distribution. It follows that Sharpe ratios should not be used for investment strategies which resemble insurance programmes and which incorporate a marked degree of optionality. For both these reasons, Sharpe ratios shown for many hedge fund strategies are more likely to misinform investors than to inform them. See Chapter 9.
Short position	Arises when investors sell an investment that they do not own. Unless the short position is established on a futures exchange, investors will need to borrow the investment to deliver it to the counterparty who bought it from them. The short seller will need to provide collateral to the stock lender when borrowing the stock (or other investment).
Skewness	A measure of the symmetry between investment returns from a market. If the returns are tilted towards the left (more negative) side of the distribution, a distribution is said to exhibit negative skewness. If returns are tilted towards the right (more positive) side of the distribution, the results are said to exhibit positive skewness.

Small cap	A smaller company by stockmarket capitalisation. In the United States a common definition is that a quoted company is small cap if its market capitalisation is less than $2bn. See Chapter 7.
SMID	Short for small or mid cap companies, a group of companies that is reckoned to be either small or mid cap by value of market capitalisation. In the United States a common definition is that a quoted company is SMID if its market capitalisation is less than $6bn. See Chapter 7.
Speculative grade	A debt issue judged by credit-rating agencies to be at best speculative or not well secured. See also **junk bond, investment grade** and Chapter 8
Standard deviation	The standard measure of the volatility of the price or performance of an investment. Common interpretations of the standard deviation derive from the normal distribution. For example, if an equity portfolio has an expected return of 8% a year and an expected volatility of 15% a year, it would be expected, approximately, to have returns of between -7% and 23% in two years out of three.
Stock selection	The allocation of investments in a portfolio within a particular market. Contrast with the allocation of investments among different markets, which is known as asset allocation.
Strategic asset allocation	Decisions, typically intended to be quite long term in nature, to manage risks and opportunities relative to an investor's ultimate payment obligations or objectives. Strategic asset allocation involves the allocation of investments between an investor's safe-haven investment and an efficient diversity of other market risks. See Chapter 4.

Structured product	An investment or investment strategy that is typically sold with some element of principal protection and/or of leverage to give accelerated exposure to the underlying market. Structured products are sold by investment banks and typically involve either some combination of zero coupon bonds, which mature with the structured product together with call options on the relevant underlying market; or a dynamic strategy that adjusts exposure to the underlying investment and government bonds to ensure that the issuing bank will be able profitably to honour the promised capital repayment at maturity.
Sub-investment grade	A debt issue judged by credit-rating agencies to be at best speculative or not well secured. See also **junk bond**, **investment grade** and Chapter 8
Systematic return	The market return that is expected to be provided for bearing well-diversified systematic risk. Often thought of in terms of equity market return, systematic return also refers to the return that should be expected for bearing any type of market risk for which market participants are willing to pay. This includes, in addition to equity market risk, credit market risk, as well as various types of insurance and other risk transfer services. Such alternative sources of systematic return are now understood to be an important potential source of hedge fund returns.
Systematic risk	The market risk that remains after diversification. Most commonly this refers to equity market risk, but it can also refer to the risk associated with a range of different sources of systematic return.
Tactical asset allocation	Decisions, typically short or medium term, to allocate more or less of an investment strategy to different markets in the hope of profiting from expected differential performance between markets.

Tobin's Q | Named after James Tobin, a Nobel Prize-winning economist from Yale University, this is the ratio of the stockmarket value of a firm to its replacement cost. If Q is less than 1 it would be cheaper to buy the firm's shares than to expand to replicate that firm. See Chapter 11 for an application to the US real estate market.

Total return | The total performance of an investment, combining income yield as well as price performance.

Tracking error | See **relative risk**.

Tranche | A slice, specifically of a collateralised debt obligation (CDO), that has different risk characteristics from other tranches of the same CDO. See Chapter 8.

Treasury bill | Government debt with less than one year's original maturity (typically 1–6 months).

Treasury bond | Government debt with more than one year's original maturity. In designing broad investment strategies, it is conventional to treat a government bond with a remaining maturity of less than 12 months as if it were a Treasury bill. In the US, Treasury debts with between one and ten years' original maturity are called "notes". In this book, the expression "Treasury bond" refers to any Treasury security of more than one year's maturity.

Unhedged | An indication that market risk, for example from the stockmarket or a foreign exchange market, has not been neutralised using derivatives or other instruments.

Utility | An indication of satisfaction, often proxied by money.

Volatility | Fluctuations in the price or performance of an investment, typically measured by the annualised standard deviation of returns.

Warrant | An option to a buy a security at a particular price and subject to particular time constraints.

Yield curve | See Chapter 3.

Yield to maturity	The standard measure of the return an investor will receive from a bond if the bond is held to maturity. Yield to maturity (YTM) takes account of the interest income and any capital gain or loss on the bond over that time.
Zero coupon bond	Zero coupon bonds, also known as zeros, ZCBs, or pure discount bonds, pay no interest, only the repayment of principal at maturity. Their maturity is equal to their duration, and for long maturities they represent the most volatile of high-quality bonds. Prior to maturity, zero coupon bonds trade at a discount to face value.

Appendix 2 Essential management information for investors

Sometimes the management information that investors receive on their investment portfolios consists of no more than a list of holdings and their values. This makes it almost impossible to see the shape of a portfolio and gives little indication of its risk exposures. Simple management information is an essential first step in taking control of investments, and it should be easy to obtain. Investment management firms routinely provide easy-to-comprehend portfolio summaries, although the format will differ from one firm to another and some will be more useful than others. However, investors who employ more than one manager need to have reliable overall snapshots that they can drill down into to see individual positions if they wish.

Some illustrative portfolio summaries are shown in Tables 1-4 on pages 213-16. They need to be adapted to particular situations, but they provide a general impression. Investors need to decide whether the information is best presented in an aggregated form, adding together all their investments from different accounts. This will often be the best way to proceed. However, if investments are held in different accounts tied to different investment objectives with different risk tolerances, aggregating the holdings may encourage inappropriate conclusions, which take insufficient account of the objectives of the various accounts, to be drawn. Conversely, a failure to aggregate holdings could cause concentrated, inappropriate or inefficient risk exposures to be overlooked. This is discussed in Chapter 2 and needs careful consideration, preferably with the assistance of a professional adviser.

Performance measurement and monitoring for good and bad volatility

As well as transparent holdings information, investors should pay attention to how performance information is presented to them. It will normally be appropriate to aggregate all their listed, or at least frequently valued, investments to review the performance of the overall strategy. For unquoted investments, review of management information on the investments needs to take the place of review of accurate performance information. Where different accounts have been established to meet different objectives with different risk tolerances, performance against those objectives should be monitored. Even when it has not been an option to fully hedge a particular objective (because it is too expensive), it is still useful to show performance relative to the notional performance of the fully hedged strategy. This allows monitoring in terms of good and bad volatility, as discussed in Chapter 4.

A similar way of achieving the same objective is to measure how the purchasing power of an investment portfolio evolves in terms of its ability to support continuing flows of expenditure. The easy way to do this for a (very) long-term investor is to take the inflation-linked yield on the longest dated TIPS in the domestic market to generate a hypothetical recurring income from the investments. For example, for each $1,000 of investments, if the yield on TIPS moved from 3% to 2% a year, the supportable income would decrease from $30 to $20 a year. Doing the same exercise with nominal government (or municipal) bond yields will provide an apparently more reassuring level of income, but this is subject to erosion by inflation over time. How this level of supportable income changes as markets move will reflect the degree of investment risk in the investment strategy. Particularly for cautious long-term investors, this is a simple metric that could be useful.

Performance measurement is a substantial subject. One of the principal features is that the performance that matters is an investment fund's total return, which comprises price changes and net interest and dividend receipts. This should preferably be after payment of fees and taxes. When the performance of a fund is being compared with a market index, it is important that a like-for-like comparison is made. For example, if the purpose is to evaluate the skill of a money manager, the comparison should be with the total return index that best represents the market and strategy of that manager. Comparing an equity manager's performance with that of a bond index is inappropriate if the intention is to shed light on manager skill. However, comparing the performance of an equity fund with a government bond index may be useful in monitoring the ability of that fund to meet particular objectives in the future.

There are two principal measures of total return:

◪ money weighted rated of return (MWR), which is also known as the internal rate of return (IRR);
◪ time weighted rate of return (TWR).

The difference between them concerns the treatment of cash flows. The TWR enables a fair comparison between a fund that receives cash flows and the performance of a market index that does not. This is by far the most common basis for the formal measurement of investment performance. However, the MWR or IRR takes account of whether the timing of cash inflows or outflows was beneficial for the fund and is more useful in measuring the evolution of fund solvency over time. For most investors who are concerned about the sufficiency of their investments, an assessment of whether a fund's value is sufficient to hedge objectives using safe-haven investments bypasses the need for MWR calculations.

Summary risk information

All investors should try to get simplified risk information on their portfolios. There are online risk services which provide sophisticated yet accessible risk analysis, such as www.riskgrades.com. But note that the risk measures that are generated will be calibrated as if the investor is by default a short-term investor. The easiest way for investors to obtain informative risk information is to track the volatility of the monthly performance of an investment fund. This can then be used to gauge comfort levels. For example, if a fund has been performing well, how would the investor respond, and would objectives be threatened, if the pattern of volatility was translated into a corresponding, unsurprising pattern of disappointing performance?

Table 1 **Summary asset allocation**

Percentages of total investment holdings	Most recent data			End previous quarter			Year ago		
	Holdings	Policy	Difference	Holdings	Policy	Difference	Holdings	Policy	Difference
Quoted equities									
Private equity									
Real estate									
Hedge funds									
of which foreign currency									
Other alternatives*									
Fixed income									
of which foreign currency									
TIPS									
of which foreign currency									
Cash									
of which foreign currency									
Total									

* Including structured products.
Note: references to foreign currency are intended to highlight unhedged foreign exposures which would be safe haven or low to modest volatility investments in their base currency, but whose risk is magnified by foreign currency risk.

Table 2 **Equity investment allocation**

Percentages of quoted equity holdings	Most recent data			End previous quarter			Year ago		
	Holdings	Policy/ market	Difference	Holdings	Policy/ market	Difference	Holdings	Policy/ market	Difference
Quoted equities by region									
North America									
Developed Europe									
Japan									
Pacific excl Japan (developed markets)									
Emerging markets									

	Most recent data			End previous quarter			Year ago		
Percentages of quoted equity holdings	*Holdings*	*Policy/ market*	*Difference*	*Holdings*	*Policy/ market*	*Difference*	*Holdings*	*Policy/ market*	*Difference*
Total	100%	100%	0%	100%	100%	0%	100%	100%	0%
Total (cash values)									
Quoted equities by GICS sector[a]									
Energy									
Materials									
Industrials									
Consumer discretionary									
Health care									
Financials									
of which: REITs									
Information technology									
Telecommunica- tions services									
Utilities									
Total	100%	100%	0%	100%	100%	0%	100%	100%	0%
Breakdown by market capitalisation									
% of equity holdings with market cap:									
>$6bn									
<$6bn, >$2bn									
<$2bn									
Quoted equities, further information:									
Largest holding									
2nd largest holding									
3rd largest holding									
Summary style information, by region or sector compared with market, to include at least:									
Average price/ earnings ratio									
Average dividend yield									

a Global Industry Classification Standard.

Table 3 **Alternative investment allocation**

Market values	Most recent data			End previous quarter			Year ago		
	Holdings	Policy	Difference	Holdings	Policy	Difference	Holdings	Policy	Difference
Private equity									
Breakdown by type of fund, stage of development and geography									
Direct holdings of real estate properties or funds (excl REITs)									
Breakdown by type, and location									
Hedge funds									
Breakdown by strategy, and fund base currency									
Equity risk substitute hedge funds[a]									
Alternative beta hedge funds[a]									
Structured products									
List individually with concise summary of risk return characteristics									

a See Chapter 9.

Table 4 **Fixed income and cash allocation**

	Most recent data			End previous quarter			Year ago		
	Holdings	Policy	Difference	Holdings	Policy	Difference	Holdings	Policy	Difference
Cash[a]									
Average remaining maturity (days)									
Currency exposure:									
Credit quality by short- or long-term rating									
Largest non-gov holding									
Next largest non-gov holding									
Fixed income (total)									
Domestic fixed income[b]									
Breakdown by maturity band (% of domestic bond holdings):[c]									
Short dated									
Medium dated									
Long dated									
Average maturity of cash and bonds									
Average duration of cash and bonds									
% floating rate debt									
Maturity of floating rate debt									
Breakdown by issuer type (% of domestic bond holdings):									
Government bonds									
Agencies									
Pass thru mortgages									
Corporate debt									
Credit quality (S&P) (% of domestic bond holdings)									
AAA									
AA									
A									
BBB									
BB and below									
Largest exposures (% of domestic bond holdings)[d]									
Largest non-gov bond holding									
2nd largest non-gov bond holding									
3rd largest non-gov bond holding									
Foreign currency fixed income (unhedged)									
Structured debt products									
List by holding and credit rating									
TIPS holdings									
Average maturity of TIPS holdings									

a That is, liquid investments which are realisable at face value within a short period of time.   b Including foreign bonds hedged into local currency.   c Conventions on maturity bands differ between markets.   d Aggregating all holdings of an individual issuer.

Appendix 3 **Trusting your adviser**

Choosing an adviser is the most important investment decision that investors make. Good investment advice is extremely valuable, so investors must be willing to pay for it. However, transaction commissions, rather than explicit advisory fees, paid to many financial advisers and investment firms create conflicts of interest and can encourage a sales-driven rather than an advice-driven culture in the management of wealth. Investors need to know whether they are dealing with a seller or an adviser, and to manage their relationship accordingly.

Pure advice is not well rewarded, but investment sales or investment management are. A minority of private wealth advisers offer a fee-based, advice-only investment service, although this is more common for pension fund advisers. However, it is important that investors ask whether these firms receive income, such as commissions, from providers of recommended products, so that they are aware of potential conflicts before making investment decisions.

In Chapter 6 it was suggested that the existence of fiduciary boards might encourage institutional investors to follow each other's behaviour. This may help to explain some patterns of investment market behaviour, but it is a side effect of a decision-making structure imposed on institutional boards which encourages good governance and due process. This should lead to considered decision-making and a structured approach for dealing with conflicts of interest when buying investment services for their funds. Wealthy families often put an analogous structure in place to protect their interests, but the management of private wealth is almost always much more flexible and less formal than that of institutional wealth. As discussed in Chapter 6, this creates vulnerabilities as well as opportunities.

The potential for conflicts of interest between investors and their advisers is often known as the principal–agent problem. This arises because the principal (the investor) has inferior access to information compared with the agent (the investment adviser). The problem is that incentives may encourage advisers to use superior information in a way that serves their own interest rather than the best interest of the investor. Although institutional investors typically have structures that can mitigate this, such conflicts are common. Ironically, one way institutional investors can reduce their exposure to these conflicts is to distance themselves from much of the detailed investment decision-making. They can employ investment managers whose remuneration is transparent and who are (depending upon the jurisdiction) under an obligation to provide best execution to their clients in discretionary investment mandates.

However, many private clients prefer a brokerage or advisory relationship where they retain control over each investment decision. The danger is that they will get lost in detail and miss the big picture because of the imbalance of information between themselves and their advisers. It can also lead to the accumulation of a portfolio of ad hoc investments, each of which "seemed a good idea at the time". With a brokerage arrangement it is therefore more likely that responsibility for portfolio balance and risk management will be overlooked. These issues are best addressed by an investment manager, who is employed to take these detailed decisions. Private investors, with the assistance of an investment adviser, can use professionally managed investment portfolios to put distance between themselves and detailed investment decision-making. Many do not like to do this as it distances them from those detailed decisions, and so they prefer to stay with a brokerage arrangement.

In the management of wealth, an investment firm will depend on recurring flows of income from the management of assets or the sales of investment products. There will always be conflicts of interest arising from the varying profitability of different investment products. Among investment firms, there is a distinction between those where individual advisers are remunerated by their firms with salary plus annual bonus, and those where advisers are paid a lower base income supplemented with commissions for sales of investment products. Such financial advisers often have explicit "sales" objectives and may in effect be private client stockbrokers or sales executives. However, in the salary plus bonus model, the main driver of the annual bonus may be sales, so the difference between the two approaches can be exaggerated.

In all broking or sales relationships, the danger is that investors will be sold what a broker wishes to sell rather than deciding to buy what they need for their investment strategy. The best safeguard is for investors to satisfy themselves that their interests and those of their advisers are appropriately aligned, and that conflicts of interest are in the open. In practice, reassurance on this will depend more on the characters of the individuals concerned than the institutional arrangements within which they work. But the importance of those arrangements should not be underestimated.

Ultimately, no advisory business model will be successful if it fails to put the establishment and nurturing of trust between clients and their advisers first. However, investors must always be aware that conflicts of interest are endemic in the financial services industry. The key to unlocking the problem of these conflicts is to have transparency of fee arrangements and then to decide on a case-by-case basis how to proceed. The general message is "buyer, beware". For some categories of investor (or investor account) in some jurisdictions, regulators insist on disclosure of all sources of investment management or private bank remuneration from a client account. Clients should request information on the adviser's (or the bank's) financial interest in a proposed transaction, preferably in writing.

Lastly, remember that good advice is valuable, and when the going gets tough, simple hand-holding by an adviser which prevents short-term mistakes may be the most valuable service that the adviser provides. Superficially it will come for free – but there is a relationship that provides fee income for the adviser and access to advice for the investor. The do-it-yourself investor misses out on this. Know what you are paying, and review but don't quibble over each item. Make sure that you are comfortable with the overall level of fees, and do, from time to time, ask your advisers whether they would make a recommended investment on their own account. Low fees do not ensure that good advice is being offered, or that an investment strategy is sensible or that risk-taking is appropriate. And the contrary also applies.

Appendix 4 **Recommended reading**

Part 1 The big picture

1 Setting the scene

There are a number of investment classics which provide a general background to the first part of this chapter (and other parts of the book):

Bernstein, P.L., *Against the Gods: The Remarkable Story of Risk*, John Wiley & Sons, 1998.

Carswell, J., *The South Sea Bubble*, 3rd edn, Sutton Publishing, 2001

Chancellor, E., *Devil take the hindmost, a history of financial speculation*, Plume, 2000

Galbraith, J.K., *The Great Crash*, Penguin Books, 1992

Kindelberger, C.P., *Manias, Panics and Crashes*, 4th edn, Wiley, 2000

Mackay, C., *Extraordinary Popular Delusions and the Madness of Crowds*, Wordsworth Editions, 1995.

The introduction to risk draws on:

Borge, D., *The Book of Risk*, John Wiley & Sons, 2001

Kritzman, M.P., *The Portable Financial Analyst: What Practitioners Need to Know*, 2nd edn. John Wiley & Sons, 2003

Kritzman, M. and Rich, D., "The Mismeasurement of Risk", *Financial Analysts Journal*, May/June 2002

Individual investors should also visit www.riskgrades.com for an easy-to-access risk measurement tool.

2 Understand your behaviour

This chapter draws heavily on the following:

Barberis, N. and Thaler, R., "A Survey of Behavioral Finance", in Constantinides, G.M. *et al.* (eds), *Handbook of the Economics of Finance: Financial Markets and Asset Pricing*, Elsevier/North-Holland, 2003.

Other particularly useful sources were:

Lo, A., "The Adaptive Markets Hypothesis", *Journal of Portfolio Management*, 30th anniversary issue, 2004

Statman, M., "What Do Investors Want?", *Journal of Portfolio Management*, 30th anniversary issue, 2004.

3 Market investment returns: will the markets make me rich?

On the term structure of real and nominal interest rates:

Buraschi, A. and Jiltsov, A., "Inflation Risk Premia and the Expectations Hypothesis", *Journal of Financial Economics*, vol. 75, issue 2, February 2005

Campbell, J.Y. and Shiller, R.J., "A Scorecard for Indexed Government Debt", NBER Working Paper 5587, May 1996

Shiller, R.J. and McCulloch, J.H., "The Term Structure of Interest Rates", in Friedman, B.M. and Hahn, F.H. (eds), *Handbook of Monetary Economics*, vol. 1, Elsevier Science, 1990.

The equity risk premium:

Arnott, R.D. and Bernstein, P.L., "What Risk Premium is 'Normal'?", *Financial Analysts Journal*, March/April 2002

Arnott, R.D., "The Meaning of a Slender Risk Premium", Editor's Corner, *Financial Analysts Journal*, March/April 2004

Dimson, E., Marsh, P. and Staunton, M., "Irrational Optimism", *Financial Analysts Journal*, January/February 2004; and *Triumph of the Optimists: 101 Years of Global Investment Returns*, Princeton University Press, 2002

Ibbotson, R.G. and Chen, P., "Long Run Stock Returns: Participating in the Real Economy", *Financial Analysts Journal*, January/February 2003

Siegel, J., *Stocks for the Long Run*, 3rd edn, McGraw-Hill, 2002.

4 The shape of strategy: start with no frills and few thrills

The principal source for this chapter is:

Campbell, J.Y. and Viceira, L.M., *Strategic Asset Allocation: Portfolio Choice for Long-Term Investors*, Oxford University Press, 2002.

John Campbell and Tuomo Vuolteenaho's "Bad Beta, Good Beta" (*American Economic Review*, vol. 94, no. 5, December 2004) is one of those occasional articles that develops a simple investment idea that then has powerful policy (as well as investor education) implications. It is the inspiration for this chapter's discussion of good and bad volatility as well as Chapter 7's discussion of apparent stockmarket anomalies. In a similar vein is Zvi Bodie's "Thoughts for the Future: Life-Cycle Investing in Theory and Practice" (*Financial Analysts Journal*, January/February 2003), where the different strands of traditional and behavioural finance are synthesised into designing suitable strategies for loss averse investors.

In this chapter (and elsewhere) invaluable resources were provided by David Swensen:

Pioneering Portfolio Management: An Unconventional Approach to Institutional Investment, Free Press, 2000

Unconventional Success: A Fundamental Approach to Personal Investment, Free Press, 2005.

5 Implementing "keep-it-simple" strategies

An important article is Allan Meltzer's "Rational and Irrational Bubbles", the keynote address to a 2002 World Bank Conference on asset price bubbles, which sets the tone for much of this chapter (source: www.tepper.cmu.edu/afs/andrew/gsia/meltzer/).

Part 2 Implementing more complicated strategies

6 Setting the scene

The discussion of arbitrage opportunities in this chapter relies heavily on Nicholas Barberis and Richard Thaler's survey of behavioural finance (see above). The discussion of taxation makes use of:

Poterba, J., "Taxation, Risk Taking, and Household Portfolio Behavior", NBER Working Paper 8340, June 2001

Evensky, H. and Katz, D. (eds), *The Investment Think Tank: Theory, Strategy, and Practice for Advisers*, Bloomberg Press, 2004.

7 Equities

The treatment of the capital asset pricing model (CAPM) and the stockmarket anomalies draws on helpful suggestions from Steve Satchell, Campbell and Vuolteenaho's article "Bad Beta, Good Beta" (see above) and Eugene Fama and Kenneth French's "The Capital Asset Pricing Model: Theory and Evidence" (CRSP Working Paper 550, August 2003).

The discussion of equity manager style draws on Daniel Nordby's "Practical Tools for Analysing Growth Stocks, in Equity Research and Valuation Techniques" and Kim Shannon's "Practical Tools for Analysing Value Stocks, in Equity Research and Valuation Techniques", both published in AIMR Conference Proceedings (February 2002).

8 Bonds, debt and credit

The discussion of debt markets and instruments draws on market contacts and on:

Fabozzi, F. J. and Mann, S. V. (eds), *The Handbook of Fixed Income Securities*, 7th edn, McGraw-Hill, 2005.

9 Hedge funds: try to keep it simple

This chapter draws heavily on market contacts as well as scene-setting articles published in recent years, including:

Asness, C., "An Alternative Future", *Journal of Portfolio Management*, 30th Anniversary Issue 2004

Asness, C., "An Alternative Future II", *Journal of Portfolio Management*, vol. 31, no. 1, Fall 2004

Scholes, M.S., "The Future of Hedge Funds", *The Journal of Financial Transformation*, Capco, vol. 10, April 2004.

Other important articles deal with particular aspects of hedge fund risk, such as the effect on apparent risk of illiquid investments, for example:

Getmansky, M., Lo, A.W. and Makarov, I., "An Econometric Model of Serial Correlation and Illiquidity in Hedge Fund Returns", *Journal of Financial Economics*, vol. 74, no. 3, 2004 (pp. 529–610).

10 Private equity: information-based returns

Mark Anson's *Handbook of Alternative Assets* (Wiley 2002) provides a useful resource for alternative investments. His article "Trends in private equity" (*Journal of Wealth Management*, Winter 2004) provides an overview of how changes after 2000 have altered the world of private equity. Steven Kaplan and Antoinette Schoar's article "Private Equity Performance: Returns, Persistence and Capital Flows" (*Journal of Finance*, August 2005) provides recent independent research on private equity performance which is drawn on in the chapter.

11 Real estate

This chapter draws on market contacts and published resources such the *Journal of Portfolio Management*'s special real estate issue (September 2003). As with other alternative investment asset classes, Swensen's *Pioneering Portfolio Management* and *Unconventional Success: A Fundamental Approach to Personal Investment* provide useful sources on real estate investing.

Other useful sources

Arnott, R.D., Berkin, A.L. and Ye, J., "Loss Harvesting: What is it Worth to a Taxable Investor?", *Journal of Wealth Management*, Spring 2001, pp. 10–18.

Asness, C., Krail, R. and Liew, J., "Do Hedge Funds Hedge?", *Journal of Portfolio Management*, Fall 2001.

Banz, R., "The Relationship between Return and Market Value of Common Stocks", *Journal of Financial Economics*, March 1981, pp. 3–18.

Benartzi, S., "Excessive extrapolation and the allocation of 401(k) accounts to company stock", *Journal of Finance*, October 2001.

Bernstein, W., *The Four Pillars of Investing: Lessons for Building a Winning Portfolio*, McGraw-Hill, 2002.

Bilo, S., Christophers, H., Degosciu, M. and Zimmermann, H., "Risk, returns, and biases of listed private equity portfolios", WWZ Working Paper no. 1/05, 2005.

Black, F., "Noise", *Journal of Finance*, July 1986.

Bodie, Z., Kane, A. and Marcus, A.J., *Investments*, 6th international edition, McGraw-Hill, 2005.

Bodie, Z., Merton, R. and Samuelson, W., "Labor Supply Flexibility and Portfolio Choice in a Life Cycle Model", NBER Working Paper 3954, 1992.

Boyle, P.S, Loewy, D., Riess, J.A. and Weiss, R.A., "The Enviable Dilemma: Hold, Sell, or Hedge Highly Concentrated Stock?", *Journal of Wealth Management*, Fall 2004.

Brealey, R.A. and Myers, S.C., *Principles of Corporate Finance*, 7th edn, McGraw-Hill, 2003.

Brown, J.R., Mitchell, O.S., Poterba, J.M. and Warshawsky, M.J., *The Role of Annuity Markets in Financing Retirement*, MIT Press, 2001.

Brunel, J.L.P., *Integrated Wealth Management: The New Direction for Portfolio Managers*, Institutional Investor Books, 2002.

Cai, F. and Warnock, F.E., "International Diversification at Home and Abroad", International Finance Discussion Paper 2004-793, Board of Governors of the Federal Reserve System, December 2004 (www. federalreserve.gov/pubs/ifdp/2004/793/default.htm).

Calverley, J.P., *Bubbles and How to Survive Them*, Nicholas Brealey, 2004

Campbell, J.Y. and Rathjens, P., *The Case for International Diversification*, Arrowstreet Capital, May 2003.

Connolly, T. and Zeelenberg, M., "Regret in Decision Making", *Current Directions in Psychological Science*, vol. 11, no. 6, December 2002.

Das, S.R. and Uppal, R., "Systemic Risk and International Portfolio Choice", *Journal of Finance*, December 2004.

Deacon, M., Derry, A. and Mirfendereski, D., *Inflation Indexed Securities: Bonds, Swaps and Other Derivatives*, 2nd edn, John Wiley & Sons, 2004.

Dimson, E. and Jackson, A., "High Frequency Performance Monitoring", *Journal of Portfolio Management*, Fall 2001.

Dimson, E. and Marsh, P., *Hoare Govett Smaller Companies Index 2006*, ABN-Amro, January 2006.

Dunbar, N., *Inventing Money: the story of Long-Term Capital Management and the legends behind it*, John Wiley & Sons, 2000.

Eichengreen, B., Hausmann, R. and Panizza, U., "The Mystery of Original Sin", in Eichengreen and Hausmann (eds), *Other People's Money: Debt Denomination and Financial Instability in Emerging Market Economies*, University of Chicago Press, 2005.

Ellis, C.D., *Winning the Loser's Game*, 4th edn, McGraw-Hill, 2002.

Evensky, H.R., *Wealth Management, the Financial Advisor's Guide to Investing and Managing Client Assets*, McGraw-Hill, 1997.

Fama, E. and French, K., "The Equity Premium", *Journal of Finance*, April 2002.

French, K. and Poterba, J., "Investor Diversification and International Equity markets", *American Economic Review*, 81, May 1991.

Fry, R.P., *Non-Profit Investment Policies, Practical Steps for Growing Charitable Funds*, John Wiley & Sons, 1998.

Fung, W. and Hsieh, D., "Hedge Fund Benchmarks: A Risk Based Approach", *Financial Analysts Journal*, September/October 2004.

Géhin, W. and Vaissié, M., *The Right Place for Alternative Betas in Hedge Fund Performance*, Edhec, 2005.

Gibson, R.C. *Asset Allocation: Balancing Financial Risk*, 2nd edn, Irwin, 1996.

Giliberto, M., "Assessing Real Estate Volatility", *Journal of Portfolio Management*, special real estate issue, September 2003.

Graham, B., *The Intelligent Investor*, updated by Zweig, J., Harper, 2003.

Gregoriou, G., Karavas, V., Lhabitant, F-S. and Rouah, F., *Commodity Trading Advisors, Risk, Performance Analysis and Selection*, Wiley Finance, 2004.

Grinold, R. and Kroner, K., "The Equity Risk Premium", Barclays Global Investors, *Investment Insights*, vol. 5, issue 3, July 2002.

Hall, B. and Murphy, K., "Optimal exercise prices for executive stock options", *American Economic Review*, 90 (2), May 2000 (pp. 209–14).

Halstead, J.M, Hedge, S. and Schmid Klein, L., "Orange County Bankruptcy: Financial Contagion in the Municipal Bond and Bank Equity Markets", *Eastern Finance Association: The Financial Review*, 39, 2004.

Haughen, R.A., *Modern Investment Theory*, 5th edn, Prentice Hall, 2001.

Haughen, R.A., *The New Finance*, 3rd edn, Pearson Prentice Hall, 2004.

Holton, G.A., "Defining Risk", *Financial Analysts Journal*, November/ December 2004.

Ineichen, A., *Absolute Returns, the Risk and Opportunities of Hedge Fund Investing*, Wiley Finance, 2003.

Kahneman, D. and Tversky, A., "The Psychology of Preferences", *Scientific American*, vol. 246, 1982.

Kat, H.M. and Palaro, H.P., "Hedge Fund Returns: You Can Make Them Yourself!", manuscript, Cass Business School, 2005.

Kay, J., *The Truth About Markets*, Penguin Books, 2004.

Kessler, A., *Running Money*, HarperBusiness, 2004.

Keynes, J.M., *Collected Writings, Vol XII, Investment and Editorial*, Macmillan, 1983.

Kritzman, M.P., *Puzzles of Finance*, John Wiley & Sons, 2000.

Lhabitant, F-S., *Hedge Funds, Myths and Limits*, Wiley Finance, 2002.

Löffler, G., "Avoiding the rating bounce: why rating agencies are slow to react to new information", *Journal of Economic Behavior and Organization*, 56 (3), 2005.

Longstaff, F., Mithal, S. and Neis, E., "Corporate Yield Spreads: Default Risk or Liquidity? New Evidence from the Credit Default Swap Market", *Journal of Finance*, October 2005.

Lowenstein, R., *When Genius Failed: the rise and fall of Long-Term Capital Management*, Fourth Estate, 2001.

Malkiel, B.G and Saha, A., "Hedge Funds: Risk and Return", *Financial Analysts Journal*, November/December 2005.

MFA's 2005 Sound Practices for Hedge Fund Managers, Managed Funds Association, Washington DC.

Mandelbrot, B.B. and Hudson, R., *The (Mis)Behaviour of Markets: A Fractal View of Risk, Reward and Ruin*, Profile Books, 2004.

Mehra, R. and Prescott, E., "The Equity Premium: A Puzzle", *Journal of Monetary Economics*, vol. 15, 1985.

Merton, R.C., "Thoughts on the Future: Theory and Practice in Investment Management", *Financial Analysts Journal*, January/ February 2003.

Merton, R.C. and Bodie, Z., "Design of Financial Systems: Towards a Synthesis of Design and Structure", *Journal of Investment Management*, vol. 3, no. 1, 2005.

Miller, M.H. and Grossman, S.J., "Liquidity and Market Structure", *Journal of Finance*, July 1988.

Moglia, J., *Coach Yourself to Investment Success: Winning the Investment Game*, John Wiley & Sons, 2005.

Poterba, J. M., "Portfolio Risk and Self-Directed Retirement Saving Programmes", *Economic Journal*, vol. 114, no. 494, March 2004.

Power, M., *The Audit Society: Rituals of Verification*, Oxford University Press, 2002.

Reb, J. and Connolly, T., "Decision Justifiability and Regret", manuscript, 2004.

Reich, R., "Who is Us?", *Harvard Business Review*, January/February 1990.

Roll, R., "Empirical TIPS", *Financial Analysts Journal*, January/February 2004.

Ross, S.A., "Forensic Finance: Enron and Others", *Rivista di Politica Economica*, November/December 2002.

Sarnoff, P., *Silver Bulls*, Arlington House Publishers, 1980.

Scholtes, C., "On Market-Based Measures of Inflation Expectations", *Bank of England Quarterly Bulletin*, Spring 2002.

Sharpe, W.F., "Capital Asset Prices: A Theory of Market Equilibrium under Conditions of Risk", *Journal of Finance*, September 1964.

Shefrin, H. and Statman, M., "Behavioral Portfolio Theory", *Journal of Financial and Quantitative Analysis*, June 2000.

Shiller, R., "Do Stock Prices Move too Much to be Justified by Subsequent Changes in Dividends?", *American Economic Review*, June 1981.

Shiller, R., "Stock Prices and Social Dynamics", Brookings Papers on Economic Activity, 2, 1984 (pp. 457–498).

Shiller, R., *Irrational Exuberance*, Princeton University Press, 2000.

Shiller, R., "Bubbles, Human Judgement and Expert Opinion", *Financial Analysts Journal*, May/June 2002.

Shiller, R., *The New Financial Order, Risk in the 21st Century*, Princeton University Press, 2003.

Siegel, J., *The Future For Investors*, Crown Business, 2005.

Sortino, F. and Satchell, S., *Managing Downside Risk in Financial Markets*, Butterworth Heinemann, 2001.

Stanyer, P. and Long, K., "Unquoted Risk: The Art of Measurement", *Professional Investor*, March 1993.

Statman, M. and Wood, V., "Investment Temperament", manuscript, June 2004

Statman, M., "Behavioral Portfolios: Hope for Riches and Protection from Poverty", Pension Research Council Working paper, 2003-9.

Statman, M., "Normal Investors, Then and Now", *Financial Analysts Journal*, March/April 2005.

Staub, R. and Diermeier, J., "Segmentation, Illiquidity and Returns", *Journal of Investment Management*, vol. 1, no. 1, 2003.

Stein, D.M. and Siegel, A.F., "The Diversification of Employee Stock Options", AIMR Conference Proceedings, Investment Counselling for Private Clients IV, 2002.

Temin, P. and Voth, H-J., "Riding the South Sea Bubble", *American Economic Review*, December 2004.

Thaler, R.H., "The End of Behavioral Finance", *Financial Analysts Journal*, November/December 1999.

Thaler, R.H. "Mental Accounting Matters", *Journal of Behavioral Decision Making*, vol. 12, 1999 (pp. 183–206).

Tuccille, J., *Kingdom, The Story of the Hunt Family of Texas*, Beard Books, 1984, reprinted 2003.

Van, G.P. and Song, A., "Historical Hedge Fund Returns Fairly Represent Performance", Research Report, Van Hedge Fund Advisors International, January 2005.

Violi, R., "Credit ratings transitions in structured finance", Banca d'Italia Working Paper, December 2004 (source: www.bis.org).

Wang, J., Wu, C. and Zhang, F., "Liquidity, Default, Taxes and Yields on Municipal Bonds", Working Paper no. 2005-35, Federal Reserve Board Washington DC, July 2005.

Wilcox, J., Horvitz, J. E. and diBartolomeo, D., *Investment Mangement for Taxable Private Investors*, Research Foundation of the CFA Institute, 2006.

Zadeh, L.A., "Fuzzy Sets", *Information and Control*, vol. 8, pp. 338–53, 1965.

Notes on sources

The publisher and author wish to thank the following sources for the use of their website information and other copyright material:

Bank of England Quarterly Bulletin (Figure 6.1)
Barclay Trading Group (Figure 9.1; Table 9.2)
Citigroup Index LLC. All rights reserved. (Figures 8.3–5; Tables 7.1–2)
Center for Research in Security Prices, Graduate School of Business, The University of Chicago. All rights reserved. www.crsp.chicagogsb.edu (Figures 7.1–2)
Credit Suisse First Boston/Tremont Index LLC. Copyright 1999–2005. All rights reserved. This book (the "Work") is provided by Profile Books Limited, which takes full responsibility for providing it. Neither Credit Suisse First Boston/Tremont Index LLC nor its affiliates, subsidiaries, members or parents (collectively, "CSFB") have undertaken any review of this Work or any recommendations contained herein, or of the suitability of this information for anyone accessing this Work, and neither the Work nor the information contained in the Work is sponsored, endorsed or approved by CSFB. The CSFB/Tremont Hedge Fund Index, the CSFB/Tremont Investable Hedge Fund Index, and the corresponding Sub-Indices, and any information in the Work relating thereto (collectively, the "Information") is made available to you for your own internal use and may not be reproduced or disseminated in any form, nor may it be used to create, offer or sell any security, financial instrument or index. The Information is provided "as is" and any use is at your entire risk. (Figures 9.4–7; Tables 9.1, 9.3–9)
Dimson, E., Marsh, P. and Staunton, M., *Triumph of the Optimists: 101 years of Global Investment Returns*, Princeton University Press, 2002, as updated. (Figures 3.4–7; Table 3.1)
Dow Jones & Company Inc (Figure 5.1)
Fitch Ratings Global Corporate Finance (Table 8.2)
FTSE EPRA/NAREIT (Tables 11.2–4)
Green Street Advisors (Figure 11.2)
JP Morgan EMBI+ (Tables 8.5–6, 9.5)
Lehman Brothers Inc (Figures 5.2, 8.1–2; Tables 4.1, 4.4–5, 8.3–7, 9.1, 9.6, 11.2–4)

Index

Numbers in *italics* indicate figures; those in **bold** type indicate tables.